the
Property
Chain

the Property Chain

HarperCollins*Entertainment*
An Imprint of HarperCollins*Publishers*

First published in Great Britain in 2004 by
HarperCollins*Entertainment*
an imprint of HarperCollins*Publishers* London

Copyright © Wordright Ltd 2004

1 3 5 7 9 8 6 4 2

A CIP catalogue record for this book
is available from the British Library

The HarperCollins website address is:
www.harpercollins.co.uk

ISBN 0-00-717578-7

Printed and bound in Great Britain by
The Bath Press, Bath

CONTENTS

ACKNOWLEDGEMENTS

We would like to thank the following for their invaluable help in the compiling of the book:

The production team at Maverick Television; John Hay at Buildstore; Michael Bates IFA, Granville Bates; Priscilla Chase; Ian Willis IP Building Services; Keith Snook RIBA; Roger Abbott RIBA, architect; Ken Byass solicitor; The Law Society; Halifax Bank; David Bitner, The Market Place; Gill Murphy, Direct Line Insurance; Nicky Stanley, Harbour Holidays, Padstow; Kath Hanley, *The Lady* Magazine; Wendy Haydon, South West Tourism; Holiday Cottages Group; Peter Bolton King, National Association of Estate Agents; Martin Bennett, Building Control Surveyor Stratford District Council; Andrew Scholey of www.helpiammoving.com; Richard Strauss CEng MIStructE, Structural Engineer; Steve Pitts, SMP Building; Jeremy Wakeling, Chartered Surveyor; Georgina Miles, Inland Revenue; Law Pack Publishing Ltd; Peter Wingate-Saul; Linda Ashworth; Carolyn Gasson; Dick and Lynn Shone; Becky and Mike Hill; Guy King, Homes Overseas Magazine; John Howell; William Pusey; Annabel Francois, OIC Locations; Janine Watson, Lane Fox; Listed Property Owners Club; Philip Friedman; www.home.co.uk.

INTRODUCTION

Napoleon was wrong when he said we were a nation of shopkeepers. As Channel 4's *The Property Chain* showed only too well, we are in fact a nation obsessed with property. Whilst the Continentals happily rent their homes, and presumably stash away their cash in bank accounts to hand on to their children, we doggedly pursue the dream of owning our little bit of Britain. (Napoleon of course dreamed of owning it all!).

A UK land-ownership map would look very much like an intricate patchwork quilt with someone's name stamped proudly on each little portion. Being 'on the property ladder' has become a life achievement, and we pay handsomely for the privilege.

The average house price in England and Wales in 2004 was somewhere around £150,000. The situation may change – and many are predicting it will – but whatever the vagaries of the economy and interest rates, the purchase of your home will probably be the biggest single financial outlay you will ever make. The Council of Mortgage Lenders reports that the average loan taken out in August 2003 was over £100,000. This figure is so high because in recent years property values have rocketed, and nearly half the population is now unable to get even a toe on this famous property ladder. Small wonder that the number of mortgage borrowers earning between £10,000 and £15,000 per annum has dropped from 28 per cent to 13.2 per cent in the last fifteen years. Soaring house prices make it impossible for them to buy.

As borrowers, according to the Bank of England, we owe £710 billion in outstanding mortgages. But that burden is just part of the story. You will have to jump through plenty of hoops before you can even start making your contribution to this enormous borrowing figure. The property buying process in England and Wales is fraught with problems, making it, if it's any consolation, one of the most complicated in the world.

As the ups and downs of *The Property Chain* made frighteningly clear, what should be a simple sales transaction becomes stressful and acrimonious. We agonise over every stage of the process: Will our house sell? Can we afford to buy? What will the survey say? Have we offered enough? Have we been offered too little? The programmes showed the mistakes and the bad decisions we all make. But the reason for our angst is because property is an emotional issue where the heart can too often rule the head. We see a house or flat we like, we fall in love with it and begin to imagine ourselves living there.

But that's a dangerous thing to do when property law in England and Wales has a major idiosyncrasy: offers on properties are not binding right up to the point of exchange of contracts. Nothing is certain until the deposit has been paid. You had imagined yourself in that lovely cottage with the wonderful views, then suddenly the whole thing falls apart and your dreams are dashed.

The result of this quirk is that more than a million people every year find themselves part of a property chain where they are dependent on other buyers and sellers, their mortgage offers and their valuation reports, in order to move. In fact nearly half of all property sales are delayed because of it. Everyone up and down the chain is perched on a knife edge. Tempers fray and, when one sale in the chain falls through, the rest of the chain collapses around it. The Scottish system is far more sensible because offers made are legally binding.

But until England and Wales come up with a better idea, and even if they do, this book will prove invaluable in smoothing the rocky path of property purchase and sale for everyone, including those north of the Border. We'll take you from the moment you decide to buy, right through the processes you need to follow and the hitches that can occur, to the happy moment when you wave goodbye to the removers so, with a bit of luck, the whole process will be easier to bear.

There is plenty more involved in property ownership than just acquiring it, however, and you'll find information here on buy-to-let, being a landlord and tenant, raising finance, building your own home or improving the one you already live in. We've also covered making money on your property, whether it be from holiday letting or having it used in a TV programme or commercial, and we have even shown you how to spread your wings and buy a second home and a place in the sun. We've packed in barrel-loads of information, including legal details, advice from experts, tips and people's real life experiences (including those from the programme). At the end of each chapter you'll find a list of useful addresses and websites.

In the back of the book, we've given you useful listings of all the experts and terms used in property purchase and ownership, guidelines to the law, especially as regards being a landlord, and information you will need to know about taxation, plus a run-down of the Scottish property system.

Some of the same details included in the book are relevant in different situations – conveyancing, building regulations and planning permissions for example – and we have made every effort to cross reference them where necessary. The information we have included is current at time of writing, but legislation is amended all the time, and organisations change or go out of businesses. The advice too is as accurate as it can be, but every situation is different, and we strongly advise that you consult a technical or legal expert where necessary.

Where we live is important to us. It's about more than just mortgages and capital assets. We all want to come home to a place we love and enjoy, and we hope this book will make that wish come true for you.

Wordright Ltd
2004

RENTING AND LETTING

If an Englishman's home is his castle, then a landlord's is his palace. Few relationships can be as fraught with trouble as that between the rent collector (and property owner) and the rent payer. But renting can be the ideal solution for both parties. For the landlord it's a good way to earn extra income; for the tenant it's a few-strings-attached way to live without the albatross of a mortgage to contend with.

THE RENTALS MARKET IN THE PAST

At the beginning of the twentieth century, 90 per cent of property was in the private rental sector, then between the wars, with the appearance of garden suburbs and a rash of house building, the figure dropped to around 50 per cent. A good deal of rented property was council owned, but in the private sector lettings often worked in the landlord's favour, with the result that there was a rash of unscrupulous property owners letting out substandard properties at vastly overblown rents. The Rents Acts (the first came into force in 1957) changed all that, and tipped the balance in favour of tenants who could take complaints to rents tribunals to have fair rents set. These were often far less than the market rate. Many tenants also became regulated or controlled tenants, which protected them from eviction and huge hikes in their rents. For many this was a long-overdue change in legislation.

The flip side, however, was that for landlords it was a disaster. Many landlords were losing out, unable to secure viable rents and unable to get rid of their tenants however badly they behaved. Some properties even had to be put on the market with sitting tenants paying peppercorn rents. The result was a huge drop in the number of people willing to take the risk on buying properties to rent. Add to that the difficulties in getting a mortgage for a second home to let, because of mortgage lenders' fears of sitting tenants, the low interest rates and mortgage relief under the Tory government of the 1980s, which made it easier for people to buy their own homes, and it's not surprising that by 1989 only 7 per cent of housing in Britain was in the private rented sector.

For those landlords who did take the risk, many would agree short 'Holiday Let' contracts with tenants, which could be renewed over and over again. These were outside the law but, ironically, during the early 1980s 'yuppie' boom many business people were being relocated by their companies and had substantial properties to let (especially in the South-East) and, conversely, many were looking for properties with their rents being paid by the company they worked for. A large number of letting agencies appeared to cope with this demand, and the result was the formation of the Association of Residential Letting Agencies (ARLA) in 1981.

The rental market changed radically on 15 January 1989, however, when the implementation of the Housing Act coincided with the beginning of the recession. The new legislation made the rental market fairer for both tenant and landlord, implementing notice periods for the end of tenancies, regulating the quality and safety of furniture and fittings, and introducing the assured shorthold tenancy, an agreement whereby properties could be let out for six months at a time, with leeway for contract renewal (*see page 22*). The collapse of the property market also left many homeowners in a negative equity situation and, unable to sell, many decided to earn income on their properties through letting. More high-quality, rentable properties appeared on the market.

The Housing Act was amended in 1996 and, though people who took on rentals before the further amended Housing Act 1989 still hold on to their protected tenancies, most agree that the situation post-1989 is fairer and safer for both parties.

THE RENTALS MARKET TODAY

One factor has revolutionized the rentals market over recent years: the buy-to-let scheme, initiated by ARLA and introduced in 1996. Prior to this, people were not allowed to buy a property just to let it out – unless they had the express permission of the mortgage lender. The only way to do it was through a high-interest bank loan or commercial mortgage. But buy-to-let has proved to be hugely successful – small investors can now invest in a handful of properties, with the mortgage repayments (one hopes) covered by the rental, and with a bit of luck have a bit of (taxable) profit left over. It has flourished too because of a growing demand for properties to rent. The stigma attached to renting has disappeared (though we are still behind the Continent as a 'renting' nation). Types of renters include:

- those whose employment is fluid and who need to relocate often, including those who need a pied-à-terre during the week if they work away from home;
- those who want the flexibility of renting without the burden of mortgage repayments to worry about (because rents are set and can be budgeted for without the fluctuations of mortgage interest rates);
- and those who sell their home and, with cash in the bank, want to look around for their next home as cash buyers.

Renting out property can be lucrative, though nothing is sure in this life. However, the average rental return in Britain hovers around the 6 per cent mark, and capital appreciation on a property is likely to match, if not exceed, inflation for the foreseeable future. As a rule of thumb, you should ensure that gross rents are between 130 per cent and 150 per cent of the monthly mortgage payments – in fact, lenders will insist on it (*see page 4*).

This yield does not include any borrowing costs, building service charges, repairs or maintenance, which will reduce it substantially, but it's a useful calculation to do in your head when looking at potential property to buy.

WILL IT PAY?

How you work out the gross yield on a property (i.e. the relationship between rental income and the cost of the property) is critical. Here's a good way of working it out:

Property cost: £130,000

Rental: £270 per week

£270 ÷ 52 weeks = £14,040 revenue per annum

Divide this by the cost of the property:

$$\frac{14,040}{130,000} \times 100 = 10.8\% \text{ gross yield}$$

At the time of writing there are over a quarter of a million buy-to-let investors – though they only represent 10 per cent of the 2.5 million properties in the private rental sector. Of course, the property market changes all the time, and the recent dotcom crash has resulted in an oversupply of properties to let, especially in London. But in some areas there's a shortage of suitable properties. Do your research right and buying-to-let is in many cases still well worth while considering. The recent concern over pensions has also made investing in 'bricks and mortar' even more attractive than ever.

But more on that below. There's a certain type of landlord who has been around for ever, and who earns a great deal of money out of a large portfolio of property (usually in major cities), but it's unlikely that you would be reading this if you fitted into that category. Let's assume you're about to become a landlord, or are about to rent for the first time. What do you need to know now?

BEING THE LANDLORD

What Sort of Person Becomes a Landlord?

Because of the rather chequered past of the rentals sector, the word 'landlord' seems to sum up a rather seedy character who lets out damp, squalid housing and then appears every week with a rent book to demand huge sums from the poor, exploited tenant. But thanks to the 1989 legislation, this stereotype has virtually disappeared and the landlord of the twenty-first century is a completely different kettle of fish.

The growing number of private landlords today are people like you who, for one reason or other, have or want to acquire an asset from which they hope to make some money and which, with a bit of luck, will represent a sellable asset. You might:

- have inherited a property from a relative, which has no mortgage owing, and which you don't immediately need to sell (an ideal situation because any income is a bonus);
- have decided that bricks and mortar is the safest place to invest your money, when pensions are not looking as promising as they once did and the stock market is subject to fluctuations (though property is not always a golden goose – witness the property crash of the 1980s – but in the long term it has always proved to go up in value);
- be having to move out of your home for job reasons (permanently or temporarily), and have decided to hang on to your property and rent in the new location;
- be unsure where you want to live, so are renting a property yourself, but keen to have a property asset;
- have children at college or university, and want to invest in a place for them to live during their time there, so you know they're safe and living in habitable conditions;
- have a part of your house that is self-contained (this sort of letting is subject to a different tenancy contract (*see Chapter 10*)).

So you have the property – or at least an idea of becoming a landlord – but it's not as simple as that. Letting is not rocket science but it has its complications. Here's what you need to think about:

What Type of Person Makes a Successful Landlord?

The best landlords share certain characteristics:

- *They're familiar with buying and selling property*: a successful landlord is not just someone whom it's nice to rent from. It's someone for whom renting is financially worthwhile, which usually comes because he or she has invested in a property people want to live in. Any property purchase is a gamble, especially if you're buying as an investment (buying one's own home can be more of an emotional choice), but you can lessen the gamble if you have experience of the property market, and know what to look for when buying your property to rent (*see below*).

- *They're organized*: able to deal with problems concerning the property (either practical or involving paperwork), and up to speed with the documentation and legal issues surrounding property rental.

- *They're interested in property*: so they market a property that is attractive to live in – the yardstick is whether you'd live in the property you're proposing to rent.

- *They're good with people*: you may rarely meet your tenants, and indeed an arm's-length relationship is often the healthiest one – but where people live is an emotional issue and you need to be able to deal with problems fairly, pleasantly and quickly, whether directly with your tenant or with a letting agency, if you're using one.

What to Buy

You may already have a property you can let (perhaps your parents' home, which you've inherited), and you'll have to test the market to see if it's the type of place people want to rent. But let's assume you're going to invest in a property. What's the best type to invest in?

Typical tenants these days are young (20–30), professional, usually single, looking to rent for short periods, and renting because they don't want the hassle of owning and renovating their own property. This suggests that five-bedroom country properties with large gardens are going to be less popular, and one- or two-bedroom flats in attractive blocks with good-sized rooms will be the most popular. As a rule of thumb this is true, though many larger properties have been rented out successfully, but sensible landlords will want to be sure that their property is occupied as much as possible and the smaller, easier-to-maintain flats and houses often return the best yield.

However, it's swings and roundabouts: London landlords snapped up studio flats in the 1990s. Then the economy faltered, and there was suddenly a glut of such properties. In other parts of the country, studio flats could not be rented for love nor money.

The best advice for potential landlords is to speak to letting agents in the area in which you're interested in investing. Ask what sorts of people come to them looking to rent. Find out the demand. Keen on buying a three-bed house? It's pointless if local tenants are looking for studio flats.

If you're not keen to rent out your new purchase through a letting agency, you can still pick their brains, and any agency worth their salt will do all they can to persuade you to use them. More about using agencies later.

So the overriding considerations are location, location, location. Thatched cottages in the middle of the countryside may be beautiful but, unless you're

> TIP *If the most popular rental properties in a certain area are beyond your budget, look a few miles down the road or in the next town. Demand changes area by area.*

very lucky and find an unusual tenant, are unlikely to be popular. Bright, attractive flats in towns where there's plenty of employment may be a better bet – for nearly half of all tenants proximity to work is the main consideration. One experienced landlord advises: 'Don't be emotional when looking for property; you don't have to live there. Decide on your criteria and stick to them.' Think about the following:

- How easy it will be to live in: if you're buying a flat, it's worth investing in one on the first floor, so tenants don't have flights of stairs to contend with. Ground-floor or basement flats are often perceived to be a security risk, and top-floor flats are hard to get to. If you're buying a house to let, consider if the garden is easy to care for (because tenants may not have green fingers, and you may need to provide garden maintenance). Is the bathroom and kitchen a decent size? Is there an area for a table to eat from? Is there plenty of wardrobe space, any storage for suitcases and boxes?

- Local amenities: the typical tenant will want easy parking, local shops, a station or underground close by (at most 15 minutes' walk away), pubs and restaurants. They may well want to be near a good motorway or road network, or even an airport.
- The locality: is it reasonably quiet? If you wouldn't want to live next to a railway line, why should anyone else?
- Costs to you: buildings with lifts, door porters, leisure facilities and so on may be attractive to tenants, but will often mean hefty service charges, which you'll have to meet and which will cut substantially into your rental income.
- How far away it is from your own house: if you're managing the property yourself, you won't want to be driving 100 miles each time something needs repairing.
- How well you know the area: it can be a good idea to purchase property in an area whose characteristics you already know well – even if it isn't your home town. It helps to be familiar with local council practices as regards planning permission etc. if you're planning to do work on the property, the local community and the fortunes of big local employers.

The Risks

Though it's important to like the property you're letting out, the overriding consideration is that it makes good financial sense. Buy a house for yourself and it may be an emotional decision: you love the house or the location, it'll be nicer when you've spent a bit of money on it, you intend to live there for years and may well see your money back, so you might just pay a bit more than you budgeted for. Buy to let out, however, and you need to be more hard-headed. Ask yourself:

- Can I afford to refurbish it to a good enough condition to rent?
- How much rent will I get for it?
- Will the rental cover fluctuating mortgage repayments (if there are any),

service charges, insurance, maintenance costs, utilities and council tax, unforeseen costs (like a new roof)?

- Will there be any profit left over after costs and tax have been deducted?
- What would happen if your tenant did not or could not pay the rent?
- Could you meet mortgage repayments and utility bills if the property was empty for a period?
- Is it sellable if you found yourself in a position where you had to sell, or if the style of property became less popular to potential tenants in this area?

To help lessen the risks:

- Contingency: do your figures on the assumption that the property will be empty for at least one month a year, and have an emergency fund of at least three months' rent to draw on if you have to.
- Avoid periods when the property is empty if at all possible: it's better to reduce the rent and have the property occupied than hold out for a higher rent and lose valuable income.
- Loss of rental: tenants may default on the rent either maliciously or because they've lost their job. Make sure you've taken out very thorough references before signing a contract with them and, if you're on a tight budget, look into taking out one of the specific insurance policies offered by letting agencies. Be warned, though: the premiums you have to pay may exceed the actual loss of rental.
- Damage: cover yourself for accidental (or careless) damage to the property, and ensure your insurance cover for the contents is adequate for any furniture you're providing.
- Capital value loss: only by keeping ahead of the game can you be sure you won't lose capital value on the property. Choose the area you buy with care, and keep an eye on how busy estate agents are in the area, and movements in the local rental market. If you suspect things are

beginning to slow down, or your property is looking less marketable, that is the time to think about selling and investing elsewhere.

- The tenant who won't budge: it's impossible to insure against tenants who refuse to leave at the end of their tenancy period, and it will take a court order, about three months and probably no rent paid, to get them out. Again, think about having an emergency fund to cover this eventuality.
- Your liabilities: insure yourself against the risk of being sued for not fulfilling your obligations by ensuring you've complied with all the safety regulations (gas, fire etc.) in the property (*see pages 20–1*).

Buying Property to Rent

You know what type of property you want to buy (having thought about all the above of course!), now you need to pay for it. Before you start, though, decide whether your aim is to generate regular income, or capital growth. The ideal property is one that will be attractive to tenants, but in a location and of a type easy to sell if and when you have to.

Cash Buyers

If you're lucky enough to be a cash buyer, the process is the same as that for buying any property, except there are certain tax issues connected with owning a second home (*see Tax and Costs*). You'll need to factor in professional and legal costs, such as conveyancing and surveys, though the latter are not always essential if you do not have to satisfy a mortgage lender. Surveys are a sticky issue. Some people find building surveys unnecessary, and are happy to proceed using their own intuition about the state of repair of a property, but if you're at all uncertain, a survey could save you an awful lot of money if it reveals some horror you might have overlooked.

Buy to Let

As we said earlier, this scheme was initiated by ARLA in 1996. Prior to the scheme, those wanting to buy to let had to take out expensive loans with surcharges or commercial mortgages at high interest rates. ARLA persuaded mortgage lenders that the new Housing Act had removed the worry about sitting tenants, and that there was a burgeoning market for lettable properties. A lot of young people had been burnt in the 'rush to buy' mentality of the 1980s, finding themselves in a negative equity situation and unable to meet their mortgage repayments. They were likely to play safe and rent. ARLA argued that mortgage lenders would be wise to encourage maturer investors to buy property for rental, as they were more likely to be a safer lending risk.

There are now nearly 50 mortgage lenders who offer buy-to-let packages.

BUY TO LET MORTGAGES

Mortgage rates are not the same as in the residential market – lenders consider buy to let a greater risk and demand a greater return:

 Their buy to let rates can be up to one percentage point higher than residential rates. The deposit required is also higher. Most lenders ask for at least 20 per cent of the value of the property, and this can rise to 50 per cent on properties valued at £1 million or over. If you arrange your mortgage through a broker, you may have to pay up to 1 per cent of your mortgage value in broker fees. You'll also have to pay for the survey and legal fees, as with any property purchase.

 Conditions vary from lender to lender, so shop around: some will want you to prove you've a minimum income (usually around £20,000 for a single person), some will want proof that you can service your residential mortgage, but all will do a credit check to ensure you have no mortgage arrears on any existing mortgage you may have (*see page 30*).

 Buy to let mortgages are not based on your income and ability to pay: they're based on the rent received from the property or properties. Most lenders will want to ensure that the rental income is at least 125 per cent of the mortgage repayments, so that there's enough leeway to cover running costs and periods when the property is empty. But the question is 125 per cent of what? Lenders will base it on the interest-only amount: on the standard variable rate or on the other type of rate you're using: tracker or fixed rate. So some properties with the same rent may have a different demand on their repayment percentages.

 Some lenders will lend not more than 75 per cent of the property value, some will go to 85 per cent, and some will set a limit to the number of properties you can borrow against, or set a maximum value. But there's no restriction on the number of different lenders you can use. Big-time landlords will shop around for the mortgage that suits the property they want to buy at that time.

 Repayment periods can be up to 25 years, though the minimum term for borrowing is 5 years. The minimum age is usually 25 and the maximum 75.

 You'll be able to set off some of the maintenance and running costs against tax. Mortgage interest payments, for example, can be set against rental income.

(Information courtesy of Charcol, www.charcolonline.co.uk.)

Buying at Auction

This is a popular way for investors to purchase property, but the same principles apply for buying a property at auction to let as they do for buying one to live in yourself. Such properties often come up for auction because it's hard to sell them any other way: they may have squatters, be in a very poor state, have short leases left on them or be in an area earmarked for road building or nearby shopping development. You'll need to carry out very thorough research before putting in a bid – searches, surveys and so on – and be ready to exchange contracts immediately, because the property will be yours at the fall of the hammer (*see Chapter 3*).

Buying a Property with a Tenant in it

This is not the same as investing in a property with a sitting tenant. An existing landlord may wish to sell the property as an ongoing concern and, so long as he has no problems with the existing tenant and you and your solicitor are happy with the details of the tenancy agreement, it's a perfectly viable way of investing in a property to rent.

Tax and Costs

Like all income, profit from rental income (after deductions) is subject to income tax under Schedule A, and, unlike the sale of your main residence, the sale of a second home is liable for capital gains tax. Each individual is allowed £7,500 income tax free per annum (2003) – £15,000 if you're married (you should check these allowances as they change each year). This constitutes your total capital gains tax allowance for the tax year and assumes you've not used up the allowance on other capital gains. It's important to keep a record of all income and expenses so you can include them on your annual tax return. Go to www.inlandrevenue.gov.uk/pdfs/ir150.pdf for details of taxation on property income. It provides guidance about what income is within Schedule A, what expenses can be set against that income and how to arrive at the taxable profit or allowable loss of a tax year. It also covers income from overseas property (*see Chapter 7*).

Landlord Costs

You'll need to make provision in your calculations for:

- agency letting fees (*see page 19*);
- utilities;
- maintenance costs;
- service charges (if you're not the freeholder);
- council tax, if there are several people occupying the property (i.e. students). Under the Local Government Finance Act 1992, however, the tenant is obliged to pay this tax and the landlord is not liable. For information on council tax in Scotland see the contact details at the end of the chapter.

Improvements

What constitutes 'improvement', and is it tax deductible? This is a tricky one. Broadly, if the property is in a lettable state when you purchase it, then any redecoration costs can be set off against rental you receive. If the property is run down and needs considerable renovation before it can be occupied, then it's counted as a capital expense. Expenditure must also be 'wholly and exclusively' for the purpose of your rental business, so you can't set the cost of painting your own home against tax.

Loans

If you've taken out a loan to buy a rental property, the interest paid on that loan is also allowed against rental profits, as is interest on an overdraft, so long as it was to fund your rental business.

Preparing a Property to Let

There's little difference nowadays whether a property is furnished or unfurnished, in terms of security of tenure – though it wasn't always so – so the decision whether to furnish your property is up to you. However, potential tenants often make a decision on first impressions. If your property is in an area, like London, where there are a huge number of rental properties to choose from, you're more likely to get a tenant if the property looks attractive, light and appealing rather than bare and unwelcoming.

TIP *As the financial and tax details surrounding rental property are complicated, it's a good idea to consult your tax advisor who will be familiar with the details. That way you can be sure you're claiming all your allowances.*

Don't forget the typical tenant profile: under 30, single and professional. They may not have furnishings and furniture of their own, and would welcome a comfortably furnished home to move into straight away. The other typical tenant is the professional who works away from home Monday to Friday, and who will not want the bother of buying beds and sofas when he or she has a well-furnished home elsewhere.

Perhaps the best argument for leaving properties unfurnished is to secure tenants who've sold their own home and wish to rent (usually a house) before getting back on the property ladder. They'll need the space for their furniture, and unfurnished properties will be top of their list of requirements. However, finding tenants for unfurnished rather than furnished properties usually takes longer, so there are more likely to be periods when unfurnished properties are empty. But you may find that you end up with a tenant who rents your unfurnished property for a longer period. Again, it's swings and roundabouts.

What Type of Furniture and Decor?

Long gone is the rental property with second-rate cast-off chairs, bumpy beds and whirly wallpaper to disguise dubious walls beneath. Since buy to let was introduced and renting became popular again, the quality of rental property on offer has improved considerably, and you'll need to bear this in mind when you come to choosing fixtures and furniture.

But furnishing a property attractively (and safely) does not need to make a huge dent in your budget. Many stores sell modern furniture and accessories (all meeting legal regulations – see below) at very reasonable prices, and they look attractive. Furniture must look and be in excellent condition, so junk-shop buys are not a good idea, and can even be dangerous.

- Keep walls a neutral colour – whites and pale creams create the freshest impression and are easy to touch up when they get grubby.
- Paint finishes are easier to maintain than wallpaper, which can get damaged.
- Good-quality curtains are essential. Don't scrimp on them – would you want thin ones that let in the early morning light?
- Floors need to be hard wearing, and in good condition, whether hard flooring or carpeting. If you do take the unfurnished option, the quality of the floor will be the only thing the tenant sees when he or she comes to view!
- Hard floors are popular – tenants aren't keen on other people's old carpets – but they need to be of high quality, as they can be damaged easily. Avoid carpets in the bathroom and the kitchen.
- Kitchens should be spotlessly clean and include a cooker, washing machine (with separate tumble-dryer if there's room), dishwasher (for two- or three-bed properties), large fridge freezer, and microwave. You

should also supply enough crockery, cutlery and glasses, a kettle, ironing board, cleaning equipment and so on – take a look around your home kitchen and make a note of what you need to survive daily life. Note:

TIP *Make sure tenants know the location of essential items such as the fuse box and the mains water inlet tap – and how they work.*

any electrical goods you supply will need to be tested annually (*see page 20*).

- Bathrooms should reflect the quality of the property – one with a high rent in a good area should include a power shower and bath, and good-quality fittings.
- Bedrooms should have plenty of storage space and, if you're providing a bed, it should be the biggest and the best quality you can afford.
- Supply as much furniture as you would need if you lived there – bedside tables, lamps, coffee table, enough dining chairs and so on.
- Leave a copy of appliance instructions, local information and details about the house – it all helps to secure a tenant.
- Bear in mind that tenants might not be as careful with your property as they would with one they owned. It's worth going that extra half mile to buy furniture, kitchen worktops, sanitary ware that are durable and hard wearing, and the same applies to paint finishes.
- First impressions really count. Make sure the property is clean and smells nice, and clean the windows.
- However, don't spend more than you'll be able to reap back in rent.

TIP *If you're unsure as to the level you should be refurbishing the property, especially if it's one that will command a high rent take the advice of a letting agent. Even if you're not intending to use them, they should be helpful with advice and may well do a strong sales pitch on you.*

REAL-LIFE ACCOUNT

Lydia Hatchard owns eight flats in east London. She runs the business with two partners as a limited company and the properties were bought with a commercial mortgage. Lydia and her partners manage the properties, but they're let through a letting agent who deals with all the administration and credit checking. The tenancy agreements ensure that sharing tenants are 'joint and severally liable' should one of them default on their rent.

'We identified a specific property type in east London – ex-local authority maisonettes – because we realized that in these areas close to Canary Wharf there's an abundance of expensive property to rent for City high-flyers, but very little for people who worked there, looking for cheaper property to rent. We calculated our best market was young professional sharers, so we pinpointed very spacious flats that had at least three bedrooms, with some able to be converted to four bedrooms.

'Most of the properties were fairly grotty when we bought them, but we established a renovation formula as we went along. We always ripped out the kitchen and replaced it with a clean-looking simple one from IKEA. We took out carpets and laid wood-laminate floors, recarpeted the bedrooms and decorated in white or off-white. At the windows we put up aluminium blinds which made it look modern and fresh. All the furniture we bought was new, though not expensive. It's best to assume you'll get two to three years' wear out of it and then replace it when it starts to look shabby. We also incorporated plenty of storage, as sharers need their own space.

'Our tenants really look after the flats, and though we stay at fairly arm's length, and let the agency have most of the contact, they do know our names, have our mobile numbers and we chat to them on the phone. We rarely meet, but because they know we are real people, this helps in ensuring that they look after the properties.'

Finding Tenants

Though every landlord would like to find the perfect tenant who causes no trouble, is clean, tidy, careful and pays the rent on time, it's not always possible. Hard as you try, you may not end up attracting the type of tenant you imagined. That doesn't mean they'll be the devil personified, but you can increase your chances by offering an immaculate property in an ideal location, with a watertight tenancy agreement. With a bit of luck, a professional person with all the above credentials will turn up to view and take on the property.

Advertising

The wording you use when you advertise or the brief you give a letting agency can all help secure the type of tenant you want. You might want to specify a professional person with a full-time job (a good idea if you're terrified of rent not being paid). You can specify no children, no pets, non-smokers, type of profession (no musicians, for example, if your property is in an apartment block), or no housing benefit tenants or students. These details will all help define the profile you require. You can also go on gut reaction: your decision is final. If you have worries about a potential tenant, for whatever reason, you can simply say no.

Three ways to advertise your property effectively:

- Local newspaper: this is often the first place potential tenants will look, especially if they're new to an area and want to find out local rental rates. Small ads can be expensive, so keep the details to the minimum, but stress location, size of property, type you prefer (non-smoker, no pets etc) to save wasting your time with unsuitable applicants. Adverts placed in local newsagents/gyms/leisure centres can work, but they'll not have a wide audience. Adverts in publications like *The Lady* (which specializes in small ads) will guarantee you a high-quality

TIP *If you choose to advertise for a tenant, ensure that you always check references of potential tenants. Also, it's a good idea to arrange for rent to be paid by standing order into your account. (Only the tenant can arrange this, but it will speed things along if you supply a standing-order mandate form for the tenant to fill in and return.) Cash payers suggest a lack of commitment. Always ensure the initial deposit and rental cheque has cleared before granting the tenancy, and you should ask to see copies of the past few payslips and an employer's reference (write to the employer yourself – don't rely on pre-written references provided by the tenant).*

> TIP *Remember: letting agents also like properties that rent out quickly. If they know that your property always gets a spring clean and a lick of paint between tenants, they'll show it first and you'll have a better chance of securing a tenant.*

response, but adverts placed in national papers are probably a waste of time, because the readership is so broad geographically.

- Companies and colleges: these are ideal if you're looking for corporate clients or students. Large local employers often help new employees who've recently relocated or are on longer-term placements. The rental is usually covered by the company, which is a comforting thought for any landlord, and companies can often produce a rich seam of tenants. Ads in student publications or notices pinned up in colleges are obviously only a good idea if you're happy to let to students, and you'll probably have two or more individual tenants, which can have implications for you as landlord (*see pages 20–1*).

- Letting agents: these suit the landlord who lives far away or who wants to let a property at arm's length as, for a fee, the letting agency will market the property, find a suitable tenant (to your brief), obtain references, do credit checks, prepare the tenancy agreement and arrange for it to be signed. For a further fee, they'll also collect the rent and deal with repairs and maintenance of the property. They may also charge to chase up rent arrears. Some agencies will charge nothing to market the property – the 'no let no fee' system. The obvious downside of using a letting agent is the cost, but being a landlord can be very time consuming. It could be money well spent if the agency's service saves you from a lot of hassle and inconvenience.

- Visit a few agents before deciding where you want to place your business – the cheapest is not always the best – and membership of a professional body (like ARLA) should guarantee a reasonable standard of competence and will give you the opportunity to appeal if you end up in dispute.

Your Responsibilities

There's a great deal more to being a landlord than providing a decent property, and then waiting for the money to roll in. Failure to comply with your responsibilities can leave you vulnerable to legal action:

- Gas safety: all gas appliances, flues and installation pipework in a rented property must meet 1994 regulations and be properly maintained and serviced at least once a year by a registered, qualified engineer. You must keep hold of the certificate of maintenance and be able to show it to tenants before they move in.

- Though gas is the cheapest fuel option, many landlords opt for electricity instead, though of course these appliances must be safe and checked too. Electrical equipment between 50 and 100 volts a/c should be safe and tested regularly.

- Smoke detectors: building regulations regarding fire protection are being updated all the time. As a general rule, smoke detectors are required in common areas such as shared lobbies and staircases, but not in self-contained accommodation up to two stories high. Any building built after June 1992 must have functioning smoke detectors installed on each floor, but as a responsible landlord, you should include them anyway, and use mains wire-connected ones with battery back-up if at all possible.

- Furnishing and fire safety: if you're providing furnished accommodation, all upholstered furniture (including mattresses, bed bases, cushions and chair covers, nursery furniture, pillows, loose covers) must meet 1988 furnishings regulations and have a label saying as much. You can obtain details of guidelines from your local authority or Citizens' Advice Bureau. It's worth investing in new furniture, as it should comply with the regulations if it's from a reputable dealer. Furniture manufactured before 1950 is exempt from the regulations. (*See appendices for information on these and other obligations.*)

- At the time of writing, there are plans to change the regulations for properties occupied by several people (i.e. students, nurses etc.) and landlords may be obliged to provide facilities such as fire escapes. If your property is occupied by more than four unrelated occupants, you should inform your local authority – your property may have to be inspected and registered as a house of multiple occupation.

- Both you and the tenant should read the electricity and gas meters at the beginning and the end of the tenancy, and have the accounts put in the tenant's name.

- It's the landlord's responsibility to insure the building and the contents *he* has provided. There are special policies available for landlords, as well as insurance policies for loss of rental income.

- Public liability insurance: your buildings insurance policy should cover injury and death through accident to persons staying in a property belonging to you, but you should check with your insurer or broker that you're adequately covered, and you may want to make extra provision by taking out public liability insurance.

- You should give your tenant 24 hours' notice of a visit for non-emergency repairs, as entering a self-contained property unless for an emergency is unlawful without permission from the tenant.

- It's also your responsibility on modern tenancy agreements to maintain the building and the facilities of the property. If you fail to, the tenant has a right to 'self-help', whereby he can have the work done and deduct the cost from rental payments.

Types of Tenancy Agreements

The 1988 Housing Act (amended in 1996) changed the way tenancy agreements worked, and tightened the law to benefit both landlords and tenants. (*See below for agreements made prior to that.*) But if you're planning on renting out now, you'll be offering an assured shorthold tenancy. This provides a contractual term (usually six months) of rental, after which the tenant has no security of tenure, and ensures that the landlord is sure to obtain possession on or after the end of the shorthold term you've agreed. The landlord will have to go to court, and give the tenant at least two months' notice in writing if he or she is still occupying the property after the end of the shorthold, but the landlord does not have to give a reason for wanting repossession (not the case in the past). In certain circumstances (like non-payment of rent) the landlord can also obtain possession of the property during the period of the shorthold.

The advantage of shortholds to the tenant is that if they believe the rent to be excessive, they can go to a rent assessment committee, who'll decide the appropriate rent for the property.

The Law in England and Wales in a nutshell:

- *Tenancies granted before 15 January 1989*: tenants still have full security of tenure and control over the amount of rent they pay.
- *Tenancies granted after 15 January 1989 and before 28 February 1997*: tenants have ordinary or fully assured tenancies with full security of tenure, except in cases where the landlord created an assured shorthold tenancy for a minimum of six months, after which period the tenant would have no security.
- *Tenancies granted after the amended Housing Act came into law 28 February 1997*: these are automatically deemed to be assured shorthold tenancies, unless (and this is rare) the landlord granted an ordinary or fully assured tenancy.

However, despite recent changes in legislation, including the Commonhold and Leasehold Reform Act (2002), the legal situation between landlord and tenant is a tricky one, and those involved need to proceed with care. Tenancy agreements will also change if the agreement is held 'joint and severally' between two or more tenants, or if you're letting to students. Reputable letting agencies will have copies of the tenancy agreements (*you'll find samples in Appendix 2*), but you're advised to consult a lawyer.

Short Lets

These are an alternative to the assured shorthold tenancy, and are popular in the corporate rental sector when tenants often only want to rent a property for a few weeks or months. In this sector, rents and the quality of properties (and decor) is often higher. Business people want clean, furnished, well-equipped, well-located properties that they can use somewhat like a hotel – only for longer.

BEING THE TENANT

Why Rent?

General opinion used to be that renting was throwing good money down the drain. It's true you won't be on the property ladder and will have no 'bricks and mortar' asset to realize, but renting is the ideal option for people who:

- cannot get on the property ladder with house prices so steep;
- want to live without the obligations and pressure of a mortgage;
- are unsure where they want to settle;
- need a place to stay during the working week;
- have sold their home and are waiting to buy again as cash buyers.

Thanks to the assured shorthold tenancy (*see above*), tenants are in a much stronger position than they once were, as they cannot be evicted by landlords without good reason (non-payment of rent being one), and have a security of tenure for the agreed period of the shorthold tenancy.

SCOTTISH LAW ON LETTING

In Scotland the law on letting and tenancy agreements (including landlord responsibilities) varies from that in England and Wales. The property or any part of it can be furnished or unfurnished, and the tenant or tenants must be an individual or individuals (i.e. not a company or partnership). It gives special rights to the landlord to repossess the property and special rights to the tenant to apply to a rent assessment committee for a rent determination in certain circumstances. A short assured tenancy must be for at least six months initially and before the tenancy begins, the landlord must also give the tenant a signed notice (Form AT5) stating that the tenancy is a short assured tenancy. An inventory should also be prepared of the furnishings or equipment included in the let.

The form AT5 must be served on a prospective tenant by the landlord before the tenancy begins. The AT5 informs the tenant that the tenancy is a short assured tenancy in terms of Section 32 of the Housing (Scotland) Act 1988. The form must be served personally to the tenant or be sent by recorded delivery to the tenant's last-known address. If at the end of one short assured tenancy the landlord offers the same tenant another short assured tenancy of the same property, he need not serve another Form AT5 and the tenancy may be for less than 6 months.

Go to www.scotland.gov.uk/library3/housing/msst-04.asp (*and to Appendix 2*) to see a sample of a Scottish short assured tenancy agreement and www.scotland.gov.uk to find out more information about private tenancies.

What you Need to Know

- A property is usually let 'as seen', so what you see is what you can expect to find in the property when you move in. You can make a request for anything obvious that may be missing (an ironing board or even a bed!) but you cannot demand one. When you receive the inventory check it thoroughly before you sign it as you cannot complain afterwards.

- You'll need to provide details of referees: your bank, an employer and a previous landlord, but you cannot provide a reference ready written – it could be a fake. You may well have a credit check run on you through a credit reference agency, and you'll have to pay for this (*see page 30*).

- It's the landlord's decision whether or not you can rent the property and if he refuses to have you, for whatever reason, then you had better look elsewhere!

- Once you receive the tenancy agreement, look at it very carefully and read every word, because, once you've signed it, it's binding in law.

WHEN THINGS GO WRONG

If you're careful and your tenancy agreement is watertight, your landlord–tenant relationship should run smoothly. But there may be reasons why you want to evict a tenant – rent arrears being the most common one. The technical term is 'a possession order' and there are three major factors to consider when possession is required:

 In order to grant a possession order, the tenant must have been given two months' notice in writing beforehand by you the landlord. This is known as the Section 21 Notice, which is served on all tenants on an assured shorthold tenancy two months before the tenancy expires.

 Notice must be given in the right way, which informs the tenants of their rights and the procedure you as the landlord will be taking. A Section 8 Notice is a notice sent by you to the tenant notifying them of your intention to take court action against them for a breach of the tenancy if they do not comply within a certain timescale. The form is designed to inform the tenant of the specific grounds for possession.

 A court order takes time, and there's a fixed procedure to follow in every case.

You'll need to attend court to give your reasons for issuing the possession order, all paperwork will be requested beforehand and during the hearing. It's very important that you have all the relevant paperwork ready and in order, because the smallest error or omission may be all that is needed for the case to be delayed and you'll have to be relisted for a court hearing at a later date, which can mean a two-month delay. The possession order process may take six to eight weeks.

Once the court date has been granted, the judge will then make a decision, based on the case and the paperwork before him, as to when the tenant must vacate the property. It might be as soon as two weeks, or 28 days. The rent is still due and payable during the wait for the possession notice date. The tenant still has a right to remain at the property after the possession date, but you may have to instruct a bailiff, again through the courts.

You should consult the Citizens' Advice Bureau or talk to your solicitor. If you're using a letting agency they too should be able to advise you on the possession procedure.

You'll also be expected to hand over a deposit (not less than one month's rent), the initial rent (depending on the length of the tenancy agreement), and a tenancy agreement fee if you've agreed a tenancy different from a standard assured shorthold one.

- The rent will have to be paid by standing order – few landlords will accept anything else.

- You should ensure that the utilities and the telephone have been put into your name (you'll have to pay a connection charge) and that you read the electricity and gas meters with the landlord at the beginning of the tenancy.

- You'll be expected to pay the council tax due on the property (unless you're renting with others – as a student for example – or take a bedsit in the owner's house).

- You'll also have to obtain a television licence.

- You're responsible for the upkeep and minor maintenance of the property while you're occupying it, though the landlord is responsible for major repairs. A landlord has an obligation to do these within 24 hours of your reporting them. But be reasonable – if it's a weekend, getting a contractor may be tricky.

- Ensure you take out contents insurance on any contents (including furnishings) that belong to you. The landlord is responsible for all other insurance.

- At the end of the tenancy it's up to you to ensure that all final utility bills are paid (and that you've informed the relevant companies that you're no longer the account holder), that the inventory is complete, the property is cleaned and in the same state as when you first moved in. Your deposit will then be returned, though probably not for about a week.

- A tenancy is a contract and if you decide to leave and just hand back the keys the landlord is entitled to claim back the rent due until the end of the fixed term of the shorthold.

USEFUL CONTACTS

The Association of Residential Letting Agents (ARLA)
Maple House
53–55 Woodside Road
Amersham HP6 6AA
Tel.: 0845 345 5752
Web: www.arla.co.uk

Buy-to-let information (e-book)
Web: www.let-a-property.info

Citizens' Advice Bureau (information on tenancy agreements)
Web: www.adviceguide.org.uk/
index/family_parent/housing/tenancy_
agreements.htm

The Guild of Letting and Management
15 Briscoe Road
Hoddesdon EN11 9DG
Tel.: 01992 420022
Web: www.guild-let.co.uk

The 1988 Housing Act
Web:www.hmso.gov.uk/acts/acts1988/
Ukpga_19880050_en_1.htm

Landlordzone
Tel.: 0870 765 4420
Web: www.landlordzone.co.uk

The Letting Centre (information for landlords and regulations)
Old Vicarage
Withycombe Village Road
Exmouth EX8 3AG
Tel.: 01395 271122
Web: www.letlink.co.uk

The Small Landlords Association
78 Tachbrook Street
Westminster
London SW1V 2NA
Tel.: 020 7828 2445
Web: www.landlords.co.uk

Information on Scottish Residential Letting Law
Web: www.scotland.gov.uk

MORTGAGES AND FINANCING YOUR PURCHASE

Stop before you go anywhere near an estate agent's window! Most people put the cart before the horse – decide they want to buy and then look at the mortgages on offer. It's far wiser to investigate the financing options available first, to make sure you're eligible for a loan. Not only will a little investigation tell you how much you'll be able to borrow – quite important so you know what you can afford – but how much it will cost you to borrow and the best deal for you and your circumstances.

WHAT IS A MORTGAGE ANYWAY?

Seems like an obvious question. Mortgages are so much a part of life these days, it's assumed everyone knows what they are – but this is in case you don't and were afraid to ask!

A mortgage is a loan from a bank, building society or other financial institution or lender that is paid back, with interest, over a certain period of time. The property you buy will be security against the loan – and the mortgage lender will want to be happy with the property you're buying; which is why they'll insist on a valuation survey. But because it's a security, if you fail to keep up your repayments, and after giving you notice, the mortgage lender has the right to repossess the property and sell it to recover the money it has loaned you (*see pages 48, 50*).

AM I ELIGIBLE FOR A MORTGAGE?

Your lender, if loaning you a large sum of money, will need to be sure the property is sound enough not to require huge sums to be spent on it (hence the surveyor's report). A lender will also want to be sure you're able to repay the loan and that you're a good risk. Lenders will need the following:

- Proof of your identity (e.g. passport or driving licence).
- Proof of where you've lived for at least the last year – in the form of a council tax bill, gas/electricity bills, current mortgage statement and so on. It's advisable to be on the electoral roll too.
- References and payslips to confirm your income from your employer.
- Your last three years of accounts if you're self-employed.
- Details of your current or last mortgage if you have one, or a rent book.
- A credit check through a credit agency to assess how credit worthy you are (*see below*).
- To know if you've any county court judgements (CCJs) against you – for example if you've defaulted on a loan payment. CCJs remain on your credit-reference file for six years after they've been issued. But if you paid off the debt at least a year before applying for a mortgage,

BEEN REFUSED?

There could be any number of reasons why you've been turned down for a mortgage, but you're entitled to ask for them. The lender may think your type of employment is too risky, or may have received a bad credit reference. For a small fee you can see a copy of your statutory credit report, and for a slightly larger fee, your full credit report. Ask your mortgage lender which credit reference agency they used – it will be one of three: Equifax, CallCredit Plc or Experian. You could ask for a report from all of them, and then you'll get a full picture of your credit history. There may even have been a mistake, in which case you can add a Notice of Correction explaining the mistake, which will go on your report. But don't give up – try another lender that may be more flexible about its lending criteria.

there shouldn't be a problem. When you fill in your application, make sure you're honest about these details. Lying will only work against you.

HOW MUCH CAN I BORROW?

This depends on how much you can afford to pay back. Some mortgage lenders are falling over themselves to lend money, and may offer you the earth – but be realistic. Would a large mortgage put you under enormous financial strain? And what would happen if disaster struck, and you had to find money urgently for some reason?

REAL-LIFE ACCOUNT

Dave and Maggie Sawyer were renting a property in Bristol, but had a nasty shock when they put in their mortgage application.

'We had been renting for just eight weeks, and saw a house we wanted to buy. We didn't have a property to sell, and the amount we wanted to borrow from the building society would have been amply covered by my husband's salary alone. We filled in the details, with our names and our current address, which was the property where we were renting. The whole thing, we thought, was going to be a piece of cake.

'A few days later the building society sent us a letter saying our application had been refused based on our credit rating. We both turned on each other, hurling accusations. Had one of us taken out a loan and defaulted on the repayments without telling the other? We then had to contact the credit reference agency and pay a fee to find the reason for the bad rating. It came back with details of a utility bill to our address unpaid by a previous tenant. We had no idea that it was not just your names, but the address on your application which could affect the rating, and that the onus was on us to clear our names. We had to pay to have the bad reference taken off our record.

'We reapplied and our mortgage offer was accepted, but by then the mortgage product we wanted had been replaced by a different one which wasn't so favourable. The result? For the next 25 years – the term of our loan – we'll be paying more than we should, just because of the fault of some past tenant.'

TIP *If you're finding it difficult to get a mortgage, see if you can borrow less than 75 per cent of the value of the property, because a loan of this value does not have to satisfy such stringent demands. For example you'll not need to take out mortgage indemnity insurance (see below).*

The rule of thumb is that your mortgage repayments should not amount to more than one third of your monthly income, after tax.

Depending on your age, most lenders are prepared to offer you up to 85 per cent of the value of the property (some might go higher, but the payments will also be higher as the risk is greater), and loan you up to three times your regular yearly income. This is your income net of any other loan repayments or regular payments you have to make. If two of you are sharing a mortgage, there are two ways to estimate how much you can borrow:

$3 \times$ the major income and $1 \times$ the minor income

or

$2.5 \times$ your joint income

The mortgage lender will also take into consideration:

- The type of property you're looking to buy – leasehold or converted properties can make a difference to the percentage you're allowed to borrow. Most lenders will look at how much time is left on the lease once the mortgage has been paid off (and expect between 25 and 50 years). The shorter the lease, the smaller the choice of lenders.
- How much cash you have for the deposit (*see page 46*).
- Whether a mortgage indemnity guarantee is required – which is

TIP *Several companies offer a credit-cleaning service – they claim to be able to remove or change information (like CCJs) held by credit-reference agencies, and will expect to be paid handsomely for this. It's not recommended that you employ them. If you believe that your report is wrong, then contact the credit-reference agency yourself.*

SELF-EMPLOYED?

Most lenders will want to see your previous three years' accounts, to prove that you have a good track record of trading. If you're new to self-employment, a loan may depend on whether you've worked in the same industry before. If you've changed direction completely, you may find it harder to get a loan until you have some trading history.

One problem of self-employment, though, is that your profit (as it appears on your accounts) may not be a true picture of how well you're doing in your business, as accountants (legally) can downplay your profit to put you in a better tax position. You can opt for a self-certification loan offered by subsidiaries of the bigger lenders – which means you can certify your income without actually having to prove it. The downside: interest rates can be high and you may not be able to borrow such a large percentage of the property's value. Look at flexible mortgages as another option (*see below*).

On a contract? You may have to prove your contract will definitely be renewed, or that you've had a pattern of renewals over a period of a year or two.

often the case if you're borrowing a large percentage of the value of the property (over 75 per cent).

- Your employment status – if you're self-employed or working on a contract for example, where the level of your income is not always guaranteed, then the percentage you can borrow may vary (*see above*).
- Any other loans you may have, and how much more you have to pay on them.

WHERE TO GET A MORTGAGE

The choice of mortgage lenders is enormous – actually a bit overwhelming – but the sheer competition is good news for you the borrower, because lenders need to keep their rates competitive.

Loans are available through the following:

TIP *Today's bargain may change tomorrow. Be guided by the annual percentage rate (APR), which is the interest figure you'll have to repay – but be careful! Some lenders set this very low, at a discount for a set period as an incentive, but it will return to a high rate once the honeymoon is over.*

- *High street banks and building societies*: both of these sometimes offer reduced borrowing rates for long-standing borrowers, which kick in once you've had your loan with them for a certain time. Most banks have a condition that you bank with them before they'll give you a mortgage, but it can work in your favour to ask for a mortgage from a bank with which you have a long and good banking history.
- *Internet/direct lenders*: this is armchair mortgage buying, whereby you do an internet search through a site (*such as those listed on page 51*) to find the mortgage that suits you, or deal with the lender direct by phone, complete your details and await the offer. There are not many lenders who work this way, but they can offer competitive rates as there's no middleman, but you're on your own in making the right decision.
- *Independent financial institutions*: the interest rates on your repayments may be higher, and the redemption penalties may be higher.
- *Specialist mortgage lenders*: these lenders often specialize in 'difficult' mortgages, such as those for the self-employed or those with a bad credit history. Their rates can be competitive as they do not have high street offices and overheads, but check the small print and the redemption clauses (*see page 45*).
- *Estate agents*: many are owned by mortgage lenders, so you may not be getting the best deal.

USING A MORTGAGE BROKER

With over 3,000 mortgages deals available, it's not surprising it's called the mortgage minefield. And the variations in each are numbing in their complexity. If you're not confident that you can make the right decision, then mortgage brokers will be your best bet. They'll do the legwork – find out your requirements, and then narrow down the field of possibilities for you – and though some charge a fee as well as a sales commission from the lender you eventually borrow from, many just take commission, so the whole process may not cost you a penny. Mortgage brokers may be independent financial advisors (IFAs), must be registered with the Mortgage Code Compliance Board (MCCB) (*see below*) and carry indemnity insurance, but if you're unhappy with the deal being offered, you can ask elsewhere. And before you begin, always ask your broker how he's paid.

REAL-LIFE ACCOUNT

Fran Green, 57, is a nurse and had a council house in the Cotswolds which, in 2003, she was given the right to buy from her local authority:

'I had taken time away from work to nurse my husband but, after he died, went back to work part-time. My income was only £3,804 per year and, even though the house was worth £180,000 and the local authority were offering me the right to buy it at £91,000 (a 50 per cent discount), there was no way I would have been able to get a mortgage from a high street lender on my salary.

'If I wanted to buy, I had to do so by September 2003, so I contacted a mortgage broker who is also an independent financial advisor. He looked at my earnings, took into account my £123 per month widow's pension, the state pension I would receive at 60, plus the fact that I was about to go back to full-time work, and put together a case which he presented to the Cheltenham & Gloucester Building Society.

'They calculated that to raise a mortgage to buy the property, it would cost me £300 per month, which is what I already paid in rent and, with the assurance that my daughter would act as a guarantor should I not be able to meet the repayments, offered me an interest-only mortgage.

'To qualify for the 50 per cent purchase price discount, I have to stay in the house for five years, and the discount will go down by 20 per cent each year, but after that period, I can sell it and buy a smaller house to live in during my retirement. It's worth getting the help of a mortgage broker because they know which lenders will take into consideration unusual circumstances. It's also a huge relief that at last I own my home and have an asset to leave to my daughter.'

CHOOSING THE RIGHT MORTGAGE FOR YOU

As we said, there's an alarming choice of loan options, and the one that suits you will depend on your job, income, age and so on. You're advised to seek independent financial advice; there are two types: a capital and interest (repayment) mortgage, and an interest-only mortgage.

Repayment Mortgage

This is the straightforward way of paying off your mortgage. Each month you make one payment to the lender, which is used to pay off the interest and some of the capital you've borrowed too. Keep up the repayments over the lifetime of the loan (usually 25 years), and at the end of the mortgage term agreed, you'll have paid off your debt. For the first few years, your repayments are mostly paying off the interest, but as time goes on you'll pay off less interest and more capital. It's a good choice of mortgage if:

- you're not planning to move frequently, because if you move often into more expensive properties, you'll be paying off interest for longer and not make a significant repayment of the capital you've borrowed;
- you're expecting to come into some money at a later date, which will allow you to pay off some of your mortgage;
- you want a shorter-term repayment period or are planning to live abroad sometime in the lifetime of the mortgage.

Interest-Only Mortgage

This is as it sounds. Your repayments each month pay off the interest on the money you've borrowed, but do not pay off any of the capital. At the end of the repayment period, you still owe exactly the same amount as you originally borrowed. But how do you repay the capital you owe at the end of the life of the mortgage? You set up a separate investment plan – an ISA, an endowment policy or a pension – and pay money into this. This money is then invested in the stock market, and hopefully will make more than enough to pay off the capital when your mortgage term ends. But, as we all know, the fortunes of the stock market are variable, and there's risk involved in taking out this type of mortgage.

Endowments

An endowment consists of two parts packaged together – a savings plan plus life assurance. The idea is that you make a second monthly mortgage payment that is invested by a life assurance company. If it performs well enough, you'll have enough to pay off the capital owing on your mortgage when the time comes. You may even have a cash lump sum left over. There are two main types of endowment:

- *With-profits endowment*: your premiums are pooled with funds from other investors. At the end of the year, the life company will allocate bonuses to all the investors. Once awarded, these cannot be taken away.
- *Unit-linked endowment*: buys specific units in stock-market-linked investments, which can go up and down in value daily. Unit-linked funds have the potential for greater and faster growth than the with-profits endowment. However, there's also a greater risk that the unit-linked policy may not produce such a good return as a with-profits policy.

This type of mortgage was very popular in the 1980s when the stock market performed so well, and financial advisors assumed the trend would continue that way. But it didn't. So you'll need to think about what will happen if your investments don't perform well. Endowment mortgages have had a bad press recently, both because of a poorer performing stock market and the scandal of some policies being mis-sold. Take advice from an IFA if you want to take the endowment route.

- Endowment policies can be moved on to your next mortgage if you move.
- You can take out a second endowment policy if you buy a second home.
- You can switch between a repayment and an endowment policy if the endowment is not performing well, or pay partly repayment and partly endowment.

Pensions

As well as your interest repayments, you also pay into a pension fund and, as these have a tax-free status, one hopes the money will grow quickly, and you'll be left with a cash sum to pay back the capital owing on the mortgage and have some left over. The pros: the money invested may pay back handsomely.

The cons: the investments may not perform well, and as much of your pension contribution will be going towards paying off your mortgage, you'll not have as much left over for your retirement. Again, consult an IFA.

Individual Savings Accounts

Individual Savings Accounts (ISAs) are tax-free investments, so the money invested should grow quickly. However, if investments underperform, you may be left with a shortfall in the cash sum when you come to pay off the capital on your mortgage. The advantage of ISAs, however, is that they're flexible and carry low management charges, so are a popular route to repay interest-only mortgages.

HOW IS THE INTEREST CALCULATED?

This is the rub. Once you've chosen the type of mortgage that suits you (from the above), there's the sticky question of interest calculations. You may find your eyes glazing over at this point, but you need to stay sharp because the wrong choice could end up costing you more than you should be paying. This is where the Internet comes into its own. Several web sites (*see page 51*) can search the right sort of mortgage for you once you've entered your details.

Flexible Mortgage

This (also known as Australian) suits people who are self-employed and whose income level is variable. It works a bit like a bank loan, but you pay off as much or as little as you can afford without penalty, and can sometimes make 10 monthly payments instead of 12. If you have a windfall, you can also pay off a lump sum (without a redemption penalty) and, conversely, you can take 'payment breaks' if you cannot meet the repayments for a while. You can also make withdrawals on an earlier overpayment. The interest rate is calculated monthly, and is usually just above the Bank of England base rate, so you'll benefit when interest rates are low. Some bank lenders will allow you to put your mortgage repayments in one fund with your current account and savings, which can bring the interest rate down.

Variable-Rate Mortgage

This is the swings-and-roundabouts mortgage. Your payments depend on the varying rates fixed by your lender, which change with the economic climate and the Bank of England base rate (and some lenders can be slow to adjust their rates in line). If interest rates fall, so do your repayments, and if they rise … well, you get the picture. This mortgage works well when interest rates are low, but the situation can change quickly. The downside is that it makes it harder to budget for your repayments, and some lenders will penalize you heavily if you decide to pay off your mortgage early. Proceed with caution on this one.

Fixed-Rate Mortgage

This is the gambler's mortgage. Your monthly repayments stay the same for a specified period, say up to five years, or for the duration of the mortgage and do not change regardless of whether the interest rate goes up or down, so you can win or lose. The advantage is that you can budget on exactly how much you'll need to repay each month, useful for first-time buyers, and is worth looking into if you feel that interest rates are about to rise. At the end of the specified period, most borrowers move to a variable rate.

Capped-Rate Mortgage

This should be the ideal mortgage. Interest payments are set at a 'capped' upper limit, over which you'll not pay, regardless of how high interest rates may go. You also pay less once the lender's normal variable rate passes below your limit. In an ideal capped rate, there should be a small gap between the cap limit and the lender's normal rate, so that over a period of about five years there should be plenty of time for the rate you pay to fall below the cap – but there's a risk that it will never fall low enough for you to benefit. Some capped rates also have a lower limit below which your repayments cannot drop, even if interest rates fall below that level; so in some cases a fixed-rate mortgage may be the cheaper option.

Discounted Mortgage

This type offers the borrower a reduced interest rate for a limited period of time – usually around two or three years – and is usually 2 per cent below the lender's base rate. The discounted rate changes, so you'll not be protected from rate rises, but will benefit from drops. Beware of tie-in clauses that penalize you if you cash in your mortgage, especially if the tie-in period is longer than the discounted period. This type of mortgage suits the investor who plans to invest for a long time. Discounted mortgages carry no penalties for moving the mortgage, which enables you to move it at the end of the discounted period to another lender offering a better deal (called remortgaging).

Cashback Mortgage

Cashback suits first-time buyers, who can benefit from the cash offered by the lender in return for taking on its mortgage. The cash is usually only handed over once you've agreed to stay with the lender for a certain period, and the amount of cashback offered can vary – some offer fixed sums, some a percentage of the original loan (perhaps 6 per cent of the amount borrowed). Be wary too of penalties if you try to repay the mortgage before the agreed term has ended.

Base-Rate Tracker

With a tracker, the amount you pay is linked to the base rate set by the Bank of England, plus a small percentage set by the lender, which might be just under 1 per cent. If base rates are low, you'll benefit and pay the base rate plus the percentage, but it works the other way too. These perform well during a period of low interest rates, but are a risk if economic circumstances change.

Euro Mortgage

As the name suggests, this mortgage is measured in euros rather than sterling, with the interest rate based on the lower euro interest rather than the high UK rate. The risk lies in the exchange rate staying favourable and the interest rate staying low. If the euro grows stronger against the pound, your loan will get bigger in sterling terms. This mortgage would suit people who are paid in euros, or who are earning income from letting a property in Europe. (*See Chapter 7 for more information.*)

Ecology Mortgages

These are 'green' mortgages usually offered to borrowers who are renovating or building new properties with a commitment to the environment, renewable resources and ecological renovation techniques, or who might find it difficult to get a mortgage offer elsewhere. Lenders will also lend to environmentally linked businesses. Lenders include The Ecology Building Society (www.ecology.co.uk), who offer a standard variable rate loan with low initial fees. (*See page 168.*)

REMORTGAGING

This means moving your mortgage to a new lender without moving house. It makes sense if you're paying a standard variable rate when you could benefit from a cheaper fixed-rate or discounted mortgage if you moved, and you can move without having to pay a penalty clause. Remortgaging can cost you a considerable sum in application fees, lawyers' fees and valuation fees, which could wipe out any savings you make, but competition is fierce amongst lenders to provide loans, so rates are competitive. The moral is: keep an eye on who's offering what to see if you could benefit from moving.

Note: to remortgage you'll have to change lenders, as your current lender will be offering its most competitive remortgage deals to new borrowers, poaching them from other lenders.

SELF-BUILD MORTGAGES

These are specially designed for people building their own homes (not for developers) and release money as it becomes necessary at each stage of the building process. (*See Chapter 6 for more information.*)

PENALTY/REDEMPTION CLAUSES

All the mortgage rates mentioned (except the variable rate) work over a fixed term, and you're tied into the mortgage agreement for the stated period. Break that tie-in period for any reason – for example moving your mortgage or paying off the loan – and you'll have to pay a redemption penalty. These can be painful, so you need to make sure you've read the small print of your mortgage agreement, and ensure you understand what the tie-in period is and what the penalty will be for breaking it. Terms vary depending on the lender and the type of mortgage, so it's worth shopping around. A similar mortgage may have varying terms.

If you think you want to or can repay your mortgage quickly, then avoid deals and stick to a standard variable-rate mortgage, or look for lenders who have no penalties attached. A flexible mortgage (*see page 39*) has no redemption penalties.

WHAT ARE CAT STANDARDS?

These were announced by the Government in April 2000. CAT stands for 'cost, access and terms', and is supposed to be a benchmark that a financial product that carries the CAT standard, offers reasonable value and has no hidden charges and terms. There are two CAT standards for mortgages: one for variable rate and the other for fixed-rate or capped rate. But not all CAT-standard mortgages are suitable for everyone, and not all mortgages carry the CAT standard. Nor do all lenders offer them – they're optional. It's worth comparing CAT and non-CAT mortgages to see which suits you better. Here is a summary of CAT mortgage standards:

Charges

 Interest must be calculated daily.

 Every regular payment and overpayment you make must be credited immediately.

 You may not be charged separately for a mortgage indemnity guarantee.

 All fees must be disclosed in cash up front before you take out the loan.

A broker arranging a CAT-standard mortgage for you may not charge a fee.

Variable-Rate Loans

There must be no arrangement fee.

The interest rate may be no more than 2 per cent above the Bank of England base rate.

When the base rate falls, your mortgage payments must be adjusted within one calendar month.

You must be able to pay off part or all of the mortgage at any time without penalty.

Fixed- and Capped-Rate Loans

 The maximum booking fee/arrangement fee is £150.

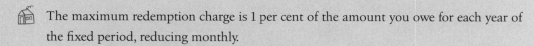 The maximum redemption charge is 1 per cent of the amount you owe for each year of the fixed period, reducing monthly.

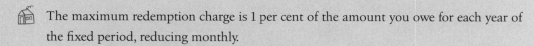 There must be no redemption charge once the fixed-rate or capped period has come to an end.

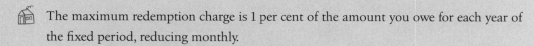 There must be no redemption charge if you stay with the same mortgage lender when you move house.

Access

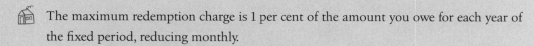 If there's a minimum amount you must borrow, this must be no more than £10,000.

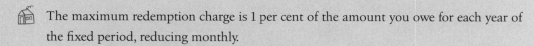 Any customer may apply for the mortgage.

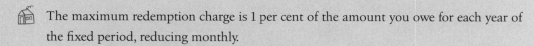 The lender's normal lending criteria must apply – there can be no special selection rules.

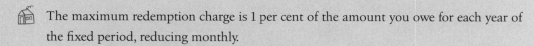 Provided the lender is happy to lend against the new property, you can continue with your CAT-standard mortgage when you move home.

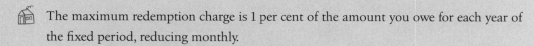 If you make regular payments, you can choose which day of the month to pay them.

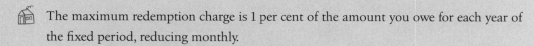 You can make early repayments at any time.

Terms

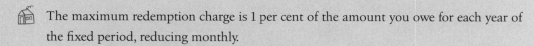 All advertising and paperwork must be straightforward, clear and fair.

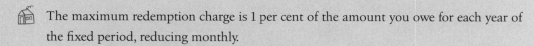 You do not have to buy any other product to get a CAT-standard mortgage.

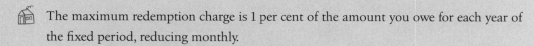 You must be given at least six months' notice if your lender can no longer offer you a mortgage on CAT-standard terms.

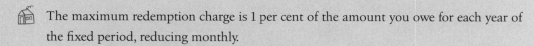 If you fall into arrears, you should pay interest only on the outstanding debt at the normal rate.

GETTING A MORTGAGE IN SCOTLAND

Before you begin house-hunting in Scotland, you need to have an 'agreement in principle' – confirmation from your lender that, subject to various conditions, they're prepared to give you a mortgage up to a certain amount. This amount will be based on your income in much the same way as it is in the rest of the UK. Without an 'agreement in principle' in place, any offers you make on properties are unlikely to be taken seriously.

You'll need to finalize your mortgage application by going back to your lender and providing details of the specific property you're planning to buy. Once this is done, the lender's valuation survey and your own structural survey (if applicable) can be carried out. In return for the loan, you're giving the lender 'standard security' over the land and buildings (known as 'heritable property'). The lender then keeps the title deeds until you've repaid your mortgage. For further information on buying in Scotland, go to:

www.icplanning.co.uk/buying_scotland.shtml (*or see page 310*).

COSTS OF GETTING A MORTGAGE

If only it were as simple as just securing a mortgage. There are other costs involved for which you'll need to budget. These are as follows:

- *The arrangement fee*: charged by the lender to cover the costs of administering setting up the loan. You may not always be charged, or some lenders will add it to the mortgage.
- *Lender's valuation survey*: lenders will want to content themselves that the property is suitable for purchase and worth the price you're paying, and you'll need to pay for the valuation survey. You may also want to undertake a full buildings or homebuyer's survey for your own peace of mind (*see page 75*), and you'll also need to pay for this yourself.
- *The deposit*: this is the initial percentage of the purchase price you pay on exchange of contracts (*see page 72*).

- *Mortgage indemnity insurance*: your lender will insist on this if you're borrowing a large percentage of the value of the property (more than 75 per cent).

- *Mortgage payment protection insurance (MPPI)*: this is an insurance policy linked to repayment mortgages (not endowment ones, which have life assurance included). It provides protection should you find yourself unable to keep up your repayments due to unemployment or long illness. It may be necessary if you have a joint mortgage (even with your spouse) and if you have dependants. Some lenders insist on you taking out this insurance, but if yours don't, like any insurance, you need to weigh up the costs of the premium versus the likelihood of your needing the cover to pay the mortgage (*see page 48*).

- *The lender's legal fees and your solicitor's fee* for handling the conveyancing.

- *Buildings and contents insurance: (see below)*.

- *Stamp duty*: this you'll have to pay if the property you're buying is worth over £60,000, whether you need a loan or not to purchase it. Stamp duty is the tax levied by the Inland Revenue on property transactions and the 2003/4 rates are 1 percent of the value from £60,000 to £250,000, 3 per cent over £250,000 up to £500,000 and 4 per cent over and above that. Go to www.inlandrevenue.gov.uk/rates/stamprates._htm for more information.

Note: It is not unknown for vendors and purchasers of properties that have a sale price close to a Stamp Duty threshold (£250,000 and £500,000) to negotiate the sale of fixtures and fitting separately. For example, a home buyer who purchases a property for £245,000 and pays separately for fixtures and fittings to the value of just over £5,000 will pay Stamp Duty at the rate of one per cent (£2450).

At time of writing, the Government plans to introduce Stamp Duty Land Tax (SDLT) that will not be payable upon completion of the purchase, but 30 days later. The individual will have to make a land transaction return to the Inland Revenue, together with a self-assessment of the tax due. Under the new system, the amount a purchaser pays for fixtures and fittings may well be reclassified as part of the property, which would push them into the next Stamp Duty bracket of three per cent. Transactions may be subject to investigation if the purchaser is thought to be avoiding tax. Consult your tax adviser.

WHAT HAPPENS IF YOU CAN'T KEEP UP THE PAYMENTS?

When a lender gives you a mortgage, your home is the security, and if you're unable to pay, then at worst the property would be repossessed to recover the loan. But what would happen if, heaven forbid, you were to die or were unable to earn money to meet your mortgage repayments? It's not obligatory, but advisable, to take out insurance policies that would cover you and your dependants in such an eventuality.

- *Life Assurance*: 'Whole of life' cover pays out a lump sum in the event of your death, no matter when it happens. The most common policies are unit linked, where your premiums are paid into an investment reserve from which a proportion is taken monthly to pay for your life cover. There are two kinds of unit-linked policy: maximum cover and standard cover:

  1 Maximum cover offers a high level of cover for a low premium, but for a set period (say 10 years). At the end of that time the plan will be reviewed, and the premium could increase substantially.
  2 Standard cover is designed so that future premium increases should be met from the investment reserve.

- *Accident, Sickness and Unemployment Insurance (ASU) and/or Mortgage Payment Protection Insurance (MPPI)*: These are insurance policies designed to cover your outgoings – usually your mortgage payments, but sometimes other living expenses – should you find yourself out of work. You pay a premium each month to the insurance company, and if you become unable to work due to an accident, sickness or unemployment, you can claim a monthly sum to cover you. If you claim on an ASU policy, the money paid out comes straight to you, but with MPPI the payout goes directly to your mortgage lender to cover your monthly repayments. With both types of policy you can specify an excess period from when you're unable to work to when the policy begins to pay out. This can range from three to nine months – the longer the period the cheaper your premiums will be. Many people go for a long excess period because they believe they'll either find another job or return to full health within a few months, but it is worth having funds available to tide you over before your policy begins to pay out.

Most ASU and MPPI policies pay out for a maximum of 12 months, and a few will pay out for up to two years. ASU and MPPI policies are available from life insurance companies, most major mortgage lenders, high street banks, building societies and direct over the phone or Internet.

If you have an endowment mortgage, then there's a life assurance policy included. (Excellent advice on insurance policies are available at www.yourmortgage.co.uk.)

BUILDINGS AND CONTENTS INSURANCE

Covering the actual *building* against damage of any kind is compulsory and your lender will insist upon your having buildings insurance – funny how they don't insist your life is covered! The policy will cover reinstatement – that is, putting the damage right or rebuilding after complete destruction – but not the market value of the property. Some lenders will sell you a policy, but you're under no obligation to take it up. You can source your own more competitive policy, so long as it's in place at the time of exchange of contracts (*see page 83*). The policy you choose should cover the standard risks (fire, accidental

TIP *Leasehold properties are usually insured by the landlord or leaseholder, and a contribution to the premiums will be added to your service charge.*

damage, subsidence, explosion etc.), but compare the small print with a couple of other policies to check how comprehensive it actually is.

It's not necessary to cover the contents of the building, and if you have nothing of great value you may feel that the cost of the premiums plus the excess you'll have to pay far outweigh any losses you may incur through theft or damage. But ask yourself what you would do if all the contents were ruined in a fire or major flood?

BRIDGING LOANS

These two words strike fear into people's hearts. As it sounds, this type of loan bridges the gap when you want to proceed with the purchase of your new property before you've managed to sell your old one. They carry a very high rate of interest. In many cases a bridging loan is avoidable – unless perhaps you have your heart set on the perfect property and do not want to lose it. Bearing in mind the pain of the repayment of this type of loan, it should be a last-resort measure.

MORTGAGE ARREARS AND NON-PAYMENT

A minority of people find themselves in a situation whereby they cannot keep up their mortgage repayments. It might be as a result of job redundancy or illness, or a change in your financial situation. But your mortgage debt is a priority, because if you fail to pay, your lender is entitled to repossess your home and sell it in order to recover the debt. However, most mortgage lenders will only do this as a last resort and are keen to help you – it's in their interests to keep you as a borrower after all – so the most important thing is to inform the lender as soon as you find yourself in difficulty.

By extending the term of the loan the lender may be able to reduce your monthly repayments until your

TIP *Take out a buildings and contents policy with the same insurer and you may well get a discount. The Internet is a good place to search for competitive policies.*

situation improves. Some banks and building societies have in-house counsellors or will refer you to the Consumer Credit Counselling Service (0800 138 1111 www.cccs.co.uk). You can also get help from your local Citizens' Advice Bureau or the National Debtline (0800 808 4000).

USEFUL CONTACTS

CallCredit Plc (consumer credit referencing)
1 Park Lane
Leeds LS3 1EP
Tel.: 0113 244 1555
Web: www.callcredit.plc.uk

The Council of Mortgage Lenders
3 Savile Row
London W1X 1AF
Tel.: 020 7440 2255
Web: www.cml.org.uk

Equifax
Credit File Advice Centre
PO Box 1140
Bradford BD1 5US
Tel.: 0870 0100 583
Web: www.equifax.co.uk

Experian
PO Box 8000
Nottingham NG1 5GX
Tel.: 0870 241 6212
Web: www.uk.experian.com

The Mortgage Code Compliance Board
University Court
Stafford ST18 0GN
Tel.: 01785 218200
Web: www.mortgagecode.org.uk

Mortgage comparison web sites:
There are many of these and you can use a search engine to source others, but here is a selection of the best known. Some contain mortgage- and loan-related information, news and advice, and may also include a mortgage calculator. Several have links to lenders who specialize in 'difficult' mortgages for the self-employed or those with a bad credit record.

Charcol Online
www.charcolonline.co.uk

Finance Search
www.financesearch.co.uk

Find
www.find.co.uk

MoneyeXtra
www.moneyextra.com

Moneynet
www.moneynet.co.uk

Money Supermarket
www.moneysupermarket.com

The Times (Your Money)
www.timesonline.co.uk

UK Mortgages Guide
www.uk-mortgages-guide.co.uk

Your Mortgage
www.yourmortgage.co.uk

BUYING YOUR HOME

When you begin looking for property, it's like starting out on an adventure. The possibilities seem endless, and surely the house you find is going to be perfect in every way. Then realities start crashing in on your dream. First you can't find anything you can afford, or anywhere you like, or an area that's got everything you want. Or you find a house you adore, but someone else pips you at the post. Within weeks you're tearing your hair out and wondering if it's all worth it. But stick with it. With the help in this chapter you'll come as close as it's possible to get to finding your very own dream home, and sail through the purchase with all the confidence of a seasoned property dealer.

Note: the information in this chapter applies to buying a house in England and Wales. The process is different in Scotland (*see Appendix 3*).

YOUR TIME FRAME

If you're in a hurry to move, your options are limited from the word go. You'll have to put speed and efficiency first in your wish list. Blitz the local estate agents, look at everything you can afford, and make sure your mortgage offer is all in place before you even start, although this will partly depend on whether you have a property to sell before you can buy. Instructing a solicitor early on in the proceedings and making sure you have a surveyor to hand before you even find a house will help speed things up too. Your priority will be to find people as anxious to sell as you are to buy, so houses that have been on the market for a while might suit you down to the ground. If you've already sold your property or are a cash buyer, you'll be very appealing to vendors, who are likely to favour you over someone who hasn't even accepted an offer yet, or who's in a chain.

BUYING IN A HURRY

Find out how much you can borrow before spending time looking at places you can't afford (*see Chapter 2*). A price ceiling will concentrate the mind on what is realistically available. Lenders will give you a certificate to say you have a mortgage agreed in principle, which should give you a head start when putting in offers.

> TIP *Don't leave viewing until the weekends when everyone else will be there. Go in your lunch hours, or make a detour on the way to or from work.*

- Tramping around banks and building societies can be a time-consuming way of arranging finance. Most major lenders can make mortgage offers in principle over the phone.
- Make sure estate agents regard you as a serious applicant. Show willing and be eager to view and you'll be at the top of the list when something new comes on the books.

If you've time to spare before completion, you can afford to be more choosy about the kind of house you consider, and you can make sure you get the closest possible fit to your requirements (*see below*). Don't let the vendors know that, though, or they might dismiss your interest as not being serious.

HOW LONG DOES IT TAKE?

In England and Wales it takes a notoriously long time for the buying process to be completed, and it's a source of immense dissatisfaction among property buyers. In most other countries it takes about half as long as in England

and Wales. The average in England and Wales is currently about 20 weeks from starting to look for a property to actually moving in. For Scotland the figure is slightly less, at 17 weeks. In England and Wales, from:

- looking for a property to having your offer accepted, about 10 weeks;
- acceptance of the offer to receiving a mortgage offer, about 4 weeks;
- having a mortgage offer to the exchange of contracts, about 4 weeks;
- the exchange of contracts to completion day, about 2 weeks.

Some buyers, however, take much longer to buy their property. For example 25 per cent take more than 14 weeks to reach exchange of contracts from offer acceptance, and nearly 10 per cent take more than 20 weeks. Leasehold properties take nearly three weeks longer than freehold.

ORDER OF PLAY

If you're also selling a property and the purchase of your next home is dependent on selling, it's strongly advisable to sell your home before you get down to serious house-hunting. If not, you could end up frustrated and disappointed, and possibly a lot poorer. Don't worry about ending up homeless between selling your house and buying the next one, because you can make it clear from the start that you're not moving out until you've found a new home. Also, once you've accepted an offer on your home, you'll know how much you have to spend on the new one.

HOW MUCH DOES IT COST?

The expenses of buying a house, quite apart from the purchase price, are quite fiddly and entail more items than if you're selling, but there's no way round it. Remember to budget for the following:

- Solicitors' and/or conveyancers' fees: at least £400 plus VAT.
- Stamp duty, calculated in increments on the value of a property over £60,000 (*see page 47*).
- Land registry fee, also based on the property value.
- Local authority searches: between £80 and £150.
- Other search fees.
- Mortgage fees (*see page 46*).
- Valuation survey fees for the lender: anything from £150 upwards (although this is for the lender's benefit rather than yours).
- Mortgage arrangement fee and possibly indemnity guarantee, if the loan is for a high percentage of the value of the property (*see also page 47*).
- Home buyer's or building survey and other specialized surveys, if necessary.
- Buildings insurance on your new property, payable in advance (*see page 49*).
- Removals costs.
- New furnishings and any alterations you have to make to your new house.

HOW MUCH CAN YOU AFFORD?

If you're selling your existing home, get a valuation so you know how much it's worth; then try various mortgage lenders to find out how much you can borrow if you're intending to trade up (*see Chapter 2*). Don't forget to factor in legal and survey fees and stamp duty, plus the other expenses listed above.

WHEN TO BUY

If you have to buy quickly for any reason (you may be relocating for your job), you won't have much choice in this. But for buyers with more leisure it's worth avoiding the traditionally busiest times: spring and late summer.

Although there are more properties on the market at that time, they're usually more expensive and agents (and all the other professionals) are rushed off their feet. In the school summer holidays and from December to March you're more likely to find sellers who are prepared to drop their prices a bit.

WHERE TO BUY

You may have a clear idea of where you want to live, and may even have narrowed it down to two or three streets, but if your budget is tight, it can be worth looking a little further afield. Estate agents should be able to tell you about fringe areas that are improving. It's important to research an area before viewing lots of homes there, or making an offer on a property there. If you decide it's not the kind of neighbourhood you would enjoy living in, then you could save yourself a lot of time and effort by doing so early on in the process. Even if you can get a bigger home for your money in an area that isn't so pleasant, make sure you really are doing the right thing.

Questions to consider:

- What is the neighbourhood like? Is it the kind of place you can imagine yourself feeling comfortable in? Who lives there?
- What kind of local amenities are there? Check out the leisure facilities, activities for kids, shops, restaurants, public transport and so on.
- If you have children, look at the local schools. Do they have a good reputation? Where do they stand in the league tables? This takes on a whole new dimension in places like London where people buy strategically depending on the catchment area of the best schools. This can inflate prices hugely.
- What is the level of crime in the neighbourhood? Ask at the local police station.
- How easy is it to reach your workplace?
- What council tax band will you be in?
- Will you have any or enough car parking space?

TIP *Remember: it's much easier to make improvements to your house than to your neighbourhood.*

- In what kind of condition are the neighbouring houses? If they're in a state of disrepair, or look neglected, it could bring down the value of your property.

Touring the area can give you a good idea of what it's like. Go at different times of day and on different days of the week. There are also some good sites on the Internet where you can research different areas and what is available there.

HOW TO SPOT AN UP-AND-COMING AREA

To make the best return on your money in the shortest time, you could take a gamble on an area that might be cheap now but that will become a property hotspot within a few years, and get in before the crowds. If you can buy before the coffee shops and tapas bars arrive, you'll get more for your money. Of course, there's always the risk that your area will remain steadfastly in the doldrums, or even goes down a little, but console yourself on not having spent too much. Although this is probably not the kind of punt you'd want to take if you have school-age children, it can be fun, rewarding and certainly colourful!

- Look on the edge of popular areas. If you can't afford the street you want, look at the map and pick out the areas on all sides that haven't been poshed up. You should get more for your money there.
- Look at the houses themselves. If a part of town has a good selection

TIP *Beat the rush: if you've targeted an area you want to move to, walk or drive round the streets every day on the lookout for new 'For Sale' or 'To Let' signs. They often go up before the property is advertised in a paper or the details have been printed, and you can get an offer in ahead of the competition.*

of solid, period homes and is near a smart area, it could be ripe for gentrification.

- Look out for projects by well-known developers, especially conversions of old industrial or commercial properties to residential use. Such companies spend a lot on research and rarely get it wrong.

- Where artists go, commerce follows – often attracted by what the pioneers have done with the neighbourhood. Look out for the arty crowd and tag along.

- Look for transport improvements. New rail links and roads will provide a boost to property values, and can open up whole new areas to commuters. Track existing rail services out from city centres and choose the next station on from the last area to be gentrified. For example, the trains that run south from London Bridge go through areas of south London that are on the verge of rocketing in value.

- Take a look at planning applications at local council offices, and find out about regeneration projects planned for city centres or rundown industrial areas.

- Red-light districts in city centres are being cleaned up rapidly, with the introduction of closed-circuit TV and other initiatives. With pressure for office space becoming so intense, central areas cannot be allowed to sink any more and once the area is cleaned up, prices often rocket. Property you buy there is likely to be pretty rundown, though, and may cost a substantial amount to renovate.

- Look out for skips. They often mean that rundown properties are being renovated by people who care. But they also show you aren't the first to spot the area's potential, so move fast.

WHAT TO BUY

Time for some serious thinking. What kind of property do you want and what can you reasonably afford? What you end up buying is likely to be a compromise between these two, so establish your criteria and prioritize them. Don't forget to include all family members in this decision. It's a time when rifts in taste can open up unexpectedly, so start discussions early.

- Do you want a new or an older house? If you're buying a very old one, make sure you have a proper survey before you buy (*see pages 75–7*), and look into the quarterly bills. Heating older properties can cost a bomb. Newly built homes demand premium prices and you may have to commit before they're fully built, but maintenance and decoration will be cheaper, and extras such as carpets, curtains and fitted kitchens are often included in the price.
- Do you want a terraced, semi-detached or detached house, or a flat? If you want a flat, do you want a purpose-built one or one in a conversion?
- How many bedrooms will you need?
- Is a garden critical to you?
- How much decorating or improvement do you wish to make to a property? A fixer-upper will be cheaper, but can you bear to live in a building site for six months?
- Do you want a leasehold or freehold property? (*see pages 68–9*).

THE BUYING PROCESS SIMPLIFIED

Below is a list of all the tasks that must be carried out during an average property purchase:

- Work out how much you can afford.
- Get a mortgage agreement in principle.
- Choose your home.
- Hire a solicitor/licensed conveyancer.
- Make an offer.
- Have a survey and valuation done.
- Do any necessary legal work.
- Arrange for life assurance or MPPI.

> TIP *Be flexible: what you eventually buy may well be nothing like your original spec. Try not to dismiss details estate agents will mail to you once you're on their mailing list, because, on closer reading, the property may well be in a good location or have a good sized garden or low running costs or be close to the school of your choice or have potential for conversion or renovation.*

- Finalize your mortgage.
- Exchange contracts.
- Organize your move.
- Finalize your contract details.
- Move in.

Put like this, it seems so simple, doesn't it? But no transaction is average and there's plenty that can go wrong, particularly if you're trying to organize the sale of your own property that depends on the sale of someone else's. *The Property Chain* was ample proof of that. Just make sure you action each stage as swiftly as possible, and at least you'll know you've done all you can to move the process along.

FIRST FIND YOUR PROPERTY

Considering all the above, let's suppose you've narrowed down the specification. How are you going to go about finding property for sale? This depends on how much time you have versus how much money, whether you're already local to the area you want to live in and how confident you are in your ability to strike out on your own. You could find a property to buy in a number of ways:

- Use estate agents.
- Look at the property pages in local newspapers.
- Contact house-building companies for details of new properties being built in the area.

- Contact home-search agents: businesses relocating premises and employees often use these. But a growing number of private buyers pay home-search agents to do the legwork, particularly if the buyer's moving a long way away. Most agents charge a retainer, but that would be deducted from the final purchase price.

GETTING THE BEST FROM ESTATE AGENTS

Estate agents see lots of people who drift in through their doors, pick up a few details and are never seen again. But to get the best from agents you'll need to register with them, let them know what you're looking for and give them plenty of feedback on the properties they suggest.

Estate agents' registration forms are frequently rigid, with boxes for houses or flats, or homes with or without gardens. It's a fine line between coming over as a serious buyer and ruling out homes that might be ideal, but don't tally with the details on your form. The agent wants to sell properties, so try to be flexible in your answers.

TIP *Talk through what you're looking for with agents and they'll tell you whether or not it's feasible. They should know the area well and could give you useful advice, but remember that they're acting for the vendors who have instructed them, and not for you.*

Prioritize the points on your list, and see where you're willing to compromise. A single house might struggle to meet all your needs, so go through the agents' property details and score them against your lists. If one point is vital to you, make sure the agent knows it, otherwise you'll waste a lot of time looking at property that doesn't meet your needs. Could you consider a modern home, which offers more rooms for the money? Could you live within cycling or driving distance from the station? Could you take on more renovation and updating work?

FIRST-TIME BUYERS

The trend of price rises in the UK property market makes it difficult for first-time buyers to finance buying a home. Over half the working population now cannot afford to buy a home, and first-time buyers can't even get a toe hold on the property ladder. But there are some pluses to being a first-time buyer – mortgage interest rates are low and, as you're not part of a chain, you're an attractive prospect to sellers.

Boost your Buying Power

If you can't afford to buy on your own, consider buying with a friend or sibling. Your joint income will increase your buying power (*see page 32*) and give you an increased choice of property and area. You can apply for a joint mortgage for up to four people, but most lenders will base how much they'll lend on the incomes of only two people. You also need to get a legal agreement drawn up by a solicitor to take account of how much each party is putting into the property, both in terms of contribution to the deposit and the mortgage payments – essential when you come to sell, or if one of you decides to move out.

New Horizons

As a first-time buyer, you may be better off buying a new-build property. Developers often include fitted kitchens and some appliances, new houses are cheap to maintain and you can do without a building survey. Many building companies offer generous deals to first-timers with financial inducements and extras like carpets or curtains included. Also, some local authorities have a starter home initiative that prioritizes local first-time buyers, and will only grant planning permission to developers who factor in a certain amount of social housing in their developments. Talk to your local authority.

WHAT TO LOOK FOR AND ASK WHEN VIEWING

Viewing can be exhausting and dispiriting. A property looks marvellous on the details, but the photograph conveniently misses off the sewage farm next door. Stick with it, because you'll find your gem when you've almost given up hope.

- See as many houses as possible: this gives you a flavour of what's on the market.
- Take someone with you: they may spot something you miss.
- Take a notebook to record your thoughts.
- Take your time looking round a property: don't let yourself be rushed by the owner or agent.
- Don't be put off by furnishings or decor which are shabby or not to your taste. These things can be changed easily and cheaply. Focus instead on the condition of the property, the aspect, how light it is and the size and layout of the rooms.
- Check out the surrounding area and nearby amenities.
- Return for a second or third look – especially at different times of the day. If you visit in the morning, the neighbours may be at work. Visit in the evenings and you might hear them throwing all-night parties. Drive past at rush hour and at weekends to get a clear picture of what it's really like.
- Think about how it will be at other times of year. Without leaves on the trees, for example, what will the view be like? Will you be over-looked?

It's important to find out as much as you can about the property – after all, it's the biggest investment you'll make in your life. You're entitled to ask questions of the vendor, so make the most of the opportunity:

- Why are they selling the property?
- How long has it been on the market?

- How long have they lived there?
- How much are the services and running costs?
- What is the neighbourhood like (especially your direct neighbours)?
- Are they in a chain?
- What's included in the sale (e.g. cooker, curtains, carpets)?

It's in their interest to sell you the property, so you may get a rosier picture from them than is entirely the case however, they are obliged by law to be truthful.

If you see a property you like, inform your solicitor or the agent right away and ask to be informed of any other offers being made or a closing date for sealed bids or offers that have been. Don't get too attached to a property until you know it's definitely yours at exchange of contracts. This helps you keep an open mind on other places you look at and will help protect you from disappointment.

BUYING AT AUCTION

Properties are sold at auction if they've been repossessed by mortgage lenders, housing associations or councils, need large-scale work that will deter buyers going through conventional estate agents, have a short time to run on the lease, or are unusual and difficult to price, will attract buyers from a wide area.

Most auctions take place in hotels and are advertised in local newspapers by participating estate agents and valuers. Contact them for a catalogue of properties going under the hammer at the next auction (often this is done via a premium rate telephone line). The catalogue will contain photos of the properties, details of tenure – mostly 'full vacant possession', meaning there's no chain – and guide prices, which are normally the minimum the vendors will accept.

If you like the look of a property, visit it well before sale day. Auctioneers will arrange group viewings for potential buyers or ask local estate agents to do individual viewings. Some vendors and their estate agents have 'pre-sale surveys' done and will give you details. These are often reliable but most mortgage lenders want an independent survey, so you may have to pay between £200 and £500 for this, which is non-returnable if you fail to buy.

Once you've decided that the property is for you, get it valued by your lender (or an independent valuer if you're a cash buyer), and get your mortgage offer in place. You'll have to get your skates on as you'll probably have only two weeks in which to organize this. At the same time do your searches on the property. Check with the solicitors for the vendor. The name and address will be given in the auction catalogue. Ask for a copy of the searches, and check that all is well (no motorways going through the property in five years' time, proper access rights, no footpaths across your back yard, all planning consents in order etc.). You'll find that a complete vendors' pack will be available from the solicitors, and they should have copies of searches available. Whether or not you trust them is up to you, and you're advised to make your own arrangements.

> TIP *The secret of successful buying at auction is to decide the ceiling price you'll pay before the bidding starts. If you think you might be tempted to overbid in all the excitement, get a friend or your solicitor to bid on your behalf.*

Before the auction day, ensure you have access to funds that would cover the price you'd be prepared to pay – research shows this is typically the guide price plus 15 per cent to be safe, or even more. Also factor in solicitors' fees, moving costs and repair work. You must pay 10 per cent of the property's sale price immediately if your bid is successful (*see below*).

At auction each property is called a 'lot'. When the lot you're interested in comes up, the auctioneer will confirm the address and details before asking for bids. The bids usually rise in £5,000 increments until they approach the guide price, when bids will rise in £2,000 or £1,000 sums.

If you're successful, you'll have to sign the memorandum of sale and pay the 10 per cent deposit on the spot. The balance has to be paid within 28 days and, if you fail to do this, the consequences can be dire – you could lose your deposit and run the risk of being sued by the vendor.

Another thing to consider is that you're responsible for insuring the building as soon as the sale is agreed. To be on the safe side, take out an insurance policy to commence on the date of the auction. You can always cancel it if your bid is not the successful one. Remember – once the hammer has come down, neither the buyer nor vendor can withdraw.

If and when home information packs (HIPs) come into use (*see Chapter 4*), experts predict that property auctions will become far more popular, as the information provided will take a lot of the risk, expense and uncertainty out of entering into property auctions. The packs will oblige the vendor to provide surveyors' reports and local authority searches. Having access to this kind of information before bidding will make life far easier for bidders, who currently pay for all the information themselves before they even enter the bidding.

> TIP *About 15 per cent of properties in catalogues are sold before the auction because a keen buyer has made a deal with the seller. If you see a property you like in the catalogue, try making an advance bid through the auction house. You have nothing to lose.*

PROBATE AND MORTGAGE DEFAULT SALES

Another route to finding a home to buy is to look for properties that form part of the estate of a deceased person (probate sale), or properties that have been repossessed by the lender.

- In *probate sales* there won't be a chain – the previous owner will have moved on to a far better place – and the property will most likely be empty. The executors of the deceased person's will should have briefed an estate agent and solicitor in the normal way, so from your point of view the sale will proceed as normal. Executors may be anxious to get rid of the property as soon as they can and this can mean a lower price, but not necessarily. You won't be able to ask the vendor the kinds of questions you might normally want to, and may have to rely on information from the agent.

- In a *repossession sale* the owners of a property will have defaulted on repayments, the lender will have repossessed the property and has the right to transfer absolute ownership, so you'll be buying from the lender. Many repossessed properties end up being sold at auction, but even when they're sold through an agent it will be difficult to gather information about the practicalities of living in the property – those questions you would have asked the vendor. A survey becomes even more essential under these conditions, as you'll have no information on what work the previous owners had done. If you do buy a repossessed property, make sure you change the door and window locks as soon as you move in. The previous owners may be disgruntled and still have possession of the keys.

FREEHOLD OR LEASEHOLD?

All properties in England and Wales are either owned freehold or leasehold and the sales details of the property will specify this. Most flats are leasehold, most houses are freehold.

Freehold means that you have full tenure or ownership of the property and full responsibility for the maintenance and repairs of the property. *Leasehold* means that the land on which the property is built is not part of the sale. You own the property for as long as is specified in the lease, and you're granted the right to live there by the freeholder who owns the land. At the end of the lease, which is basically a very long-term rental agreement, the property again becomes the possession of the freeholder. Many leases are originally granted for up to 999 years, but existing leases on properties are usually shorter. Leases that are shorter than 60 years are not a good buy and you'll have trouble getting a mortgage for a property of this type. Lenders normally want at least 20 years left on the lease after the end of the mortgage term (*see page 32*).

You must pay a ground rent to the owner of the land (the freeholder), usually a small amount each year. Your solicitor should check that the seller is up to date with ground rent payments before you sign the contract. Your responsibilities as a leaseholder are to keep your property in good order, to pay (on time) a share of the costs of maintaining and running the building, to behave in a neighbourly manner and not to do certain things without the freeholders' consent – for example make alterations or sublet.

The lease will normally require the *freeholder* to take out adequate insurance for the building and the common parts, and will give him or her the right to recover the cost of the premium through the service charges, but this policy will not normally cover contents of the properties of individual leaseholders.

A lease is a contract between you and the freeholder setting out each side's rights and duties. With a well-written lease and a properly managed building, a leasehold property should provide a perfectly good home and a secure investment. Ask your solicitor to explain the lease in detail.

MAKING AN OFFER

Making the offer simply involves telling the estate agent or seller that you would like to buy the property at a particular price, *subject to survey and/or contract* (*see page 71*). You can make an offer before you have a mortgage offer or survey in place, but you're more likely to be taken seriously if they are. It's a good idea to get a written agreement in principle from a mortgage lender to show the vendor you'll have enough money, and the process will be able to take place quickly once you've both agreed on the sale.

Before you make the offer, you should establish exactly what's included in the sale and what's not. For example, plumbing and heating installations and electrical and gas fixtures are usually included automatically. However, furniture, lights, curtains and carpets are not, unless specified.

How much you offer is up to you and may depend on how busy the market is. In a slow market, you may be able to get away with a low offer – it's human nature to try to strike a deal. But if the housing market is booming it will need to be a bit closer to the asking price, and you may even end up paying more if there are rival bidders.

In the third *Chain* programme, David and Jo Jones were at the top of their chain and had not yet found a property to buy. To prevent the process falling apart, they initially decided that they would move into rented accommodation and look for the ideal house to buy once the dust had settled and their new gallery business was running smoothly. But during the long delays caused by problems lower down the chain, they found a vacant property to buy, and had their offer accepted. At the bottom of the chain, however, Sue and Steve Aldrich did end up moving into temporary accommodation, having sold their property already. If the parties at the bottom and top of the chain are prepared to be adaptable in this way, it takes the pressure off the intervening transactions and the chain is far less likely to break down.

Your own position will also affect the sale negotiations. A couple of factors could be to your advantage:

- If you're not in a chain, the seller can be more certain that everything will be completed on time and may favour your bid over someone else's.
- First-time buyers, people who've already sold or exchanged contracts on their own property and people who've nothing to sell all have an advantage.

What happens next depends on whether or not your offer is accepted.

OFFER REJECTED

You can put in a higher offer, but it's not wise to get involved in a bidding war – you don't want to end up offering a lot more than the house is worth. There's no limit on the number of times you can make offers on a property.

OFFER ACCEPTED

If your offer for the property is accepted, the offer must be made formally, in writing, and it should state the terms and conditions. Ensure that the agent and vendor understand the terms of your offer.

Your offer must be 'subject to contract and to survey'. This means that you're not legally bound to proceed until a survey has been satisfactorily completed and signed contracts have been exchanged. This is very important, and gives you the opportunity to specify what fixtures and fittings you want to be included, and any work on the property you want undertaken before the sale has gone through. It also gives you the opportunity to pull out of the purchase or renegotiate the price if the survey and local searches are unfavourable. You can put down a holding deposit at this stage as an act of goodwill, and begin the buying process.

If you find your ideal home and it seems to be priced correctly, consider offering the full asking price, particularly if the market is rising and you want to move quickly. It means you'll be taken seriously, there won't be any time wasted and it will lessen the possibility of another party stepping in. Remember not to offer more than you can really afford!

Be realistic with your offer, but it isn't legally binding at this stage – you can always negotiate a lower price later on if a survey reveals there's work that needs doing to the property.

SEALED BIDS

When a property is very popular, and an offer race is about to ensue, the vendor may decide to (or be advised to) go to 'sealed bids'. This means that interested buyers quite literally place their best offer in a sealed envelope, and on an agreed date they're opened. The purchaser who has made the highest bid will gain the property. There are two types of sealed bid:

- Formal tender: Once the bid is accepted, the sale is binding (like at auction) and there's no leeway to change your mind, so the offer cannot be subject to conditions, and you'll have to have carried out all the necessary searches and surveys.
- Informal tender: The bid is subject to survey and contract, and until contracts are exchanged either party can pull out.

HOLDING DEPOSITS

Once the owners have accepted your offer, you may be asked to pay a small deposit to the estate agent. This is not usually more than £500. It's meant to show that you're serious about going ahead with the purchase. It's repayable if the sale does not go ahead, but is some sort of security.

If you fear being outbid, suggest paying a pre-contract deposit (*see below*), which entitles you to buy the house at the price agreed, so long as contracts are exchanged within a specified number of weeks.

GAZUMPING

This is the situation all buyers fear, when an offer is accepted by a vendor, but rejected later in favour of a larger offer from someone else. The first buyer is left in the lurch, and either has to offer a higher price or accept the loss of that property and look elsewhere. This practice tends to occur in a market when house prices are rising and there are more buyers around than sellers. Legislation has outlawed the practice in Scotland, but in England and Wales it certainly does happen and is a subject of real angst – as *The Property Chain* proved only too clearly.

The problem is that until contracts of sale have been exchanged, the sale agreement is not legally binding. Once your offer has been accepted, either you or the vendor can pull out at any time until the exchange of contracts. Unfortunately, agents are legally obliged to inform vendors of all offers made on their property, even after one offer has been accepted. However, during this period between the acceptance of your offer and exchange, you as the buyer will be spending a considerable amount of money on surveys, solicitor's fees and arrangement of your mortgage. If the sale falls through because someone has stepped in ahead of you, you do not get any of this money back, and will have to pay out all over again for the next property you make an offer on. If you're part of a chain of sales, you could even be affected by someone else being gazumped and lose your sale as a consequence.

Ways to avoid the gazumping trap:

- Choose a vendor whose agent has a policy on gazumping, if at all possible. Some agents insist that the vendor signs an agreement to turn down any offers after one has been accepted.
- Keep in regular contact with the vendor's agent, tell them when you've completed the survey and received a formal mortgage offer. This way they can be sure that the sale is progressing and are less likely to be tempted to consider any other offers.
- Make a pre-contract deposit agreement. This involves both parties paying a deposit of 1·5 per cent of the agreed purchase price to a stakeholder, and signing an agreement saying that contracts will be exchanged within four weeks. If one side withdraws from the sale, the other party receives both deposits. If you're a gazumped buyer, you therefore get some compensation. This is not a watertight agreement, as either party can pull out if they are willing to lose the deposit, but this definitely reduces the risk.
- Ask that the property be taken off the market once your offer has been accepted. Check that the board outside the house has a 'sold' sign on it, and contact the agent if it does not. To make sure the property really is off the market, get a friend to make enquiries at the estate agent's! If the agent is still prepared to invite offers, drop a note through the vendor's door asking them to contact you direct, as the estate agent's actions may be jeopardizing the sale.

If you're gazumped, emphasize to the agent and vendor how keen you are on the property. If the buyer whose higher offer they've accepted pulls out, they may contact you to ask if you're still interested. But resist the temptation to go back with a higher offer. Not only do you risk offering too much for the property: are you really prepared to trust the vendors again?

CONTRACT RACES

The vendor may accept more than one offer and instruct their solicitor to send draft contracts to more than one potential buyer. The solicitor must inform all potential buyers that more than one contract has been sent out and that the first contract returned, signed and ready for exchange, will get the house. This is known as a contract race and is quite legal. There's nothing you as the buyer can do except withdraw if you do not want to incur the necessary costs in getting the contract completed quickly.

BASIC VALUATION

Gazumping is a worst-case scenario. Let's assume your offer has been accepted and the purchase process is going through as normal. Before confirming the mortgage, your lender needs to know whether the property is actually worth the amount of money you've agreed to pay out for it. This is known as the 'basic valuation', and it will be done by a valuation surveyor acting for your mortgage firm, although you pay for it. Though often referred to as a 'survey', it's really too superficial to merit this title and is no substitute for a homebuyer's report or buildings survey. The valuation compares the property with similar ones, taking factors such as age, condition and location into account, and will point out any very obvious major faults that could affect the property's value but will dig no deeper.

If the property is valued at a price lower than the agreed purchase price, then your mortgage offer may be withdrawn. If the valuation is lower because of structural problems, the mortgage offer may be conditional on specified work being carried out first. If it does reveal that the property is worth less than the price you've agreed to pay for it, you may be able to renegotiate the price, but first double-check with the surveyor how the value was reached and that he or she is certain you're paying too much. The basic valuation takes about half an hour, and costs between around £100 to £300, depending on the value of the house. Some mortgage lenders waive the fee for the basic valuation as part of a package to attract your custom.

ARRANGING A SURVEY

Perhaps because of the expense, some people don't bother to arrange a more detailed structural/buildings survey, basing their decision to buy on the lender's valuation report. But given the investment property purchase represents, it seems foolhardy to enter into it without knowing in detail the condition of the property. A full survey might seem to cost a lot at the time, but the prospect of paying out thousands of pounds later for major repairs of faults you overlooked would probably change your perspective. If the survey uncovered major defects, you might even think again about your purchase, or you could be in a position to renegotiate the price.

You can choose between two levels of survey over and above the lender's valuation report: the homebuyer's report and the buildings survey (previously known as the full structural survey). Which you choose to have will depend on the type of property you're buying.

- *Intermediate* or '*homebuyer's report*': this gives a report on the condition of the parts of the property easy to see and to get at, and may recommend further tests or investigations – for example a specialist check for woodworm. This is particularly suitable for properties less than 50 to 75 years old, conventionally constructed, and in generally sound condition. Any issues to be discussed with your solicitor, such as parking spaces or rights of way, should be noted in the report. An estimation of the value of the property is also included. The small print will specify exactly what will be examined, so do check this carefully. You may be able to economize by asking your mortgage lender to arrange for the surveyor doing the basic valuation to carry out a homebuyer's report at the same time – so long as he or she is suitably qualified. However, if you prefer, you can find your own surveyor.

- *Buildings survey (formerly known as a structural survey)*: this is the most comprehensive – and the most costly – type of survey. It's suitable for any building, but is especially recommended for older buildings (75 years upwards), those constructed from unconventional materials such as timber or thatch, properties that have had lots of alterations or extensions or that you intend to alter or renovate.

  The surveyor will check the property thoroughly, looking at everything visible or easily accessible to examine the soundness of the structure, its general condition and all major or minor faults. More specialist surveys can also be carried out on aspects such as foundations, damp-proofing, drains or tree roots, either by a specialist within the firm of surveyors or by an independent specialist surveyor.

  The report you receive will be extremely thorough and very long as surveyors are legally obliged to inform you of all the findings of the survey. Don't necessarily be put off if it seems that endless defects are listed – every property has some defects and surveyors are obliged to detail every fault they find. One very experienced surveyor reckons that in 30 years in the business he has never seen a property with a 100 per cent perfect survey. The last paragraph of the report will generally contain a summary of the surveyor's findings so, although you should read the whole thing eventually, you could cut to that first. If the report is very negative and you do not have ample funds for renovation, think twice before proceeding.

HOW DO I FIND A SURVEYOR?

It's not hard to find a surveyor company. Asking for recommendations from your lender, solicitor or estate agent is probably the easiest way of finding a reliable surveyor, or you could contact one of the professional trade associations for details of surveyors in your area. Shop around and get plenty of quotes, as surveys are expensive and prices can vary. The amount you pay normally depends on the value of the property you're buying. It's possible that you may have to pay more than once for a survey if a sale falls through and you decide not to buy the property on the basis of the survey results and look elsewhere.

You're advised to check up on the surveyor's credentials if you're unsure whether he or she's a qualified professional. All surveyors should be members of the Royal Institution of Chartered Surveyors (*see below*).

CONVEYANCING

As soon as your offer has been accepted, let your solicitor or licensed conveyancer (*see Chapter 4*) know so they can get things moving. A great deal of the housebuying process seems to involve solicitors waiting for documents to arrive from other solicitors. It isn't being rude or pushy to keep in regular contact so that you know how far your house purchase has progressed, and it might stop your papers slipping further down the list of your solicitor's priorities.

The conveyancing process involves searches (*see page 79*). These are a variety of local checks that research whether there are any factors which could adversely affect your property – industrial development or road building plans for example. They'll also reveal any environmental problems, such as previous mining in the area or landfill sites. If you want to jump the queue for a local search, you can pay extra for a personal search. This should reduce the search time from a fortnight to a couple of days.

Before making a choice as to who will do the conveyancing, you're advised to find out the probable costs of the conveyancing. It's important to contact more than one solicitor or licensed conveyancer as there's no set scale of fees for conveyancing. You should:

- check whether the figure quoted is a fixed fee or depends on how much work is involved;
- check that the figure includes stamp duty, search fees, land registration fees, expenses and value added tax (VAT) and get a breakdown of these costs;
- find out what charges, if any, will be made if the sale falls through before contracts are exchanged.

FIRST STAGE: BEFORE EXCHANGE OF CONTRACTS

Once the vendors have accepted your offer, you exchange solicitors' details with them. Your solicitor will then contact the vendor's solicitor and receive the draft contract. The draft contract contains details of prices, the two parties involved, other information about the transaction such as deposits, and information from

REGISTERED AND UNREGISTERED PROPERTY

In England and Wales property can be either 'registered' or 'unregistered'. If property is registered, the title to the property has been registered at the Land Registry and is guaranteed by the state. The owner has a 'land certificate' instead of the usual title deeds. Buying registered property is more straightforward than buying unregistered property. If property is unregistered (this can happen if a property has not changed hands for several years), ownership is not guaranteed by the state. The title can be proved only by a copy of the title deeds, and your solicitor will check back the property's documentation over at least 15 years to certify it. With unregistered property, disputes over title are not uncommon. When you buy unregistered property, it must now be registered for the first time with the Land Registry. This will take some time, so the buying process will take longer than if you're buying registered property. Your solicitor's/conveyancer's fees will probably also be higher.

the vendor's title deeds. A property information form may also be included if the solicitors are operating the TransAction Protocol (*see Chapter 4*). Your solicitor will check the details of the draft contract and negotiate it with the vendor's solicitor. It's a good idea to check through the draft contract yourself in case anything has been missed out, such as any agreements you may have made with the vendor, so ask your solicitor for a copy if you've not been sent one.

It's the solicitor's or conveyancer's job to make all the necessary enquiries to ensure that there's no reason why you might want to change your mind about buying the property. The process, as explained by www.home.co.uk, is as follows:

Local Authority Searches

Enquiries are sent to the local authority to establish whether there are any plans for a major road to be built nearby, or whether there are any problems with the property that you would need to rectify. Your solicitor should also get checks done on nearby buildings or empty land: do they have planning permission for more buildings or development?

Enquiries to the Vendor's Solicitor

These are known as the 'preliminary enquiries'. Your solicitor will send a standard set of enquiries to the vendor's solicitor, which will include:

- whether the vendor is actually entitled to sell the property;
- ongoing disputes relating to the property;
- boundaries and who has responsibility for the maintenance of hedges and fences;
- planning constraints and whether any additions or alterations that have been made to the property have met local planning requirements and that building regulation consent was received;
- rights of way and shared rights of access with a neighbour such as a garden or driveway;

- restrictive covenants that might affect what you can do with the property;
- guarantees or insurance policies;
- warranties on a new build and building regulation compliance;
- the property's utilities (gas, water, electricity), and whether they reach it via a neighbour's property or are shared with a neighbour;
- a list of contents included in the sale;
- whether it's being sold freehold or leasehold (in which case the freeholder has to be informed of the sale).

Additional searches may be carried out if necessary, for example commons searches, coal mining searches and so on.

SECOND STAGE: EXCHANGE OF CONTRACTS

Once you and your solicitor are satisfied that everything is in order, the contracts can be exchanged. You sign a copy of the contract, which is passed to the vendor, and the vendor signs a copy of the same contract you receive. Once contracts have been exchanged (normally by the two solicitors) both parties are legally bound to follow through with the transaction. You can no longer change your mind – if you pull out it's likely you'll lose your deposit, and you could be sued for breach of contract. However, you're now free of the worry of being gazumped.

At this point you hand over a non-refundable deposit, usually 10 per cent of the purchase price, to be kept as security for the vendor in case the buyer pulls out. This will be provided by your lender, unless you're a cash buyer, in which case you'll have to ensure the funds are available at time of exchange. The solicitor or licensed conveyancer keeps this until completion, and then passes it on to the vendor along with any interest earned. If you do not have the money for the deposit at hand immediately, you can arrange for a temporary loan.

Before exchanging contracts, check that:

- you've received and are satisfied with the survey report;
- you've received your formal mortgage offer, and are happy with it;
- the deposit sum has been agreed and you have the money available;
- you've arranged life and property insurance and they're set to be in place on completion (buildings insurance must be arranged to commence from exchange of contracts if your solicitor is not using the TransAction Protocol);
- the completion date has been agreed with all parties;
- the terms of the contract have been checked and finalized by all involved.

Once contracts have been exchanged, your solicitor prepares the draft transfer document (if the land is not registered it will require a special kind of transfer or 'conveyance'). This document transfers title to the land from the vendor to the buyer. Once both parties have agreed on the draft, it's signed by the buyer and the vendor. Your solicitor will also deal with the finalization and signing of documentation relating to your mortgage, and will arrange for the money to be available on completion of the sale.

- Final searches and enquiries will be undertaken.
- Land registry checks are carried out by your solicitor, to make sure that nothing is registered against the seller (or at the land charges registry if the property is not registered).
- Problems such as undisclosed mortgages or disputes could be uncovered at this stage.

You will have to deal with various matters in the run-up to completion. There will be some documents to sign and payments to make: you must pay Land Registry fees and stamp duty. Before completion you need to make sure that all the terms of the contract have been fulfilled, such as any repairs, and start arranging your move (*see Chapter 5*).

REAL-LIFE ACCOUNT

June and Douglas Davis were moving out of London to the country. Douglas was winding down his career in the City and starting to think about retirement, and they had found a large period house in a quiet village.

'The circumstances of the sale were slightly peculiar,' recalls Douglas. 'The couple were getting divorced and the house had to be sold so they could separate their assets, but they had been running the place as a sort of commune and there were extra bodies all over the place. They had even converted the garage – quite improperly – to provide a living space for one of their mates and he was still living there. I suspect the situation was a bit offputting to some potential buyers but we were undaunted. To raise money from the contents, they arranged an auction to take place at the house between exchange and completion. I can't say we were terribly thrilled by the idea of hordes of total strangers tramping through what was soon to be our home, but the agents promised they would clean up the mess, and we felt sorry for the couple, so we agreed and even attended the sale, although we didn't buy anything.

'Now, in the garden was a lovely antique sundial, set into the ground. It was most unusual and we had specifically asked for it to be included in the fixtures and fittings. I'm sure you can guess what happened. Between the time of the auction sale and the time we moved in, someone went to great trouble to prise it up. We were livid, but the auctioneers claimed it had still been there when they left, and the vendors had disappeared as had the disgruntled bloke in the garage. We claimed on insurance, of course, but it was a unique piece and I really felt annoyed. I'd felt uncomfortable about all those people from the auction poking around the house and I'm convinced someone had come in to case the joint. I wish now I'd never agreed to it. We changed all the locks straight away and had a new alarm system installed, just in case.'

THIRD STAGE: COMPLETION

On the day of completion you receive the keys and the vendor is obliged to move out. You also have to pay the balance of the price on the house (the agreed price minus the deposit you've already paid), usually through your solicitor or conveyancer. The vendor's title deeds are now handed over to you, and arrangements are made for any outstanding mortgages on the property to be paid off. After completion the solicitor still has various details to tie up. He or she will do as follows:

- Where relevant, inform your mortgage lender, life insurance company and the freeholder that the sale has been completed.
- Register the transfer of ownership at the Land Registry. They will then send the deeds to you (if you're a cash buyer) or your mortgage lender, who will keep them until you either sell the property or pay off your mortgage. If you're a cash buyer, you're advised to leave the deeds in the safe hands of your solicitor.
- Pay the stamp duty.
- Send you a statement of completion, including a summary of the financial transactions. If you've not already paid their fees, they'll ask for these now.

HOUSEHOLD INSURANCE: BUILDINGS AND CONTENTS

Make sure you've arranged for buildings insurance cover on your new home from the time of the exchange of contracts (*see Chapter 2*) or from the day you move in if your solicitor is using the TransAction Protocol (*see Chapter 4*).

If you're not a first-time buyer, arrange for the insurance on your previous property to continue right up until the day you move out, in case the deal falls through. If your home is part of a larger building, such as a block of flats, your buildings insurance may be bought in a joint policy by everyone in the building, so you'll only need contents insurance. Or if it's a leasehold, the freeholder may have insurance. Check up on these.

Contents insurance insures all your possessions inside your home. You may be surprised how much your possessions are worth – even if you're not a big spender, they can

TIP *Often contents insurance is set up to a general limit; so if you need extra cover for more valuable items, you'll need to specify them.*

TIP *If you already have contents insurance on your previous home, make sure the cover is transferred from your previous home to your new one on the day you move in.*

be worth tens of thousands of pounds. 'Contents' refers to everything from furniture and carpets to jewellery, cameras and clothes.

To work out how much cover you need, make a list of everything in each room and how much it's worth or would cost to replace. Remember to include furnishings, carpets and other fittings, and clothes and food, as well as more obvious items like TVs and jewellery. Insurance for items you take outside your home, such as bicycles, musical instruments, sports equipment and so on, may also be included in your contents insurance.

You can reduce the cost of your insurance premium by agreeing to paying a larger excess on any claim, on both buildings and contents policies. This is where you pay the first part of any claim; for example, if your TV is stolen and you've agreed to a £100 excess, you receive the price of a new TV minus £100.

YOUR WILL

When you buy a home for the first time, you acquire a large asset. If you do not already have one, it's a good idea at this point to draw up a will to specify who will receive what parts of your estate (what you own less what you owe) when you die. There would be enormous complications if you were to die intestate (without a will), and solicitors will often draft a will at a very competitive rate to encourage people to do so. (*For more on property tax, see Appendix 4.*)

USEFUL CONTACTS

Association of British Insurers
51–55 Gresham Street
London EC2V 7HQ
Tel.: 020 7600 3333
Web: www.abi.org.uk

Building Societies Association (BSA)
3 Savile Row
London W1Z 1AF
Tel.: 020 7437 0655
Web: www.bsa.org.uk

Incorporated Society of Valuers and Auctioneers
3 Cadogan Gate
London SW1X OAS
Tel.: 020 7235 2282

The Law Society
113 Chancery Lane
London WC2A 1PL
Tel.: 020 7242 1222
Web: www.lawsociety.org.uk

The Law Society of Scotland
26 Drumsheugh Gardens
Edinburgh EH3 7YR
Tel.: 0131 226 7411
Web: www.lawscot.org.uk

National Association of Estate Agents
(NAEA)
Arbon House
21 Jury Street
Warwick CV34 4EH
Tel.: 01926 410 785
Web: www.naea.co.uk

Royal Institution of Chartered Surveyors
12 Great George Street
London SW1P 3AD
Tel.: 020 7222 7000
Web: www.rics.org

Property web sites:
www.assertahome.com
www.findaproperty.co.uk
www.fish4homes.co.uk
www.home.co.uk
www.upmystreet.com

The Leasehold Advisory Service (LEASE)
(free advice and guidance to leaseholders and landlords on all aspects of leasehold law)
70–74 City Road
London ECIY 2BJ
Tel.: 020 7490 9580
Web: www.lease-advice.org

The Law Society
113 Chancery Lane
London WC2A 1PL
Tel.: 020 7242 1222

The Council for Licensed Conveyancers
16 Glebe Road
Chelmsford CM1 1QG
Tel.: 01245 349599

Property site with searchable database and excellent background information:
www.home.co.uk

Searchable database of UK properties:
www.propertyfinder.co.uk

Searchable database of new homes for sale, covering all of UK. A wide range of property developers represented:
www.smartnewhomes.com

SELLING YOUR PROPERTY

So you've decided to sell your home? You'll have a lot of decisions to make in the next few months, so the earlier you start with your planning, the better. And preparing your home before you allow the first estate agent across the threshold will help make sure you maximize the valuation and, one hopes, the price your buyer will eventually pay.

YOUR TIMESCALE

If your move is not urgent, you could plan to make some of the big improvements that will add value to your home. Redecorating your living room, kitchen or bathroom could make your home more desirable and boost its value. Adding central heating, insulation (but not double glazing), an en suite bathroom or an appropriate conservatory can repay your investment when it comes to resale. But all of these take time, planning and money. See Chapter 9 for the most cost-effective additions; then go through your home and make a list of the things you have the time – and funds – to improve.

Before investing a large amount of money doing up a property to sell, find out its maximum potential value. It's pointless spending £20,000 improving your home if you'll add only £10,000 to its sale price. Look in local property papers and estate agents to find out the asking price for similar properties on your street.

If your deadline for moving is closer, the best you can do is a partial fix – it doesn't even have to cost that much – get that dripping tap fixed, redo the grubby grouting on bathroom tiles, have the carpets cleaned, smarten up the garden or repaint the woodwork. Do everything you can to make the first impression on a potential purchaser truly impressive (*see pages 100–2*).

WHEN TO SELL

Spring and autumn are usually considered to be the best times of year to sell, with Christmas and the summer holidays being the quietest months. You may not have the luxury of choosing when you put your home on the market, but the advantage of selling at a quieter period is that you should have more attention from your agent. If you have to sell quickly at a quiet time of year, think about placing your property with more than one agent (*see below*). Although you'll pay more in fees, you'll reach a wider market at a difficult time of year.

HOW LONG DOES IT TAKE ?

According to Government research, it takes vendors an average of eight weeks between putting their property on the market and agreeing terms with a buyer. The only certain thing is that however long it takes, it will feel much longer.

HOW MUCH DOES IT COST TO SELL?

Are you looking forward to all that lovely money you're going to make on this sale? Slow down. The process of selling itself is going to eat into your profit, so try to work out how much the selling (and moving) is going to cost. That way you'll know how much you have available to buy your next property.

- Solicitors' (or licensed conveyancers') fees are hard to predict accurately, because they'll be based partly on the value of the house, partly on how complicated the transaction is, how long it takes, how many documents have to be processed, whether or not the land has been registered (*see Chapter 3*) and how complex the conveyancing is. The

Law Society recommends that fees should be 'fair and reasonable', but that still allows for plenty of leeway. Ask for several quotes, and ask friends for recommendations of conveyancing solicitors who've handled property transactions for them. You might be able to get a written quotation, which will help you plan your costs. As a rough guide, allow up to 1 per cent of the selling price.

TIP *In a hurry? Appoint a solicitor when you first put your house on the market and not once you have an offer. This will help him or her prepare documents and ensure that your side of the transaction can move forward without delay.*

- Estate agents' commission will vary according to the deal you've struck with them, but it could be as much as 3 per cent of the price, plus VAT.

- Mortgage redemption charges can apply if you repay your mortgage early. You're likely to be charged administration fees, and possibly a sum of interest or a percentage of the outstanding mortgage (*see Chapter 2*).

- If home information packs (*see page 106*) are introduced in line with Government plans, the vendor will also have to pay around £600 to assemble the documents the pack will contain.

On top of all that will be the expense involved in finding and buying a new property (*see Chapter 3*) and removal expenses (*see Chapter 5*).

USING AND CHOOSING AN ESTATE AGENT

Most people who sell their homes use the services of an estate agent. You don't have to and, in many ways, because of the ready availability of information on the Internet, it's easier now to sell a home privately (*see page 94*). Estate agents take a percentage of the selling price of your home as their fee, typically between 1·5 per cent and 3 per cent, plus VAT, and that can amount to an awful lot of money. (Although, of course, if your home doesn't sell, they get nothing.) So you want to be sure that the agent is working hard to earn that fee.

This is what their service should include:

- establishing your sale price;
- preparing accurate details of sale;
- advertising your home in their premises, local papers/magazines and on web sites;
- passing details of your home to potential buyers;
- puttting up a 'For Sale' sign;
- arranging viewing appointments for you;
- conducting viewings if you're unavailable or don't want to do them;
- following up buyers to obtain 'feedback';
- collating relevant documentation supplied by you;
- negotiating the sale on your behalf;
- receiving and forwarding offers;
- selling mortgages, insurance, legal or other services;
- holding pre-contract deposits (sometimes paid by the buyer);
- communicating with your solicitor/conveyancer;
- keeping tabs on the progress of exchange of contracts;
- advising on the status of chains;
- holding the house keys on completion date;

Which is the best agent for you?

- Look out for 'For Sale' boards in your area, particularly on properties similar to yours, and make a note of the agents, and note how long it takes for 'sold' signs to appear.
- Ask around for recommendations from friends and acquaintances, or be pushy and ask vendors of the houses you've noted how the agent is working for them.
- Take a look at their display ads in newspapers and on the Internet. How do they look to you?
- Call into the agents and pretend to be looking for a property like yours. How are you greeted and treated?
- Make sure any agent you speak to is qualified. Contact the National Association of Estate Agents, who can provide you with a list of registered agents near you.

VALUATION

Ideally, you should ask three or four agents to visit your home to provide a valuation. Make sure your house is turned out as smartly as possible for this visit, with all repairs done, decorating finished, tidy, uncluttered and clean throughout. First impressions count. Although agents are visiting only speculatively at this stage, they should take their time and look around both inside and outside, and should show that they know and understand the area. Some agents are experienced valuers, and use the code for valuation devised by the Royal Institute for Chartered Surveyors, which states that sales prices should be based on:

- the age, type, accommodation, fixtures and features of the property;
- the construction and general state of repair;
- the siting and the amenities of the locality;
- the tenure, tenancies, service charges or other liabilities.

Agents will also factor in local conditions that might affect the price, such as:

- the prices of similar homes in your area;
- the popularity of your area;
- any improvements, such as extensions, new decor, fitted bathrooms and kitchens;
- the general market demand from buyers.

Obviously, you want the best price you can get for your property, particularly if you're buying another home based on the proceeds, so don't admit to wanting a quick sale. On the other hand, if your property is overpriced, it's likely to stay on the market for a long time while similar properties, more realistically priced, are changing hands all around. Even if you're tempted to push for a higher valuation, be guided by their expertise.

Although the criteria for valuation sound quite cut and dried, many people believe that even experienced valuers' judgements are swayed by first impressions, so take care over the way you present your home, taking as much trouble for the estate agent's visit as you would for prospective buyers (*see pages 100–2*).

SOLE OR JOINT AGENCY?

Most estate agents prefer to be the only ones marketing your home, so they'll encourage you to sign a *sole agency agreement*, which usually means you're contracted to use just them for around six to eight weeks, during which time they'll, you hope, successfully sell your home. This is the cheapest option for the vendor, because you'll be paying the agent the lowest percentage of the selling price as commission.

Another, but costlier, option is a *joint agency agreement*, which means two estate agents will market your home and split the commission, whichever of them sells it. You pay a higher percentage, but the agents get less overall.

Finally, the most expensive option is a *multiple agency agreement*, which means several estate agents will market your home, but only the one that sells it gets any money. Estate agents aren't keen on this option, because they have no guarantees they'll earn the commission.

What you really don't want to agree to, however, is a *sole selling right* clause, which some agents are starting to include in their contracts. If you sign such an agreement, it means that, even if you sell privately to a buyer you've found yourself, you'll still have to pay the agent's commission (*see below*).

BEFORE YOU INSTRUCT YOUR CHOSEN AGENT

The agents will be working for you, so make sure you're completely happy with the service they're offering and, before you ask them to act for you, check the conditions. Once you instruct an estate agent, the agreement is legally binding, so make sure you know:

- the percentage of the selling price they're going to charge you;
- when you'll have to pay them;
- how long you're tied to the contract;
- whether they agree to joint agency;
- whether they'll provide a 'For Sale' board;
- how and where they'll market your property;
- whether they have other branches where your details will be available;
- whether your property will be advertised in the window;
- whether you have to pay for extras, such as for advertising in local papers, drawing up floor plans, photographs, printing details;
- whether they'll show people round;
- if there's a penalty if you cancel the agreement early, for example if you decide not to sell, decide to change agents or appoint another agent, and how much notice you would have to give.

Your agents are working for you – and frankly, you'll be paying them enough if they find you a buyer, so check that you're happy with draft details (check they have the room dimensions right), and ask them to make any changes you particularly want before you sign off. You can also negotiate over terms before signing the contract. In many areas a shortage of properties means it's relatively easy for vendors to insist on commissions of 1 per cent to 1·5 per cent rather than the more typical 2 per cent to 2·5 per cent, and to demand short contracts of just a couple of weeks.

When you call your agent, it's a good idea to try to speak to the same person each time, so you build up a personal relationship. That way, they should be up to speed with all the developments and you won't waste time explaining everything over and over again.

> **TIP** *To ensure your agent is doing everything necessary to sell your property, ask a friend to register as a buyer looking for a similar type of property to your own and see how well your home is being marketed.*

REAL-LIFE ACCOUNT

Gerry was selling his late mother's house, having finally gained probate. The house was in a popular seaside resort and although it had been empty for a while, he hadn't removed or sold any of the furniture because he wanted it to look lived in. He had been going there regularly to open up and keep on top of maintenance and the house was in excellent condition.

'I appointed a local agent and felt rather relieved that I wasn't going to have to keep popping down, although I knew I'd have to clear the house sooner or later. The agent found a buyer within a couple of weeks and we handed over to our solicitor. Things were moving along nicely, and my solicitor came to me with a list of queries, including whether I was including any of the contents in the price. Well, my mother's furniture was in very good condition and although I didn't have room for any of it myself, I certainly wasn't going to let it go with the house, so I asked my solicitor to say no and I didn't hear any more about it.

'We were moving close to exchange of contracts, so I went down to spend some time at the house so I could arrange for a house clearance company to come in. I was doing some gardening when a woman stopped outside the house. We fell into conversation and I realised that she was the purchaser. I was gobsmacked when she said, "We were disappointed that you didn't want to sell any of the furniture. It would have been perfect for us". We quickly realised that the message had got scrambled as it was passed between the solicitors. She'd asked if I was prepared to sell any furniture, but the version I'd got was whether the furniture was included in the sale price. I invited her in, and we quickly came to an agreement about the items she wanted – virtually everything, in fact.

'I know solicitors and agents don't like their clients to talk to each other, but in this case, it saved a lot of trouble for both parties.'

DO-IT-YOURSELF

Whether you use an estate agent or sell your home yourself is entirely up to you. Do-it-yourself (DIY) selling puts you in control, but might take time to organize. If you'd rather avoid an estate agent's fee, you could join the growing ranks of people selling their homes themselves. If you know that your property has complicated leaseholds or disputed ownership that will complicate matters, then go through an experienced estate agent. But provided you're confident that the sale should be straightforward, why not give it a try? You could save as much as £3,000 on the average sale price in Britain. But you'll have to prepare yourself for some hard and time-consuming work.

Here's an overview of what you'll need to do to clinch a sale:

- Work out the price you're going to ask (*see page 91*). Check prices of similar properties in local papers or Internet sites such as www.upmystreet.co.uk, which monitor sales for different property types in each postcode. To do it properly, you could commission a chartered surveyor to give you a brief survey and professional valuation, which should not cost much above £100. It may even be worth arranging for a survey to establish if there are any major problems that might adversely affect the value of your home – damp, subsidence or roofing repairs for example. To do it on the cheap, you could go to two or three local estate agents and say you're thinking of putting your property on the market. They'll probably send someone round to value it at no cost, so you'll then have a good idea of what your home is worth.

- Decide whether or not to include any extras in the sale, for example

SELLING VIA THE INTERNET

Selling your house yourself has never been easier, with the wealth of online property-selling services available on the Internet. Typically, you pay a one-off fee, fill in your own details and provide a photo. You'll pay between £20 and £200 to register and advertise on property sites. Some services go as far as to provide you with a 'For Sale' board featuring a freephone contact number, and will take telephone enquiries on your behalf, relaying them to you so you can fix viewings at your leisure. But Internet sales, although on the increase, are still unusual, so newspapers are often more effective. Such Internet services describe themselves as 'advertising mediums' rather than online estate agencies. As such, you should be able to use these, or ordinary newspaper adverts, alongside a sole agency or multiple agency agreement with estate agents, and see which works best for you.

curtains and carpets or appliances. You can include these fittings in the asking price, or negotiate a separate price above the asking price. It's normal practice for a potential buyer to offer a lower price for the house than the vendor is asking. You might therefore want to allow for this by setting your price a little higher than the amount you would like to get.

- Advertise your home in the local press, or in the nationals if you're selling a large or unusual property. At the other end of the scale, you can put small ads in newsagents' windows for a small charge.

- Try selling via the Internet (*see above*).

- Compile a brochure or an information pack for prospective buyers, including room dimensions, features and a photograph. You could model the way you draw up the details of your home on estate agents' details. It's a tried and tested formula: include information on aspect, community charge or council tax, local facilities, fixtures and fittings (*see below*). These details can then be given to potential buyers, either before they call, or at the time they view.

- Put up a 'For Sale' sign – but make sure it looks professional and doesn't exceed the maximum legal size.

- For your own security, keep a record of all inquiries. Do as estate agents

The Property Chain

If you've done a lot of the work on your home yourself, it might be worth having a survey done yourself before you put it on the market, to highlight any problems that would be off-putting to a purchaser and that could hold up the chain at a crucial moment. Sue and Steve Jones in *The Property Chain* programme 3 would have been well advised to do this when they decided to sell their converted dairy in Somerset. Over the previous 15 years they had lovingly restored it from a shell to a desirable country house – but there were problems about which they had no idea. If they had known about the irregular access and their water supply, they could have taken steps to clarify the situation early on instead of its jeopardizing their sale and the whole chain.

do (or should do): for security, show people by appointment only, and ring back every inquirer on their landline before you arrange for them to view. Always have someone you know with you when showing people round, and keep all valuables, including keys, out of sight.

Pros and Cons of DIY Sales

The advantages are fairly apparent:

- No estate agents mean no agents' fees.
- You have the final say in pricing your home.
- You're in control of where and when you advertise.
- You arrange the viewing appointments.
- You negotiate directly with the buyer.

The disadvantages may, however, outweigh these:

- Advertising in the press and printing an information pack can prove expensive.
- Designing your own ads and packs might be difficult, although many printers should be able to help you with this, and if you can handle a computer you should be able to produce reasonable copy yourself (selling through a property web site – *see above* – makes all this easier).
- If you describe your home inaccurately in your information pack, you could be fined under the Property Misdescriptions Act.
- Finding time to organize everything could be tricky, particularly if you want to sell in a hurry.

WHAT YOU SHOULD LEAVE BEHIND
WHEN YOU SELL

There are some items you must sell as part of the house unless you make it clear to the buyer that they're not included. These are known as 'fixtures and fittings' and include such items as fireplaces and a central heating system. However, in some cases it's not always clear whether something is a fixture and fitting, so it would be useful for you to draw up a list of any items you intend to remove or are prepared to sell to avoid problems later. For example:

Fixtures and fittings included in the sale of the property:

General
Plug sockets
Door bell
Door knocker
Shutters and grilles
Interior door furniture
Exterior door furniture
Double glazing
Window fittings

Kitchen
Cooker
Cupboards
Fridge
Fridge-freezer
Microwave
Dishwasher
Spice rack
Cutlery rack
Extractor fan
Washing machine
Utensils

Curtains/blinds
Built-in appliances
Utensils

Living, Dining & Bedrooms
Curtains (including net curtains)
Curtain rails
Curtain fittings
Tracks and poles
Pelmets
Blinds
Carpet
Heaters
Lampshades/bulbs
Wall fittings (shelves, mirrors etc.)
Gas/electric fires
Burglar alarm
Smoke alarms

Bathroom
Carpet
Medicine cupboard/cabinet

Mirrors	***Outside***
Towel rail	Shed
Fitted shelves/cupboards	Greenhouse
Shower or bath unit	Trees, plants, flowers
Toilet fittings	Outside lights
Heater	Garden equipment/furniture (specify)
Curtains/blinds	Garden ornaments
Shaver fitting	Water butts
Soap and toothbrush holders	Dustbins
Shower fittings and curtain	Satellite dish / TV aerial

AUCTIONING YOUR HOME

If your house is particularly unusual or historic, you might consider selling it at auction (*see Chapter 8*). There are auctioneers who specialize in character properties, and their bidders come from far and wide, so you could reach a far broader and more receptive audience than dealing with your local high street agent. But auctions are not for the unwary. You won't be in a position to think about the offer and compare it with others.

You'll be expected to provide a seller's pack, usually put together by your solicitor, which will include searches and other relevant information, so buyers know what they're getting.

- One week before the auction, set the 'reserve price' – again, the minimum you'll accept at auction. This price will be kept confidential between you and the auctioneer.
- Just before the auction, tell the auctioneer the minimum price you'll accept.
- Once the hammer has fallen, you and the buyer are legally committed to the sale.
- If you sell your home successfully, you'll pay commission to the auctioneer – usually around 2.5 per cent of the sale price.

- Completion is usually 28 days from the date of the auction, so you'll need to be in a position to complete and vacate the property within this time.
- But remember – if the bids don't reach your reserve price, you'll have to go through the whole auctioning process again.

THE SELLING PROCESS

General tips for selling:

- Before you even ask the first estate agent into your home, take a long cool look at it, first from outside, and then moving from room to room making notes on which areas could be improved. Ask a trusted friend or family member for their opinions too, because when you've been living in the place for a long time you can often overlook problem areas.
- Get an idea of the competition: what other properties are your potential purchasers viewing and how does your home stack up against these?
- Cleaning and sprucing up the most tired parts of a house can often make a big difference. If you're very lucky, investing £500 could add £5,000 to the resale value of your home.
- Think about the type of purchasers you're targeting – first-time buyer, family or retirees? What are they likely to be looking for? Does your home meet their needs? For example if you're hoping for a first-time buyer, you should consider including appliances, curtains and carpets in the asking price. For families, make sure you have information about schools to hand.
- First impressions – before a buyer has even stepped inside, they've already formed an impression. A well-kept garden, pathway and fence and a freshly painted front door are immediately appealing, whereas a scruffy outdoor space with a litterbin outside the front door will turn many prospective buyers away.

- It's important that potential buyers can visualize themselves in your home, so depersonalize it a bit – make sure you keep the decoration clean and neutral and hide the family clutter, such as photographs and children's paintings.

- Dust and clean thoroughly from the top to the bottom of the house, from cobwebs on the ceiling to crumbs and stains on carpets and rugs. Remember to wash down paintwork and clean windows. If you're short on time, call in a professional cleaning service.

- Painting walls a pale plain shade maximizes the feeling of light and space and also enables buyers to imagine their possessions in the property.

- To prevent rooms looking too bland, use strong colours to accent walls or cushions and accessories.

- Finish off small DIY jobs such as touching up chipped woodwork and replacing washers on dripping taps.

- The right lighting can significantly improve the mood of a room. Choose a variety of different lights to suit the particular space, from downlights and lamps in the living room to task lighting in the kitchen. A room looks much cosier with a few table lamps rather than bright central lighting.

- Clean your windows inside and out so your home catches as much light as possible. Even better, if you have a log fire, make sure it's lit for the perfect homely touch – though perhaps not in August or if it smokes.

- If you have a dark hallway, hang a mirror at eye level to make it seem more spacious, and increase the levels of light in the room.

- Most buyers simply like the smell of a freshly cleaned and aired room. Open the windows every day to bring fresh air into the house. Choose cleaning products with a 'natural' rather than a harsh chemical smell. The old trick of brewing coffee is often perceived as being just that, a trick to create a homely feel or even, perish the thought, to cover up the smell of damp!

- If you have pets, it's a good idea to take them out during viewings or to ask friends and family if they can look after them temporarily.

- Fresh flowers and a bowl of fruit will brighten up a room and provide a pleasant scent. However, make sure you replace them regularly as rotten fruit and wilting flowers are not attractive!
- Organize rooms so they each have a specific purpose – this will help make the property more appealing and let buyers see the property at its full potential.
- Developers spend thousands of pounds 'dressing' show homes to encourage sales and they have it down to a fine art. Visit a couple of local show homes for some ideas of how you can display your rooms to the best advantage. Don't forget these show homes may be your competitors.

Conducting Viewings

Some potential buyers prefer to be shown round, on their first viewing at least, by the agent rather than the owner, so check with the agent to see if they've expressed a preference.

A second viewing is when you can swing into action. If they're really interested, they're more likely to listen to your opinions than those of an estate agent. So give some thought to what you may want to say.

- Before the visit, prepare yourself for viewers' questions about your home and the area. If it helps you remember, write down all the possible questions and answers on such topics as running costs, schools, shops and public transport.
- Explain why you're moving – your viewers will want to know it's not because the house is falling down.
- Give them some space and time to look around on their own.
- Make sure you have recent utility bills and council tax bills to hand to give an idea of the costs of living in your home.
- If you've had any major work completed in the house – such as damp-proofing or timber treatment – show the guarantees.

- Explain what you're leaving behind, such as curtains and carpets.
- Answer any questions as honestly as you can. If you don't, you may be held responsible for providing false information.
- Remember what you liked about your house when you bought it – and explain these features to the viewer.
- Don't stand in front of a window – this will block out some of the light in the room.
- Don't look desperate. Keep your cool, otherwise potential purchasers will be put off or may feel they can put in an offer considerably below the asking price. Be positive about your home.
- Know your property – measure the rooms, find out about local amenities and so on. You may not use public transport, but your potential buyer may wish to.
- Don't be too matey and don't talk too much.
- Let the viewer walk into rooms first, and avoid following them into small spaces, such as the toilet, where you may have to invade each other's personal space.
- If you're embarrassed about any area of your house and want to distract prospective buyers, play some background music in that part of the house. Classical music creates a more sophisticated feel than pop, but can seem a bit contrived.

Surveyors' Visits

Potential buyers will usually want a valuer and/or surveyor to inspect a property, and will have to if they're borrowing the money to buy. It's a good sign that they're serious, because they're paying for the survey. You'll have to allow the valuer/surveyor to look round the property if you want the sale to go ahead, so be as helpful and cooperative as you can.

Accepting Offers

When someone views your home and decides it's for them, they'll make an offer either to you, if you're selling yourself, or through your estate agent. If you're lucky, the offer may be for your full asking price, or just below. But normally, people offer a lower figure to start with. Here are some possible reasons why:

- They may feel your home isn't worth the asking price.
- Their mortgage lender won't let them borrow enough money.
- They want to gauge your reaction to the offer.
- They're trying their luck.

Remember: you don't have to accept the first offer you get. If you feel confident about selling your home, you may wish to insist on more or wait until a better offer comes along. In a very popular area, or when the market is rising, you may have prospective sellers increasing their offers to secure the property.

If an offer is less than you expected, you need to find out more about prospective buyers:

- Are they first-time buyers and able to move quickly?
- Are they selling a home? If so, is it already on the market?
- Have they accepted an offer on their home?
- How soon do they want to move?
- Do they intend to pay by cash? If not, do they have an agreement in principle to a mortgage?

If your potential buyer isn't ready to move, this could mean delays and complications later. So, it may be worthwhile keeping your home on the market until your buyer is in a stronger position – or you get a better offer.

If you're using estate agents, it's often easier for them to find out this information from the buyer, and to handle competing bids. This is where good estate agents are worth their weight in gold. They'll advise you when an offer is worth accepting (or rejecting). They know the market; so trust them.

Once you've found a buyer, the rest of the process should be handled by your solicitor, unless you're intending to handle the conveyancing yourself. The first thing you need in either case is a letter from the buyer's solicitor confirming the offer.

Even if you've accepted an offer, there's nothing in law to prevent you from changing your mind at this stage and accepting a higher offer from someone else, but imagine how you would feel if this happened to you. You should also bear in mind that when an offer is made and accepted, the potential buyer can also withdraw – for example they may not get a mortgage, or the survey may show up some structural problem.

If you're selling yourself, it may be a good idea to keep the names and addresses of all potential buyers who make offers, in case the one you accept falls through.

Sealed Bids

(*See page 71*)

REAL-LIFE ACCOUNT

Anna Orme was just married and had to sell her south London house so she and her new husband could buy a property in Nottingham, where they were renting.

'The housing market was very slow and there had been precious few viewings. It didn't help that I wasn't living there full-time, and had let a cousin stay in the property. I couldn't be sure what state it was in when people came round anyway. It might have been left messy – despite my request that she kept it tidy – which could have been putting off potential buyers.

'Eventually I had a phone call at work to say there had been an offer from a cash buyer who was keen to move quickly. The offer was below the asking price, and I was very disappointed. However, the agents I had instructed were south London specialists and knew the market and the area well. They advised me I would be very foolish to turn the offer away, so I bit the bullet and accepted it. I had made a bit on the value of the house since I had bought it, so I think I was perhaps being greedy. You get so used to a prevailing market that it's hard to imagine fortunes will change.'

WHAT HAPPENS IF YOU FIND THE BUYER YOURSELF?

You may have found your own buyer for the property who has not come through the estate agent – for example a friend may want to buy the property. You're entitled to sell to a buyer this way, but you may find that you'll still have to pay the estate agent's commission. What you have to pay will depend on the contract with the agent. But since some people try it on as a scam to get out of paying fees, you can expect agents to look into the situation thoroughly in order to satisfy themselves that the private sale is bona fide and not just a 'deal' between you and a buyer who did actually find out about the property through the estate agents' marketing. In most cases, the agents will seek to recover their costs at least, and the vendor will end up paying a proportion of the agreed commission.

Some agents, however, are starting to include 'sole selling rights' clauses in their contracts. If you sign such an agreement, it means that if you sell privately you're still obliged to pay the agent's full commission (*see page 92*).

HOME INFORMATION PACKS

Once known as sellers' packs, this long-discussed Government initiative is intended to improve the drawn out and often painful process of buying and selling property in England and Wales, and seems set to become law in 2006.

PLAYING BY THE RULES

It's unlawful for vendors or their estate agents to discriminate against a prospective buyer on grounds of race, sex or disability, either by refusing to sell the property, or by offering it on less favourable terms.

Some organizations welcome the initiative, but many interest groups are dissatisfied with the Government's current recommendations and predict a massive slow down in the market as a result. But what exactly are home information packs (HIPs)?

HIPs will be bundles of information about a property gathered by the vendors and given to potential buyers who express interest. They're intended to replace the current system, where potential buyers make an offer, often after a brief viewing, and then pay for a survey, searches and other investigations. In 15 per cent of cases, the information these investigations reveal results in a withdrawal of offer, after great expense and wasted time. So, rather than buyers getting the information they need gradually, once they decide they're interested in making an offer, vendors will have to assemble it all at their own expense before the house is even on the market. This system will make it difficult and costly for vendors simply to 'test' the market to gauge demand for their property, and quick, spontaneous property sales will be virtually impossible.

The estimated cost of £600 may seem a small proportion of the price of an average property in London, but it's a tidy sum for a modest ex-council terrace in less expensive parts of the country. The cost may put off many prospective movers entirely, particularly if they do not absolutely have to move but would like to if they could find a willing buyer at the right price.

The HIP will have to be given free of charge to anyone interested in buying, and is likely to include copies of the following documents:

- terms of sale;
- evidence of title;
- replies to standard preliminary enquiries made on behalf of buyers;
- copies of any planning, listed building and building regulations consents and approvals for new properties;
- copies of warranties and guarantees;
- any guarantees for work carried out on the property;
- replies to searches made of the local authority;
- Home Condition Report (HCR) based on a professional survey of the property, including an energy efficiency assessment;
- an environmental report.

For leasehold properties this will also need to include the following:

- a copy of the lease;
- the most recent service charge accounts and receipts;
- building insurance policy details and payment receipts;
- regulations made by the landlord or management company;
- memorandum and articles of the landlord or management company.

But there are downsides to this initiative. About 75 per cent of purchases require mortgages, and the lenders have an obligation to base their loans on a strict valuation of the property involved. The home condition report (HCR) will be carried out by so-called 'home inspectors', who will not have the qualifications of surveyors and whose work may not be fully insured. Lenders will be under no obligation to accept the Home Information Pack (HIP), so buyers may still have to pay for a valuation report. Moreover, buyers may not trust information compiled by vendors, who've an obvious vested interest in painting the property in the best possible light – and would end up paying for a survey of their own anyway.

Exchanging contracts without an HIP in place will break the law and sellers who fail to produce one could be fined or even imprisoned.

The aim is to speed up the property-buying process by helping to reduce the time spent by buyers and their solicitors compiling documents. But with advances in 'e-conveyancing' and the availability of information on local authority searches and Land Registry information from the National Land Information Service, many experts feel HIPs will be rendered unnecessary.

CONVEYANCING

Conveyancing is the legal and administrative work involved in transferring ownership of land or buildings from one owner to another. The conveyancing process starts after an offer has been made and accepted for a property, and solicitors' details have been exchanged by the vendor and buyer. So once you've accepted the offer and you're ready to move ahead with the sale, you need to appoint a solicitor or conveyancer (England and Wales only) who will:

- ask for your home's legal documents – called the title deeds (if you don't have them, your mortgage lender or solicitor probably does);
- ask you to complete a questionnaire on your home;
- prepare a contract for the sale;
- ask your mortgage lender how much they need to settle your mortgage;
- pass the buyer's deposit to you;
- communicate with the buyer's solicitor or conveyancer to agree a moving date;
- make sure any necessary payments are made to complete the sale.

Usually the same solicitor cannot act for both the buyer and vendor of a property, but two solicitors from the same firm may, as long as there's no clash of interests between buyer and vendor. You should hire a solicitor or conveyancer as soon as possible when selling your house so that they'll be

THE LAW SOCIETY TRANSACTION PROTOCOL

This is a Law Society scheme used by many solicitors in the conveyancing process to speed up the conveyancing process. If your solicitor is operating this scheme, he or she may offer the buyer's solicitor a package at the beginning of the process that includes the following:

 The draft contract.

 Copies of previous title deeds (registered/unregistered – see above).

 A property information form, giving key property information (this saves the solicitor from wasting time with many of the preliminary enquiries).

 Fixtures, fittings and contents form, telling you which fixtures, fittings and other items are included in the price and which will be removed on completion. You should agree with the vendor what is to be included, and make sure everything is correct in the form.

ready to step into action as soon as you accept an offer, or make one on another property. The faster you can start conveyancing, the better.

Licensed Conveyancers versus Solicitors

There's no difference between a licensed conveyancer and a solicitor when it comes to moving home. Conveyancers are legally qualified and have the powers to do the same work as a solicitor. There are even advantages in using conveyancers over solicitors, one of which is that conveyancing work is all they do. If you use a solicitor, he or she may well be involved in other cases and could be away in court for the day.

Conveyancers are also very experienced and can use this to your advantage.

DOING YOUR OWN CONVEYANCING

Legally, there's no reason why you can't do your own conveyancing. In fact, in recent years DIY conveyancing has become increasingly popular. Doing it yourself means you'll save hundreds of pounds on solicitor or conveyancer fees but there are good reasons for leaving it up to the experts. Here are some:

 Many mortgage lenders will insist on employing a solicitor to protect their interests. They do not want to risk having shoddy conveyancing work.

 There's a higher risk of things going disastrously wrong.

 The purchasers involved may not be happy with you doing your own conveyancing, and may even withdraw their offer on this basis.

 Some parties to a sale (like the lender) may charge you higher transaction fees anyway to cover potential mistakes on your part, so savings are limited.

With some properties DIY conveyancing is particularly inadvisable – for example if it's being sold by a divorcing or separating couple (this requires specialist skill or knowledge), if it's not a freehold or not registered, or if it's not a house.

A solicitor will usually have taken an exam in conveyancing and may not have had as much first-hand experience. Most firms of solicitors offer a conveyancing service. Although all solicitors can legally do conveyancing, it's advisable to choose a solicitor who has experience of this work. Licensed conveyancers are not solicitors but are licensed by the Council of Licensed Conveyancers. If you want to find out if a local conveyancer is licensed, you can write to the Council of Licensed Conveyancers (*see page 117*).

Before choosing who will do the conveyancing, you should find out the probable cost. It's important to contact more than one solicitor or licensed conveyancer, as there's no set scale of fees for conveyancing. You should:

- check whether the figure quoted is a fixed fee or will vary if more work is required;
- check that the figure includes expenses and VAT, and get a breakdown of these costs;
- find out what charges, if any, will be made if the sale falls through before contracts are exchanged.

The Main Stages of Conveyancing

There are three main stages to the process, although the order may vary from transaction to transaction:

1   Before the exchange of contracts: when the draft contract is received and negotiated, enquiries are made and the formal mortgage offer is received.

2   Exchange of contracts: when the contract is signed and the buyer hands over a deposit (usually 10 per cent of the sale price) to the vendor's solicitor. Final accounts are prepared and the mortgage deed requested for you to sign. Final searches are made.

3   Completion: when the keys are handed over and title deeds transferred to the new owner. The buyer and his or her mortgage lender pays the balance purchase price, and the transfer is arranged at the

Land Registry. Stamp duty is paid by the purchaser. Any interest earned on the deposit during the period it was kept by the solicitor or licensed conveyancer should now be passed on to the vendor. The vendor may need to ask for the interest, as it's not always passed on.

(For further information on this process see Chapter 3.)

Exchange of Contracts

From this point onwards the legal implications get more serious. You and the buyer are legally bound to go ahead with the deal. If either of you pulls out now, you'll both incur big costs. The 10 per cent deposit paid by the purchaser will remain in your solicitor's account until completion. At this stage, the solicitors will arrange the 'completion date' – the date when your home transfers to the buyer (four weeks after you exchange contracts is what most people aim for, but this varies greatly).

Once contracts are exchanged and, before completion, there's plenty to do. *(See Chapter 5 for more information on what has to happen at this stage.)* The buyer may wish to visit the house, for example, to measure up for carpets or to get an estimate for building work. However, you should not allow any work to be done by the buyer before completion.

THE PRICE OFFERED IS REDUCED

A buyer may decide to reduce the offer made for the house (known as 'gazundering'). If this happens before contracts are exchanged, it's up to you as the vendor to decide whether or not you want to accept this lower offer. However, once contracts have been exchanged a buyer is legally committed to paying the price stated in the contract. If he or she tries to drop the price at this stage, you do not have to accept this lower price. If the sale is not completed, a buyer forfeits the 10 per cent deposit paid when contracts were exchanged and you could also sue the buyer for any additional loss.

Completing the Sale

Finally, completion takes place, but that is not the end of the matter. Almost all completions now take place at a distance and the vendor's conveyancer sends the completed documentation to the buyer's practitioner through the post or DX system. Documentation may take a few days to arrive at the offices of the buyer's conveyancer. Only when all these formalities have been dealt with can the conveyancer make application to the Land Registry to register their client as owner of the land in question. Even then, registration is not automatic. Requisitions may be raised by the Land Registry if it identifies problems or irregularities with the produced documentation. On the day of completion, the balance of purchase monies has to be transferred to the seller's conveyancer. This is usually done by electronic bank transfer, but difficulties can and do arise in chain transactions.

Once everything has been sorted out, your solicitor will let you know when the money has arrived in your account. Then either you or the estate

> TIP *If you're planning to buy a new home, remember to exchange on your current home first. Otherwise, you might need to take out a loan before you can buy the new one!*

The Property Chain

In the fourth programme in *The Property Chain* series, we saw buyer Stevie Ledger start work on the house she was proposing to buy before contracts had even been exchanged. The house was vacant, and the owners, Tony and Jane Fairclough, were in Switzerland and had no idea this was going on. Using keys the estate agent had given her so that she could have quotes for work to be done once they had completed the purchase, Stevie had a carpet replaced, redecorated and made alterations to the garden. What she did was illegal and when the chain started to falter, she realized how dangerous her actions had been.

Vendors should never allow purchasers to have free access to their property before completion. After exchange, they can be allowed to measure up and seek quotes for work that will be done later, but they should be accompanied by the estate agent if the house is empty, or should sign for the keys and return them promptly.

> TIP *Cut the time between exchange and completion. There's no legal reason why there should be a gap of several weeks between exchanging contracts and completing. If everyone involved in the sale is amenable and there are no other complications, you could press the solicitors to carry out the completion details soon after the exchange, or even on the same day.*

agent must hand over the keys. And that's it. You've sold your home. Just time for one last fond farewell . . . let's move on to the next! Your solicitor will receive the rest of the purchase price from the buyer and pass this, together with the deposit, on to you.

INSURANCE MATTERS

Remember to continue buildings insurance cover on your property until contracts have exchanged, at which time it becomes the buyer's responsibility. For peace of mind, most solicitors advise vendors to maintain cover until completion, just in case purchasers have not arranged cover themselves, with an option to continue it in case they drop out at the last minute. If your solicitor uses the TransAction Protocol (*see page 109*), the responsibility for buildings insurance usually remains yours until completion anyway.

SURVIVING THE CHAIN

As we already know, chains are the bane of any property sale or purchase. If you can steer clear of one, so much the better, but that's not easy to do. Here are a few precautions to take, which may keep things moving.

 Sell to someone who has already sold his or her house, has moved out and has been paid for it.

 Sell to a first-time buyer.

 Sell to someone who has sold 'subject to contract'.

 Keep in touch with your solicitor and check up regularly on the state of play.

 Pay for a personal search and reduce the search time from a fortnight to a couple of days.

HOW YOU LEAVE YOUR HOME

Legally there's no stand on how clean a property should be left. You'll be contractually obliged to make sure that the property is empty of all its contents as agreed ('vacant possession'), but specifying 'cleanliness' is too subjective: what may be clean to one person may not be to another.

 Don't remove light bulbs, door handles, light fittings, fireplaces, fitted cupboards, or anything planted in the garden or cemented down unless it has been agreed that you can.

 Leave a property in the condition in which the purchaser first saw it – but cleared of all items not included in the purchase price or bought separately by the new owner.

 Do as you would be done by – clean the property and dispose of your rubbish and the skipload of unwanted bits and bobs that have been cluttering up your attic, cellar and garage for years.

 Don't forget anything: the new owner can claim that the items you left behind are now his and they could be very hard to recover.

Contents insurance remains your responsibility until completion day. If you're intending to change to a different policy or insurer, don't cancel your existing policy until after the move.

HARD-TO-SELL HOUSES

Even if you put your property on the market at the best time of year, you can't predict how long it will take for a suitable offer to come along. It depends on so many factors. How long it takes before you get the right offer depends on how well the property market is doing at the time. If it's buoyant, it could take anything from a couple of days to a number of weeks. If it's flagging, it might drag on for months. Other factors affecting how long it will take include the asking price, competition from other houses on the market, the type of property and the geographical location.

You could consider one of the options below:

- Take the property off the market and try again later.
- Stick with it and hope a buyer comes along.
- Reduce the price in the hope of stimulating interest.
- Improve 'property appeal' (*see pages 100–2*).
- If selling via agents, change the agent or consider a multi-agency agreement.
- If selling privately, improve your marketing and sales methods or consider using an agent.

To Reduce or not?

A price reduction does not always work in your favour and certainly doesn't guarantee a sale. Taking the property off the market, and then trying again, perhaps with another agent, may be better.

If your agent is urging you to reduce when you don't really want to, think what they have to lose, relative to you. On a property worth £180,000 with agency fees of 2 per cent, a reduction of £10,000 would be a major reduction to you, but for the agent it represents a loss of only £200 in commission, the difference between £3,600 and £3,400. If you suggest going to another agent, you might find it focuses their minds wonderfully.

Another trick when trying to sell a small property is to change to an upmarket estate agent where your property will be the cheapest on their list. Yours will stand out and your details will reach a lot of wealthier people who may well be considering an investment or purchase of 'something cheaper for the children' – as well as people the agent usually regards himself as 'unable to help, too poor'. One vendor did just this with his three-bedroomed semi, which had been stuck on the market for two years with other agents, just by placing it with his local 'mansion retailer'. He was delighted: 'There was no extra commission. In fact his fees were lower than some of the others, the service was excellent and we found a buyer within three weeks.'

TOO MUCH INFORMATION

Information on local area risks – landslip, flooding, industrial pollution, local landfill or subsidence – is now available on the Internet. Other sites are offering information on local schools, crime rates, and average property prices. Buyers have access to much more information about your area and property than they used to, and at an earlier stage in negotiations, simply by surfing the Internet. Some are using this as a bargaining tool. Make sure you know what they know by taking a look at www.homecheck.co.uk or www.upmystreet.com. Outline information is available free of charge by entering a postcode, and more detailed reports are also available for a small fee.

USEFUL CONTACTS

The Council for Licensed Conveyancers
16 Glebe Road
Chelmsford
Essex M1 1QG
Tel.: 01245 349599
Web: www.conveyancers.gov.uk

The National Association of Estate Agents
Arbon House
21 Jury Street
Warwick CV34 4EH
Tel.: 01926 496800
Web: www.naea.co.uk

Surveysonline
Web: www.surveysonline.co.uk
(*See also Chapter 3*)

Online property advertising:
www.houseweb.com
www.propertybroker.co.uk
www.thelittlehousecompany.co.uk
www.realestatedirect.co.uk

MOVING IN

Popular wisdom has it that moving home is one of the most stressful things you'll ever do – it tops the angst league with bereavement and divorce – so everyone expects the worst. But does it really have to be so bad? Certainly, it's a huge upheaval with the added pressure of huge financial outlay and endless information to exchange before you can take possession and create a home. And it's not really an art that people get to practise very often: once every seven years, on average, and that's long enough to forget everything you might learn from your mistakes.

Of course there's a huge amount to organize, but planning ahead is, as ever, the answer. With a cool head and the information gleaned from this chapter, you should be well on your way to making your move as simple and straightforward as possible.

FIRST STEPS IN MOVING HOUSE

So you've agreed your purchase, and maybe a sale as well. There are two main things to sort out now, assuming you've got the money in place and legal arrangements are ticking along:

- moving everything to your new home;
- letting everyone know you're moving.

When you exchange contracts (*see Chapter 3*) you'll agree your completion date and it will be specified in the contract. (If you're buying a new-build property, the date you can move in may not be fixed at this stage, but the builder will agree in the contract to give you notice so you can organize your move in plenty of time.) The time between exchange of contracts and completion is how long you've got to get everything for the move sorted and, although you'll be busier than you ever thought possible, your solicitor will also be very active, so stay in touch regularly to make sure everything is proceeding as it should.

If you're not a natural list maker, by the way, you'll have to force yourself to be. It's the only way to ensure everything gets done. Buy yourself a big note-pad or a clipboard, some coloured pens, highlighter pens and coloured sticky labels – you're going to need them both now and later on.

INSURANCE AND OTHER DOMESTIC ADMIN

The first thing to establish is who is taking care of insuring the property you're moving into (*see Chapters 3 and 4*). The mortgage company will need to know this and it's vital that it's in place.

ACCESS TO THE PROPERTY YOU'RE BUYING

This is a good time to take accurate measurements of the property you're buying, say for curtains or carpets or to plan where furniture is to go when you move, so you can give your removers the clearest possible instructions and label your boxes and crates accordingly. Some vendors are quite happy with this – you've committed to buy the property, after all, but you may have to use concerted charm to get your way. If you're selling, your buyer may want the same from you.

Most sensible vendors will insist on keeping their keys until completion, as vendors will want to be present when you visit. If the property is vacant, they may agree to the agent giving the keys to you for the duration of your visit, but you'll have to sign for them. No one wants a buyer to move into the property before the sale is completed, so it could be that the agent will accompany you on your visit. Don't take exception to this: it's normal procedure. If you were the vendor, you'd want to take precautions of this type.

Similarly, if you're moving out of a property and are covering buildings insurance until completion, make sure you have the option of continuing to pay the premium in case the purchaser drops out at the last moment. (*See Chapter 3 for more advice.*) A list of other admin you'll have to deal with is included in the countdown below.

THE REMOVAL COMPANY, OR GOING IT ALONE

The next thing you have to decide is how you're going to move all your worldly goods from where they are now to where you want them to go. This decision will be based on how much stuff you have, how far you're moving, how many strong mates you have, whether you're moving straight into your new home or putting your possessions into storage.

In absolute terms, it's cheaper to handle your own move in most cases, but the fact is that the extra stress it causes may simply not be worth it. A good removal company is worth every penny you pay them. Don't forget, they're dealing with the logistics of moving heavy furniture every day, whereas, for you, it may be the first time. Remember too that your effects (and any damage they cause anyone else) are insured by them while in transit.

ANY DAY BUT FRIDAY

Did you know that Friday is the most popular day of the week for moving house? Well, it's logical, isn't it? People want the weekend to get things straight. But Friday is the very day to avoid, if you can. For a start, because of the extra activity, banks and building societies are completely overloaded and the BACS system used to transfer money from one account to another can be plagued by delays – the last thing you need on moving day, when timing is all. Removals are also more expensive on Friday and the companies will be more stretched and may have to bring in part-timers. Many removal companies offer discounts for moves earlier in the week to counter the Friday effect, so get smart and arrange your move for another day – provided it's not over the weekend or a bank holiday, which are just as bad!

CONTACTING REMOVAL COMPANIES

The choice of removal company is an important one. You're inviting their employees into your home and entrusting your treasured possessions to their care. Their attitude and professionalism will have a big impact on how

---

REAL-LIFE ACCOUNT

Ben and Tracy Gillett were moving from a cottage in Worcestershire to a bigger family house about four miles up the road.

'It was one of the smoothest sales transactions you can imagine. We had sold the house in about five minutes, and the agent hadn't even had time to complete the property details. Our buyer had no property to sell, and the people we were buying from had a very easy purchase too.

'It took the removal company two days to pack, but we had been very organized, had made plenty of visits to the new house, so had marked up our boxes as we should. They were swift, polite and efficient. We set moving day for a Friday. The children were being looked after by friends, and when the solicitor rang just after lunch to say completion would take place in the next hour, we handed the keys to the agent, waved a tearful goodbye to the house and jumped in the car to follow the two removal lorries up the road. Something had to go wrong – and it did.

'As we were driving along, my mobile phone rang. It was the solicitor. The mortgage lender – Barclays Bank – were refusing to release the balance of the purchase because they had no confirmation that buildings insurance was in place. We were gobsmacked and almost drove into a tree. Not only had we had it in place since exchange of contracts, but the insurer was none other than Barclays Bank! The insurance department (based in one town) had not communicated with the mortgage department in another.

'We pulled up outside our soon to be new home, and went inside to talk to the vendors. They were fuming. Their lorries were waiting to move. Ours were sitting in the road outside. Our children were about to arrive at what they thought was their new home. Two cleaners had arrived to clean the house. The chain had ground to a halt minutes before completion and the banks were due to close in about an hour. The previously cordial relationship had turned distinctly icy. After frantic phone calls between solicitors, and the banks, a bank official had to run up Worcester high street carrying a banker's draft for the balance of the sale. We finally completed with about five minutes to spare.'

smoothly the move goes, so choose with care. It's too late to have qualms when a battered and dirty van turns up in your drive, with staff that make your skin crawl. Contacting the companies either in person or over the phone will let you get a feel for them and will also give you a chance to ask them any questions or advise them on any special requirements you have.

Personal recommendation is the best way of finding a removal company you can rely on, but it's always best to get a number of quotes: say three or four from your local area or from the area you're moving to. It can sometimes work out cheaper to use a company based near your destination, as they'll be ending their day's work close to home. If you're asking a number of companies for quotes, make sure that all the companies are offering to do exactly the same things, or you'll receive quotes that not only vary widely, but are for completely different jobs. Something else you'll need to decide is whether you're going to be doing your own packing (often an easier option, as you can do it bit by bit, and make decisions about what to throw out as you go), whether they'll be doing everything for you, or whether you'll go for a partial option.

Note: if you do pack your own boxes, there's a good chance the insurance company will not insure them during transit (*see page 124*).

Even if you're contemplating doing the move yourself, it's worth asking for a quote. Removal experts are trained to notice all the little problems that you don't and you may realize, once they start asking questions, that the job is really too big for you to take on yourself.

Whatever you choose, don't leave it too long. Removal firms get booked up well in advance, particularly on Fridays. The really smart way to do it is to contact removers before the sale is even agreed, so you have your quotes in well in advance of exchanging contracts. Some removers will allow you to make a provisional booking and give the exact date once you have a completion date. Providing it isn't a Friday, this shouldn't be a problem. Good removal companies specialize in being flexible!

INVENTORIES

Many removal companies will quote in the first instance on the basis of an inventory form they'll send you to fill in yourself. If you're filling in your own inventory, be honest so the company will be able to give you an accurate quotation. Even the smallest thing could affect the time spent on the removal. If you already know that the wardrobes and beds had to be taken into the house through the bedroom window or that you've altered the stairs since the furniture was taken up, tell them and they'll be happy to bring along tools, ladders, and extra men if necessary. Also remember that the amount of furniture and belongings you write down on an inventory form will dictate

REMOVAL INSURANCE

Some household contents insurance policies will insure your possessions for the period of the move. If yours doesn't, you should take out extra insurance cover for any mishaps that occur during the move. Most insurers will extend your cover for the removal period, for an additional premium, normally around £25, to cover the increased risk. But it's difficult to obtain this cover from insurance companies with whom you do not already have an insurance policy. Check what the policy covers and the time limit within which a claim must be made. The policy probably will not cover the following:

 scratches and dents;

 banknotes, shares, bonds, deeds, stamps and securities;

 loss or damage due to strikes, weather conditions, or delay;

 goods that are not professionally packed (ensure everything is packed, and unpacked, by professional removers or your claim may be jeopardized).

Removal firms may offer insurance as part of their contract. If they do, check the limit on what compensation you'll be able to claim, as it's often quite low. Ask to see in writing exactly what will be covered and the time limit for making a claim. With most removal insurance, you have to pay a part of any claim – the excess – which is usually £50 or more.

the number of containers allocated to your move. You wouldn't want a lorry arriving that is too small. Any missing information will lead to delays on moving day, and time is one thing you won't have to spare.

REMOVAL CHECKLIST

Try to think things through before the removal representatives come, so that you're providing the most accurate information. Here is a checklist to get you started:

- Arm yourself with a pen and paper to make notes, and always start from the top of the house.
- If you have a loft, check it over first. Nothing you keep there is likely to be in constant use and therefore can be boxed up well in advance.
- Are the contents of the loft to be brought down by you or the removal men? There may be Health and Safety regulations to consider, but the companies will be able to tell you about this.
- Go through everything, deciding what you would like to keep, throw out, sell or give away. If you separate these things into various piles, it's easier to see what you have. Be ruthless. Better to throw away now than have to pay for it all to be transported to the new house, only to throw it out later.
- In the bedrooms, who is going to dismantle the wardrobes, and the beds if necessary?
- Self-assembly furniture isn't designed to be flattened, moved and reassembled, so usually isn't covered within the insurance the removal companies offer. No matter how hard they try, sometimes this furniture will not go back together perfectly after a move. *Remove it whole.*
- Ask if your washing machine and dishwasher can be disconnected by the removal men, and whether they can lift and transport any carpets that are going with you.

- Don't forget the contents of the garage, any outbuildings and garden furniture that you're taking. Some plant pots and troughs can be extremely heavy, but if you point these out, they'll be all taken into account.

- Any flammable substances like old tins of paint, creosote, paraffin, matches, gas bottles and similar things will not be allowed to go on the van, as this will invalidate any insurance cover. So you'll have to remove any fuel from garden machinery.

- Take a moment to think about where they're going. Remember: you're the only one who has seen the property you're moving to. Warn the removers if you expect any difficulties with getting furniture into your new property. If you don't, you might end up with your bedroom furniture in the lounge of your new house.

- If there's any change in what you're planning to take, let the removers know. The van and staff assigned to your move are calculated on the basis of what the representative has been shown or what you've stated on an inventory form – you can't assume there will be spare capacity for, say, the wardrobes you had originally planned to leave behind.

To give the most accurate quote, the removers will need to know the following:

- exactly where you're moving to;
- what access is like for parking and unloading;
- the date you wish to move;
- whether the vendors are moving out on the same day;
- whether the purchasers are moving into your old property on the same day, and the timings;
- if you need a packing service;
- if you have fragile objects to be packed;
- if everything is going to the same location;
- if you need to put some of your possessions into storage;
- if you'll need them to provide cartons and packing cases.

The cost of your move will vary, depending on how far you're moving, how many staff are needed, what kind of service you're having, whether there are any tricky items (like pianos), access to the properties, the day of the week, the number of vans and the cubic capacity needed for your possessions. You may well end up not choosing the cheapest quote. In removal, as in most things, you get what you pay for. Most people go for the company that makes them feel comfortable. It's a tough process, and you need to feel that the removers are on your side.

Once you have a definite date for your move, let your first choice of removers know. If they're booked up you at least have some more quotations to fall back on. Ask about the logistics of the move, the time the van will arrive and the estimated time to finish loading up and time of completion. Even after you've had the estimate, telephone the removal company to check the date is confirmed before sending out the deposit. Some companies will want either a deposit or full payment before the removal, and some will want paying on the day after the job is done. If you've booked a day and have to cancel, check the small print on the 'terms and conditions', as you may have to pay a cancellation fee – sometimes as much as 60 per cent of the removal cost.

GOING IT ALONE

- If you'd rather not pay for a removal company, and you're not moving too far away, then a DIY move becomes a possibility. Provided you don't have too much furniture, you can hire a van, enlist the help of some muscular friends and do all the work yourself.

- Call some van rental companies for quotes. All you'll need is a full driving licence to hire a van, one other proof of identity and be over 21. But when you book it, check the company include unlimited mileage in the deal. If they don't, you may find that you're paying over the odds for trips back and forth between your old and new homes.

What's more, you can't blame breakages on anyone else. Make sure your home insurance covers you for belongings damaged during the move. Measure the doors of the van and compare them with your largest items of furniture. If the furniture wins, admit defeat and call a removal company, quickly. Whatever you choose to do, the packing tips will be particularly useful to you.

STORAGE

You might find it convenient to put some of your possessions into storage, and there are specialized firms that deal with this, although most large removal companies offer this facility. Most firms use containerized storage: large wooden boxes that can be moved about using a forklift. Unless you have particular access problems at your home, these will be loaded outside your house, sealed in your presence, and not opened again until they arrive at your new home. This cuts down on the amount of times your belongings are handled, and reduces the risk of damage to them. If some or all of your possessions are going into storage, you need to think and plan ahead.

- Even if the duration of storage is only a few days, you should keep any personal papers and documents with you. So invest in a lockable document case and check through your drawers and desks before you consign them to the warehouse.
- Check with the company representatives about what they can and cannot store. They may vary, but foodstuffs and flammable items like paint or petrol will certainly not be allowed to go into storage. If they are included, this will completely invalidate any insurance cover.
- It's usually possible, for a fee, to search through your belongings in store, but to find documents and small items can be very time consuming and difficult.
- Any large items, like ladders, carpets and large furniture, that won't fit into a container can be stored separately. So don't panic.

- If there are things that are not to go into storage, like clothes and personal items, put them all in a separate room and shut the door. Tell the team leader what is to go/stay as soon as the removers arrive.

- Don't make the mistake of saying, 'It's all to go,' because the removers will take everything that isn't fastened down. Unloading containers to find the items you never meant to go in there in the first place will slow things down terribly. If this happens, you'll definitely have to offer them another mug of tea and probably a biscuit too.

- Keep walkways in the house clear. When furniture goes into store, the team have a lot less space to work in, and will need to pick and choose more carefully what they take to the van. This is why packing for storage takes longer than a straight move. The removers will be going from room to room looking for that piece of furniture that will fit exactly – a bit like a giant jigsaw puzzle.

- White goods should, of course, all be emptied, disconnected, washed out with detergent to avoid unpleasant odours and then be thoroughly dried out. You don't want your freezer defrosting inside the container surrounded by your beds.

- If most of the things you've stored in drawers will be going into store, just leave them there. This saves a lot of space within the container and saves you having to pack. If a chest is very heavy but the drawers and legs are strong enough, the removal team will take out the drawers, carry the chest into the van and then replace the drawers.

- Remove any breakable items from drawers, as they'll roll about as they're being moved.

- Electrical goods are best packed in their original boxes, if you've kept them. If not, pack in a carton bigger than the equipment and surround it with bedding or clothes that will protect it. Mark the boxes 'Fragile' as clearly as you can.

SELF-STORAGE

This is a simple, cost-effective and safe way of storing your possessions, which can be delivered either by you or a removal company to the storage facility and placed in a sealed room/unit big enough to take everything. You'll be the only person to have access to the keys for your room or unit.

Most self-storage companies will send out an assessor to help work out how much space you'll need, calculated in cubic feet. It's very hard to work out yourself, as everything will be piled up. Obviously, the more you take the more expensive it is, so you don't want to take more than you need.

- Visit the storage facility beforehand to get a feel for the place. Check the opening hours so you have an idea of the times you're able to gain access.
- Remember that it could take several hours to unload your belongings into your room/unit, so don't arrive at the store minutes before they close.
- Your storage rooms may not be on the ground floor and, although most self-storage companies have large lifts, you may still have to manhandle your belongings. Barrows and sack carts will usually be freely available to help with this.
- As before, flammable goods, explosives and perishable foodstuffs are not allowed in self-storage units.
- Lay down plastic sheeting on the floor of your unit before you start loading.
- If you have a large enough unit, leave a walkway either down the side or the middle so you can gain access to items without having to unload everything.
- Place any valuables towards the rear of the unit.
- Try to pack it to the ceiling by placing heavier items like drawers and wardrobes on the floor and lighter, more fragile items on top.
- Fill any spaces or gaps with small items or soft items like bedding.

MOVING YOUR PLANTS

It's very important to show the removal company all the plants to be moved inside and out. Believe it or not, plants take up the most room in the back of a removal van, because they cannot be stacked on top of each other.

- If you have plants to dig up, wrap the root ball in plastic sheeting, making sure the soil is moist.

- Most garden pots and troughs are never moved, and therefore any frost damage is not discovered until the removal men pick it up and it falls to bits. This is quite common, so you'll find that the removal company will not be liable. If you're worried about this, empty the contents out to take some of the strain from the pot. The removal men will take great care, but outside pots tend to be covered in moss and if wet are extremely difficult to lift: there's often a large thorny branch waving about, usually in your ear!

- For obvious reasons plants cannot be put into storage, although some of the smaller removal firms will take them for a short period. They'll probably be stored loose so they can be watered, and outside plants are often left in an outside compound.

- Removal companies will always try to handle your plants with great care, but because plants are living organisms they'll not be covered under any insurance policy. Liability for loss or damage is also probably excluded under the terms and conditions. You can find details on the back of the acceptance forms that you'll have received.

MOVING CHECKLIST

Ready? Steady? Get that clipboard and start making your lists. This countdown to moving day is only a guide – every move is different – but here are the basics:

Four to Six Weeks before Moving

- Confirm the date when you'll be moving in and make sure you know what your new postcode is going to be – you'll need it for all the utility companies, for a start.
- Book time off work before and afterwards.
- Decide whether you're going to move yourself or use a professional removal company, and book them.
- If you're moving from rented accommodation, notify your landlord and check how much notice you have to give. Contact your telephone and utilities companies to tell them about the move.
- Have a clear out of anything you don't need: organize trips to the charity shops and tip.
- Start gathering what you'll need for packing your belongings.
- Plan your journey, especially if you're moving far away and will need to book overnight accommodation.
- Call your telephone company and arrange reconnection or installation in your new home. You may be able to arrange to take your existing number with you. If not, most providers offer a call redirection service. Make sure you arrange to transfer any ADSL or ISDN services at the same time.
- Inform the utility suppliers (gas, electricity, water) that you're moving so you can arrange for final readings.

The Property Chain

Packing for a move takes a long time, and you may be tempted to start before your sale is agreed. Don't pack too early in the process, however, or you could be setting yourself up for disappointment. In the first *Chain* programme, Jonathon Linn and Tineke Bosma were so keen to get going on the move from their Manchester loft flat to Waterside Cottage that they started packing their possessions before they had exchanged contracts with London solicitor Roy Ledgister, the buyer at the bottom of the chain. When the sale and subsequently the whole chain fell through, they had to unpack at least a proportion of their belongings to dress the flat to make it ready to attract another buyer.

- You should also inform the person at the council responsible for council tax, or in Northern Ireland, the Rate Collection Agency responsible for rates collection.
- You'll have to inform all the businesses and organizations you're in contact with of your change of address. Here's a list to get you started:

Banks
Brokers and financial advisors
Building society
Credit card companies
Dentist
Doctor
DVLA
Electricity company
Employer
Family
Friends
Gas board
Hire purchase companies
Hospital if you're having regular
    treatment as an outpatient
Inland Revenue
Insurance companies
Magazine subscriptions
Mail order companies
Mobile phone account providers
National Insurance office
Opticians
Post office, and arrange for your mail
    to be redirected
Private healthcare provider
Professional organizations
Rental companies
Schools
Share registrars
Sports and social clubs
Store card companies
Motoring organizations (RAC/AA
    etc.)
TV licensing authority
Vet
Water company

Two Weeks before

- Have your car/cars serviced, particularly if you're moving a long distance away.
- You'll need to renew your driving licence and vehicle registration document, as failure to notify the DVLA of a change in address is an offence. For the Vehicle Registration Document complete the appropriate changes section on your registration document and return it to:

DVLA
Swansea
SA99 1AR
Tel.: 0870 2400010

- You'll need a driving licence with your new address on it. Complete Section 1 of your paper licence (DVLA no longer issues paper licences. Photocard application packs are available from the post office) or the paper counterpart (D740) and your photocard licence and return them both to:

DVLA
Swansea
SA99 1BN
Tel.: 0870 2400009

For more information go to www.dvla.gov.uk.

- Tell your bank of your change of address and maybe consider transferring your accounts to a branch nearer to your new home. If you have anything retained for safe keeping with your bank or solicitors don't forget these.
- Store and credit cards have change of address forms, usually on the reverse of the statement. Don't forget to notify any card protection insurers you may have.
- Let your child's school know when you intend to leave, and advise the new school when you intend your child to start.
- When you notify your local tax office, you'll need to quote your reference number. This is on your payslip/P60 code notification.
- Contact your broker or the individual companies for your life, motor, medical, pet and contents insurance. When contacting your house contents insurers, check with them to see what cover you have

regarding moving house. You may find you're fully covered and have no need to take out extra cover with your removal company.

- Sort out TV licence and rental, if appropriate. Fill in the change of address part of your existing licence. Contact your rental company. If it's a large national firm, you can normally take your items to your new address and your records will be transferred to their nearest branch.

- If you're intending to book your pets into kennels or a cattery, do so now. Arrange for the transfer of pets' records to the new vet.

One Week before

- Finish packing items you won't need to use before the move.

- Confirm your move with the utility companies. Inform them of your new address and the date you're moving. They'll need at least 48 hours' notice, so don't leave this any later.

- Check that your removal company has directions to your new address. You can print out a map from the Internet if you really want to be clever.

- Put any important documents – such as your passport, birth certificate and driving licence – in a safe place.

- Label all your boxes with the room the items are going into (*see page 141*).

- Contact land and mobile phone providers and your Internet service provider (ISP), informing them of your change of address and the date you wish your new number to operate from. Make sure you have a way to contact your solicitor and estate agent and vice versa if your phone is to be disconnected.

- Return any library books and rented videos you find, and advise the lenders of your new address.

- You can have your mail redirected by the post office. This can be arranged by post. Just pick up a form at the post office. Redirection requires seven days' notice.

- Arrange for change-of-address cards to be printed, or print some out on your computer, and send them to everyone on your Christmas card list. Don't forget to do some for your children to hand out at school.

- Settle all outstanding milk and newspaper accounts and cancel further deliveries.
- If you've arranged to have carpets/curtains and so on delivered to your new address, confirm that the companies have the correct delivery address, date and time. If you have to have your carpets fitted on the day of the removal, remember that you'll have removal men walking in and out of your new house, so tell your removal company and arrange for the carpets to be put down as soon as you receive the keys.
- If possible, arrange for the children to be looked after on removal day.
- Pick up your dry cleaning.

Three Days to Go

- Pack a bag with a change of clothes and a survival kit for the other end, including things like light bulbs, toilet rolls, candles, a few tools, matches, cash and a list of important telephone numbers. In fact, include anything you might need for the couple of days after moving day. You can put jewellery and valuables in this bag and, on the day of the removal, lock it in the car.
- Do a last-minute laundry.
- Check that the keys to your new home are going to be available and sort out your old keys so you can deliver them to the solicitor on completion. Clearly label any spare keys and leave where they'll be seen when you leave on moving day. The kitchen worktop is usually good, as this is the first room the new people will settle first.
- Also leave a folder of any guarantees and instructions for appliances you're leaving behind – for example damp-proofing guarantees, boiler instructions and service agreements, with the necessary contact numbers. It's also thoughtful to leave a stash of menus from local takeaways, taxi service phone numbers, and other useful contacts for your area.

- Check with neighbours and resolve any parking problems. The average removal van is the same size as a double-decker bus. You need to leave room for the lorry to manoeuvre into position. The removal team will usually want to have the back doors of the wagon as near to the access point as possible.

Two Days to Go

- Empty, defrost and dry out your fridge-freezer. This is particularly important if your furniture is to go into store or you're moving a long distance.
- If you've been quoted to have your freezer moved with the contents, put the food into polythene bags so they can be lifted out while carrying the freezer and placed back inside with the minimum of fuss.
- Go through the kitchen cupboards and throw out anything out of date. Also make sure all the packets, bottles and jars are sealed tightly to avoid spillage.
- If some of your furniture is to be delivered to more than one destination, confirm with the receiving parties the delivery date and time.

One Day to Go

- Book a cleaner to clear up as you pack, and to follow you to your new home to clean up there before you unpack.
- Aim to finish the packing today, apart from a few essentials in the kitchen and bathroom. You'll feel so much better when you can see the end is in sight.
- Unless you've arranged otherwise with the removal company, you'll be expected to dismantle any furniture that cannot be moved out whole.
- Take down curtains and any fixtures you're intending to take with you.

PACKING

If your removal company has agreed to do the packing, make sure you're clear about exactly what they're going to do. It can range from packing every last thing to just the glass and china. Also check to see if they'll be coming around the day before to pack or will do it all on the day. This can depend on the time you have to vacate your house.

 If you're doing the packing, begin as early as possible.

 Before the move, collect all the newspapers, tissue paper, boxes, cardboard, wrapping and padding you can find. The removers will provide some, but supermarkets, greengrocers and electrical goods suppliers are a good source.

 Protect your valuables with bubble wrap.

 Clearly label boxes with fragile items – and load them into the van last.

 Take extremely delicate items with you in your car.

 Make sure you use suitable boxes that are strong enough. Always fill the box to the top and then close the lid, so you can stack boxes in the removal van. Always use tape to fasten both the bottom and the top of all your boxes. Clearly write which room you would like the box to end up in. If you do this on the tape, the removal team will know that these are your instructions, and will also keep the boxes in better condition, allowing them to be used again and again.

 Place heavy and bulky items in the bottom of a box; then lighter stuff on top.

 Use small boxes to pack books, these are the heaviest things you'll have to pack, and therefore keep the overall weight of the box down.

 General items are packed into boxes about the size of a tea chest. Linen boxes are bigger because the contents are obviously lighter. Robe units or hanging garment carriers are used to hang your clothes in (portable wardrobes). Your removal company will supply you with these, usually on the return of your acceptance form.

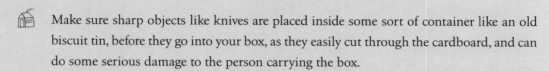 Make sure sharp objects like knives are placed inside some sort of container like an old biscuit tin, before they go into your box, as they easily cut through the cardboard, and can do some serious damage to the person carrying the box.

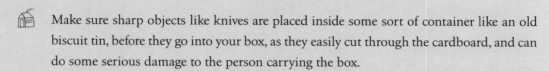 Write on the labels which room the boxes are going to. Stuck on the side as well as the top, colour-coded sticky labels are the simplest solution.

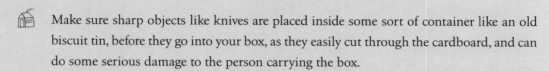 Keep your stereo speakers away from your TV – the speakers contain magnets that can damage it.

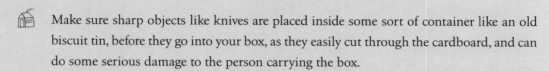 Put one or two heavy items in each box so they weigh roughly the same – check the weight is even throughout the container.

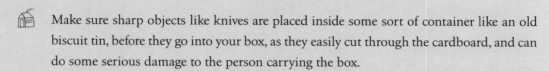 Before you lift a box, test its weight. Put it down straight away if it's too heavy.

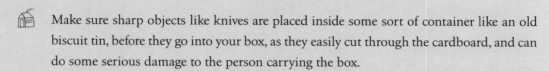 Finally, ask someone to help you on the day of the move. It may be too much to tackle on your own.

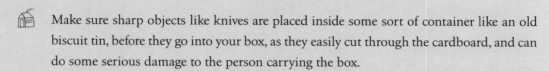 To make unpacking easier, carpets and rugs should go in the van last so at the other end they can go down first before any furniture.

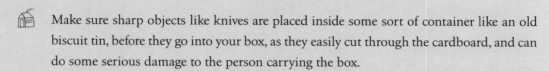 To protect furniture during the move use rugs to cover anything that could be scratched or damaged.

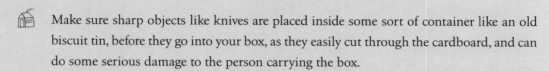 Protect your hands while packing and unpacking – wear gloves.

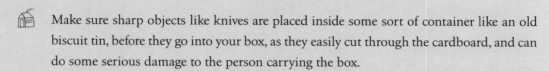 Bin bags are very useful for placing bedding and so on into. This even helps with the packing of the van or containers as they squash and fill all the awkward gaps.

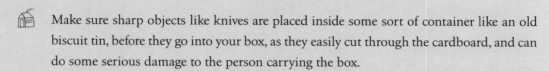 Protect china plates by packing a paper plate in between each one.

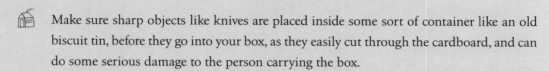 Draw out a floor plan of your new house and photocopy it for the removers. If, using coloured stickers, you colour-code the rooms and the boxes to go into them, you'll reduce mistakes and the removers will be able to get on without having to ask you what goes where all the time.

- Make sure you've disconnected the washing machine and fit transit brackets to secure the drum.
- Make up a box of refreshments for the next day, bearing in mind that your cooker may be disconnected or in the back of a removal van. Include tea, coffee, sugar and so on and, the most important item of all, the kettle. You'll have to keep the refreshments flowing as moving house is thirsty work. A selection of cold drinks is also a good idea. Mark on the box 'kettle things', which will be guaranteed to be last on and first off the van. Slip in a bottle of champagne so you can start off life in your new home in style.
- Make up a box in the bathroom and put in the toiletries you won't need before the move. Leave this box open to put in all the other toiletries the next morning, so you can then seal it up after everyone has got up.
- In case of rain try to put anything moveable outside either into the garage or in a dry place.
- If you have difficulty parking outside your house, it could be a good idea to park your own car or cars there overnight; then move them as the removal van arrives. Remember: the van needs more room than its own length to manoeuvre.
- Make sure your mobile phone is fully charged up for the next day – you're probably going to need it.
- Pack a box of emergency items for the actual day of the move. You'll also need cleaning equipment and lots of bin bags.
- Don't run out of money on the day – you may want to buy a takeaway meal, make an emergency dash to the shops for supplies, buy a bottle of wine or even tip your removal men!
- Keep a note of the telephone numbers of utility companies in case there are connection problems at the new property.

Moving Day

- Make certain that curtains are easily accessible. You'll need them to cover windows on the first night.
- When the van arrives, show the team leader around the house and explain exactly what is to go and what isn't.
- Once the van is loaded, take a walk around with the team leader to ensure that all the items to be moved have been placed on the van. Check behind doors, in cupboards and on the walls. Don't forget to take the clock or anything else still hanging on the wall.
- Once the removal van has left, read all the relevant meters, make a note of the readings and load up your cars/car. Check when you leave that all the windows and doors are locked.

At your New Home

- Make sure the entrance hall is protected from dirty footmarks as people tramp to and fro with furniture and boxes.
- Inform your team leader which rooms are which.
- Check that the utilities companies have connected your gas, electricity and phone.
- Have someone stand at the main entrance that the removal men are using and direct them to the appropriate rooms. If you're having boxes unpacked, the contents will usually be placed on to a table or appropriate surface for you to put away.
- Check around the house and if you need anything heavy moved, ask the removal men to do it for you. But don't take advantage.
- You'll get more out of your removal men if you offer them an incentive when they finish, like fish and chips.
- Make the beds. The main thing to do tonight is to go to bed and get a good night's sleep.

- If you're moving with children, make sorting their rooms out a priority so that they have their familiar things around them. Don't underestimate how unsettling it is for them to be uprooted.
- Make sure you have a TV licence before you switch on.
- Set yourself achievable goals for unpacking and sorting. Tackle it room by room, rather than piecemeal.
- Change the front and back door locks, just in case there are spare sets floating around that the previous owner forgot to call in.
- Get spare sets of keys cut as soon as you can.

USEFUL CONTACTS

Packed with information, and run by an ex-removal man who understands the problems first hand:
Web: www.helpiammoving.com

Provides the postcode of any address you key into it. If you're not sure of your new one, check it before you start filling in all those forms:
Web: www.royalmail.com/paf

Provides a map centred on the postcode or address you key in. Useful if your removal company isn't sure where to go:
Web: www.multimap.co.uk

Useful to find out your credit rating:
Web: www.checkmyfile.com

Sort out your TV licence online:
Web: www.tv-l.co.uk

Online service to let you inform the companies and organizations you need to tell about your change of address:
Web: www.ihavemoved.com

Energywatch (energy watchdog site with lots of consumer info)
Web: www.energywatch.org.uk

Save on Your Bills (find the best deal for services to your home)
Web: www.saveonyourbills.co.uk

Unravelit (compare prices for energy, insurance and financial products)
Web: www.unravelit.com

uSwitch (information and impartial advice, allowing you to compare, choose and obtain the best services deal on line, including mobile phones)
Web: www.uswitch.com

National Guild of Removers and Storers (companies vetted, approved and bound by the Guild's Code of Practice)
Tel.: 01494 792 279
Web: www.ngrs.org.uk

Self Storage Association (SSA) (trade organization representing companies that operate self-storage centres, with a list of nationwide members)
Tel.: 07071 224235
Web: www.ssauk.com

Cartons Direct (sell extra-strong boxes, tape, bubble wrap and so on for moving house)
Web: www.cartonsdirect.co.uk

E-pack (over 1,500 packing materials can be ordered online – cartons, polythene, tapes, strapping, cushioning, postal products etc.)
Web: www.e-pack.co.uk

BUYING LAND AND SELF-BUILD

Searched the country and just can't find your dream home? One option is to build your perfect house. Most recent figures show there are about 20,000 self-builds or renovations each year – making self-builders more prolific than the country's biggest building firm.

The market for self-build land and housing has generally been on the increase for the last few years. The Government's new house-building targets for various 'development areas' has stirred interest and demand in several parts of the country, especially as house prices levelled off during 2003.

Self-build tends to be more prevalent in less urban areas and where the market for speculative house building is relatively small, and the typical self-builder is well off and looks for a more individual home. A change in the way self-builders can borrow money has helped too.

'Self-build' is, however, a misleading word, as only about 5 per cent of people actually do the building work themselves. That is for the very brave. Most self-builders may find the building plot themselves, then commission designers and architects, and select builders, often with site managers, to oversee the build.

But in any circumstance, self-build is not the answer for the faint-hearted. Before you start, ask yourself some questions:

ARE YOU THE TYPE TO SELF-BUILD?

- Can you afford to build and live somewhere else while construction work is carried out?
- Are you able to oversee the project yourself, or do you need to budget for an architect or site manager to do it for you?

- Are you a calm person? Building work can be stressful and you need to be a problem solver not a panicker.
- Are you good at explaining exactly what you want? You'll be asked many questions by designers and builders during the process and you need to be decisive and have thought out the end result before you have to deal with queries.
- Are you flexible? Self-builders need to compromise when restrictions stop them doing exactly what they want.
- Are you good with money? You'll need to keep a very close eye on costs as the project progresses so you stay on budget.
- Do you have a basic knowledge and understanding of building processes? Not essential but it helps!

WHY SELF-BUILD?

Most people choose to self-build for the following reasons:

- They can have a home in a location of their choice (so long as a building plot is available).
- They can choose a house design that suits them and their family.
- It usually costs less to build a house than to buy one.
- Self-build homes can be constructed at a cost far less than any major house builder can match – around 30 per cent cheaper.
- They can incorporate ecological and energy-efficient schemes into the project.
- The satisfaction of doing it.

It's true too that self-build homes are a good investment, because they tend to be built with more care and innovative design than houses built by standard developers. This means that they could see stronger price appreciation than other properties – on average a self-built house is worth 25 to 30 per cent more than it cost to build – though of course there are no guarantees.

IS IT REALLY CHEAPER TO SELF-BUILD?

This table compares the cost of the average four-bedroomed developer's house
with the cost of a self-built four-bedroomed house around the UK:

County	Developer-built	Self-built	Saving
Greater Manchester	£146, 873	£108,765	26%
Essex	£309, 995	£192, 157	38%
Kent	£234, 995	£213, 267	9%
Glamorgan	£179, 995	£100, 949	44%
County Down	£168, 500	£128, 892	24%

Source: Buildstore (www.buildstore.co.uk) 2003

Three other bonuses:

1   With no property developer involved, there's no developer's profit to
    be factored into the costings on the project.
2   VAT reclaim: VAT can be reclaimed on building materials bought
    from a VAT registered supplier. This is done at the end of a new build
    and is the big advantage over renovating or extending your existing
    house. If you use a VAT registered contractor, all invoices for labour
    and materials should be zero rated (*see page 166*).
3   Stamp duty: on a self-build project stamp duty is paid only on the
    land, and then only when the purchase price is over £60,000 (duty is
    levied at 1 per cent on the amount over this – *see page 47*). No stamp
    duty is levied on the cost of the build.

BUDGETING THE PROJECT

Like any major purchase, you need to work out what you can afford – a very
important part of any self-build. There's no point in dreaming about a huge
modern construction, with five bathrooms and a jacuzzi, if your budget is

> TIP *Calculate the value of the finished property. Though you're no doubt self-building to create the house of your dreams, it does make sense to find out how much the house will be worth in the end so you aren't tempted to overspend. Take the plans to local and experienced estate agents, and ask them to calculate a value, were they going to market the finished house. They'll be cautious, as these are only plans they're looking at, but don't be overoptimistic yourself. From the estimated figure they give you, take off the cost of the plot, the cost of the build, plus a contingency for overspend of at least 10 per cent.*

only going to stretch to four bedrooms and a shower room. The average self-build costs about £147,000, with 15 per cent costing over £225,000, including land (2003).

The first step is to find out how much your existing house is worth and then how much you can afford to raise or borrow (*see below*).

The average self-build takes between one and one and a half years, which should help you work out your budget for living costs in the interim. As an incentive to complete the work, the indemnity policy and site insurance usually run for a maximum of two years.

The second step is to work out how much materials and goods will cost in relation to the size of the property you have in mind. You can find an excellent calculator on the Homebuilding & Renovating web site at www.homebuilding.co.uk. Click on 'Beginners Guide'. The company also publishes a magazine.

Self-build Mortgages

In the past self-build mortgages were notoriously hard to find. Lenders were not keen to lend on properties that were being self-built, because of the risk that, if the build was not completed, they would have to repossess and try to sell a half-built house. However, the situation is easier these days – several lenders specialize in this type of loan. Some lenders will lend you money to purchase land, typically 75 per cent of the purchase price or value, whichever is lower. The main difference between this and a traditional house-buying mortgage is that the rest of the money is then released in stages as the build progresses, rather than in a single sum.

There are typically five stages:

1   Preliminary costs and foundations.
2   Wall plate level or timber frame erection, or wind and watertight if it's a conversion/renovation.
3   Wind and watertight for bricks and mortar or timber framed, or plastering and services stage on a conversion/renovation.
4   First fix and plastering for brick/timber buildings, or second fix for conversions/renovations.
5   Second fix to completion and completion of a conversion/renovation.

At *first fix* stage:

- Electrician has placed cables and metal boxes for switches and sockets.
- Plumber has fitted carcassing (pipework).
- Floor joists and stud work for walls complete.
- Door frames are in place.

At *second fix* stage:

- Sockets are on walls and the electricity supply has been made live.
- Sanitaryware has been fitted and radiators hung.
- Boiler has been fitted.
- Plastering is complete, and skirting and architrave fixed.
- All doors have been hung.

TIP *Some lenders release the funds after each stage has been completed, which can cause you cash-flow problems. It would be better to find a lender who has an advance-stage payment method so you have the funds before each stage starts.*

The Accelerator Mortgage

This is a special self-build mortgage launched by a company called Buildstore (www.buildstore.co.uk). It can direct you to a lender who will provide 95 per cent of the value of the land and 95 per cent of the value of the build, so you may not have to sell your existing home in order to buy your plot and start building. In effect you're paying your existing mortgage alongside the new-build mortgage, which sounds hairy, but the logic is

- you would be having to pay rental on accommodation anyway while funding the build, which may well be as much as a mortgage repayment each month – if not more;
- you only pay interest on the increments you borrow (the money to buy the land), and then the money to complete the build, which is paid out in stages.

This type of mortgage works in a similar way to a purchase mortgage, with varying interest arrangements, though one lender, The Mortgage Business, offers a ten-month payment holiday (at time of writing) which would be an advantage. The accelerator mortgage includes an indemnity insurance policy, through Lloyds, which costs a one-off payment of between £400 and £500, which covers the lender against the project failing.

Ecology Mortgages

These are 'green' mortgages, usually offered to borrowers who are renovating or building new properties with a commitment to the environment, renewable resources and ecological renovation techniques, or who might find it difficult to get a mortgage offer elsewhere. These mortgage companies will also lend to environmentally linked businesses. The best-known lenders include The Ecology Building Society, which offers a standard variable-rate loan with low initial fees and an accelerator mortgage.

The Cash Self-builder

As self-build is so much cheaper than buying a property outright, you may be in the fortunate position of being able to use the profit from the sale of your previous home to finance the building project. You still need to live somewhere while the work is going on, but many self-builders buy or hire mobile homes and live literally 'onsite' surrounded by scaffolding and rubble. Only you can decide if this sort of existence is bearable (don't forget how long the average self-build takes), or if it would save your sanity and your marriage to rent a house in the meanwhile.

If you take the cash-build route, it's going to be up to you to ensure that you have enough cash flow. Builders rely on stage payments simply in order to pay for materials and subcontractors. Before the work begins, have a meeting with your builder and find out what payments will be due and when (*see page 149 for the typical stages*), and ensure that the money is available when the invoice comes in. If there's a hitch because of your poor cash-flow management, it will hold up the continuity of the build and will not help harmonious relations with your builder.

Other Costs in Self-build

- Don't forget services: unless you're buying a serviced building plot, connections to services such as water, drainage, electricity, gas and telephone can be surprisingly expensive. Depending upon the area the self-build land is located in, these can come to £5,000 or more.
- You'll have to pay for planning and building regulations in any situation, but you'll also have to pay for other professional services as required by your lender. These will include some form of professional certification. For example a site survey may be required and soil samples taken by a surveyor or a structural engineer. The involvement of these kinds of professionals on sites with complex issues (such as difficult soil composition and conditions or poor drainage) is largely inevitable, since they'll be needed to design the foundations.

> **TIP** *The single most important piece of advice for any self-builder is* keep an eye on costs. *Building projects notoriously run over budget, as unforeseen circumstances emerge. You may well also be tempted to add details to the specification as the plans are transformed into bricks and mortar. Make sure you factor in a sensible contingency sum – between 8 and 10 per cent – either from your own funds or by incorporating it into the amount you borrow.*

- You'll need to budget for the architect at design stage, a project manager, who may well be the architect, and an architectural technician if you use one.
- Landscaping the area round the property will also have to be budgeted for, especially driveways and terracing, garden and lawns, fencing and gates (*see page 169*).
- If you have a self-build mortgage, you'll have to factor in living costs while your house is being built, unless you have an accelerator mortgage.
- On top of all this, you'll have your own legal fees (including local searches – *see page 79*), and the mortgage arrangement costs.

LOOKING FOR LAND

Finding and buying the right plot is the hardest part of any self-build scheme. You may be lucky enough to have found a plot already, or may want to build on your own land (subject to planning permission of course!). But if you haven't, what should be the considerations? Location is critical – and the same criteria work here with buying a plot as they do with purchasing a house:

- Do you want a rural/urban setting?
- Are local amenities important?
- Does it need to be near a school or college? Or your place of work?
- Is it too close to another property that might be noisy and disruptive?

Not all land for sale can be used for building development. The ideal plot will be for sale with outline planning permission (OPP), which means the local authority has agreed in principle to the building of a house, but you'll need to check the OPP carefully to see what size of property they'll allow (*see below*). Most advertisements will mention that OPP has been granted – if it's not mentioned, then ask the vendor, or contact the planning department at

> TIP *Because self-build works out cheaper, it has the distinct advantage of enabling you to live in an area where you could not afford the current house prices.*

the local authority who will be able to tell you if the plot is likely to get planning permission. Some land is sold with detailed planning permission (*see below*).

Replacement Dwellings

This can be a good route to finding an ideal plot for your self-build: finding an existing property – perhaps a small bungalow or rundown shack made from timber or corrugated iron – that can be demolished and replaced. It's a wise move too as the land may already have access to a road, and mains services such as water and electricity, which would save you money. These types of properties are often on the market with detailed planning permission (DPP) meaning detailed drawings of a property have been passed in principle by the local authority. The proposed replacement building may not be what you had in mind, but you can always resubmit plans to your own design. But once again it's essential before you go any further with a purchase that you contact the local planning office and find out what restrictions they would put on a rebuild. They may only allow certain materials, a certain design and, most importantly, may only allow for a 'footprint' rebuild. This means the same size property in the same place as the previous one.

Conversions

Buildings with scope for conversion into homes offer people with imagination a fantastic opportunity to create something unusual and original. It might be a barn, an old church, a cow shed, a disused telephone exchange –

> **TIP** *Check that there's suitable access to the plot. Some land may be ideal for development, but access may be over someone else's land, in which case you'll have to negotiate rights of way. These can be complicated.*

the opportunities are wide and varied – and will give an architect something to get his teeth into. Though this is not strictly self-build-from-scratch because, like a replacement dwelling, there's an existing structure of some kind to work on, conversions are considered as 'development' by the local authority. You'll naturally need planning permission, which should include an application for change of use, and the structure may well be listed too. The building and site details, however, remain the same as for self-build (*see Chapter 8 for more information on buying unusual properties*).

Who's Selling it?

There are several places where land for sale is advertised:

- The local newspaper.
- Estate agents.
- Land agents: though many are keener on dealing with developers. Some plots are advertised in specialist magazines such as the *Estates Gazette*.
- National Building Plot Register: this is a comprehensive listing of self-build opportunities, updated daily. It can be accessed online via Plotsearch at www.plotsearch.co.uk, which has a small lifetime access subscription.
- www.plotfinder.net: an online resource of plots of land and properties for renovation and conversion with an annual subscription.
- PropertySpy: land and property experts who sell plots of land where there's a chance of getting future planning permission. Go to www.propertyspy.com.

You can do your own research too:

- Study ordnance survey maps for houses on very long or wide plots of land. The owner may be interesting in selling part of the plot for development – this is called 'Back Space' development.

- If you live in or want to build in a town, look for gaps in the street and find out who owns the land by consulting the Land Registry at www.landreg.gov.uk (or in Scotland www.ros.gov.uk). Look out too for disused lock-up garages.

- Water, electricity, telephone and gas companies sometimes have disused buildings around the country. Contact the estates department of the relevant body once you've identified your potential plot. Your planning permission application will have to include change of use (*see Chapter 8*).

The Cost

A simple way to calculate the price of land for sale is to find a similar plot for sale in the area you've earmarked that already has a property built on it; then find out the market value of that property from a local estate agent. The value of the land should equate to about 45 per cent of the market value of the property. Prices will vary from area to area, with the highest prices in the south-east.

CONVEYANCING AND A PLOT OF LAND

There's no difference in the conveyancing process when you buy a plot of land from when you buy a property, because the principle of conveyancing is that you become the owner of (officially 'have title to') that *plot* whether or not there's a property on it. If you buy a plot with a derelict building 'Rose Cottage' on it, for example, and you then demolish the derelict cottage and build a grand new house called 'Rose Manor', simply inform the Land Registry and they'll change the address on their register.

PLANNING PERMISSION

This can be a sticky issue, and many self-builders believe that planning officials go for 'safe' design and are stricter with self-builders than with other developers. It's a distinct advantage to buy land that already has outline planning permission (*see above*), but it may well be more expensive. The OPP will have certain restrictions, and you need to look closely at the fine detail to check it suits your requirements. There may be restrictive covenants on the land, and in some cases, where the land lies over mineworks or old tunnels, building on the land may be very expensive. Before you proceed with the purchase, you should organize a site appraisal of the land with a qualified planning development/land surveyor, who can give his or her opinion on suitability for building. You'll have to pay a fee, but it could be money well spent. To find a suitable surveyor in your area, call the Royal Institution of Chartered Surveyors contact centre on 0870 333 1600.

Some land may be sold with detailed planning permission – illustrative drawings including elevations – indicating that detailed plans have already been submitted and agreed to by the local authority for the erection of a specific type and size of house. Again you need to look very closely at the specifications for restrictions and convenants.

Once you've bought the property with OPP, in the knowledge that you can build on it, you can move to appointing an architect (*see page 152*). If you use a local architect, he or she should be familiar with the restrictions imposed by your local planning authority, and this will stop time being wasted by submitting plans that will never be accepted in a million years.

If the plot you've bought includes DPP, and you aren't keen on the design, you can always resubmit plans, with minor or major amendments (you'll have to pay a fee when you submit plans for planning permission).

> TIP *Get friendly with the neighbours: the people who live close to your proposed plot are the second most important people after the planning office, because they have the right to make an objection to any plans you might submit. Be friendly and talk through your ideas with them – but most of all, get them on your side.*

Have these drawn up bearing in mind restrictions that may have been imposed which enabled
them to be provisionally passed by the local
authority in the first place. Be realistic: if the DPP
was for a four-bedroomed, brick-built house,
you're unlikely to have plans accepted for a six-
bedroomed stone-built one – but it's always worth
a try! Many local authorities are clamping down
on the development or building of large new
properties in rural areas, and are demanding that

TIP *Make sure you note the time
restrictions on any planning permission granted. Some may last two years,
others five. If the plot has been on the
market a long time, and the planning
permission expires in two years, you
may have a very short time before you
need to start your building project.*

new builds are on the 'footprint' of any previous building that was on the
plot (*see page 153*). They'll also want to ensure that any new build is in keeping with the local area in terms of height, materials used and design.

For information go to www.onlineplanningoffices.co.uk.

The Office of the Deputy Prime Minister web site also provides information about planning permission and how to apply for it: www.odpm.gov.uk.
For information on Scottish Planning go to www.highland.gov.uk.

(*For more information of planning permission*)

DESIGN

The biggest advantage of self-build has to be in the possibilities for design it
offers you. Why else would you do it? Of course those pesky people at your
local planning office may place certain restrictions on the external design,
but undoubtedly your house will be more innovative and interesting than
any developer-built property you'll find. You can arrange the interior almost
any way you choose, so long as it's within building regulation guidelines, and
you have a blank canvas on which to incorporate the flooring, heating,
doors, windows, staircase, kitchen, fireplaces and lighting that *you* want –
not that you've inherited from someone else.

The obvious expert – and you must consult an expert – is the architect,
and you should ensure he or she is a member of the Royal Institute of British

Architects. In fact, the word 'architect' is a protected term and only qualified architects can use it. Their costs will depend on their level of involvement (*see page 152*), but you should negotiate the fee right at the beginning and have in writing what it will cover. Commission him or her on certain work stages: sketch proposals, full planning application, building regulations drawings ('full plans approval'), finding tenders for contractors, and administration of the contract (or overseeing the project until competition). Some architects make better designers than project managers and you can dispense with your architect at any stage, though you may have to renegotiate the fees. To find an architect, you can go to the RIBA web site (*address on page 168*) or ask friends or other self-builders who they've used, and in which area the architect excels. Word of mouth is the best recommendation.

Before briefing the architect, make a list of exactly what you want to achieve:

- Look carefully at the site, because it may dictate some aspects of the design. You may need to consider other houses and buildings nearby. Is there a view you want to exploit?
- Where does the sun rise and set? You may want to position bedrooms facing east and a sitting room facing west. Are there rooms that may get too hot in summer?

KIT-BUILT HOUSES

This is a viable self-build option, and there are a growing number of kit-house companies. You work with the company designer to find the style of house to suit you, or buy one of its standard designs 'off the shelf'. The timber structure is then made elsewhere and literally delivered on the back of a lorry once foundations and services have been put in place. Kit houses come in various shapes, sizes and budgets, and can be erected quickly. Another big advantage is that you buy all the details such as staircase and window frames up front, so you don't need to make compromises later on.

- Where will services like drains and electricity come on to the property?
- Do you want chimneys and open fireplaces?
- Think carefully about the entrance, as well as access to the property. Once you've established where the front of the house will be, you can work out the ideal plan for location of the rooms.
- How many bedrooms and bathrooms would be ideal?
- Do you need a downstairs loo? Legislation in 2004 regarding disabled access may make this essential, and your architect should be aware of this.
- How many reception rooms are necessary? Could you incorporate a kitchen-cum-dining room to create more space?
- What would be your ideal exterior material (though there may be local restrictions – *see page 153*). Brick, timber frame, stone, render . . .?
- Do you want plenty of garden/terrace, or a large parking area?
- Do you need to incorporate plenty of storage space?
- Is light a priority? Could you include a conservatory?
- Do you have certain large pictures or mirrors that you need a large wall space to include, or even a piece of furniture that needs to be incorporated?
- Could the loft space incorporate another bedroom/office/study? Even if you can't afford to develop this space now, think about where a staircase might go at a later date, and ensure the loft is built to the right building regulations for conversion to living space.
- Do you need a garage or workshop area?
- Are you keen to incorporate solar power or ecological schemes?

This will help the architect to put together a picture of what you need, and a framework around which he can work a design. It may also help to provide him with pictures of properties you admire, though once again restrictions on what will pass through planning vary from area to area, and what is acceptable in Cumbria may not wash in Somerset, for example. If you're dead set on a certain style, you may have a battle on your hands to persuade the planners, but it's worth a try – and you might achieve your dream.

> **TIP** *It's better to build the best and biggest house you can within your budget, even if it means delaying to a later date the erection or completion of other areas (such as the garage or the loft) you can't afford now. Put your money into quality and don't skimp on important materials – that is, use good-quality bricks on a simple shape, rather than cheaper bricks in a complicated shape, and install timber-framed windows rather than uPVC.*

Some architects are full-service designers and will produce schemes for the interior detailing too, but if yours has strengths in house design only, then use other specialists – heating and lighting designers, kitchen planners, specialist carpenters and so on – for their experience and flair in these areas. They'll be able to work from the architect's plans. As with briefing the architect, scour magazines and specialist publications (and borrow ideas from other people's houses) to give you a broad idea of what is possible, so your designer will know what you have in mind. If any of these experts seem unsure about your ideas or have never worked in that way before, find someone else who is more confident.

BUILDING REGULATIONS

Full planning approval is not the same as planning permission, but concerns the actual fabric of the house and sets the minimum standard the building work (materials, workmanship, depth of foundations etc.) must meet to satisfy the guidelines laid down by the building control department of your local authority.

The main reason for these regulations is to ensure the property is built safely, but they also cover energy conservation, access to the property and other matters. This doesn't mean you can't exceed the standards, if you decide you want larger joists, improved levels of heating and ventilation and so on. In fact, self-build houses are usually built to a better specification than developer builds.

Once you've received planning permission, you'll need to arrange for separate (building regulation) drawings to be drawn up showing all the constructional details, and these should be submitted in plenty of time to be approved before the project starts. The drawings can either be put together by your architect or you can have them done yourself by an architectural technician, depending on the contract you have with the architect. These experts are often the cheaper option. Your architect will hold copyright to the original drawings (which show the design of the property) but it's quite acceptable for you to take his drawing elsewhere to be prepared for building regulations.

You'll have to pay a fee to the local authority when you submit the building regulations drawings, and then they'll either be accepted or rejected within a certain time limit (usually within five weeks). They may also add certain restrictions to their approval. You can appeal if the plans are rejected, and you should ask them what the procedure is for this.

Once you have the approval, and the project is underway, the build will be inspected at regular intervals by a Building Control Officer or Surveyor. Your builder will inform the officer when he has reached a certain stage, and he cannot proceed until approval at each stage has been given. The officer will make his or her final visit upon completion and, once satisfied with the work, will issue a Certificate of Completion, which you should keep safely with your title deeds, as it will be needed once you come to sell the property.

STRUCTURAL ENGINEERS

Your architect may budget for and include the services of a structural engineer to do calculations about the construction of the property. He or she will

TIP *There will be a huge number of decisions to make about everything, right down to the style of electric socket, so you'll need to be methodical and give yourself plenty of time to think each element through. Then be decisive. Mistakes are expensive to put right later. However, you must be the one who makes the decisions after taking advice. You've gone to all the trouble of building your own house, so make sure it's the way you want it to be. When it's finished it will be too late for regrets.*

REAL-LIFE ACCOUNT

Nick and Carolyn Gasson, who have a farm in South Warwickshire, seven years ago self-built a six-bedroomed, three-bathroomed house on their land.

'We had been living in a bungalow in Hook Norton and Nick was involved in the family farm, which folded. When they paid him out, we had to use all the money to buy farmland which had no farmhouse, so we bought a mobile home and had to earn enough from the farm before we could afford to build. We had a 13-month-old baby, and by the time we had built the house four years later, we had another child and one more on the way! There was no mains electricity to the mobile home – just a generator with seven hours of power on it before we had to refuel, so in the winter months it was freezing.

'We borrowed a certain amount to start the build, but put it onto the general farm borrowing. At first we wanted to convert a stone barn, but the planning department said there was no way. It was too prominent on a hill. When they had given us permission for the mobile home, they hadn't come to see where we had put it – again high on the hill – but when we put in for the house, they came to see and were horrified. No way could we build there! The driveway was in fact three quarters of a mile long to the proposed plot, and in the end we were given planning permission to build 400 yards from the road, which on reflection was much more suitable in terms of access.

'Our architect was an old friend, and I literally drew him a picture as a child might of a very simple house with chimneys at each end of the roof. It did seem to match local farmhouses quite well, but throughout the process when we went to people's houses we spent the whole time looking at their architraves or skirting boards for ideas! We talked it through very thoroughly and went back to the drawing board many times to change details. We didn't want doors in the middle of walls into rooms for example – it cuts a room in half – and we wanted to use the loft space for the fifth and sixth bedrooms and put in dormer windows. I'm good at imagining things off-plan which I think helped a lot.

'We employed a jack-of-all-trades-type builder as project manager – you have to have someone oversee the job – and he would tell us when we needed the next tradesman in the chain. But we did all the ordering, and were very busy going off to collect things. I even had rolls of lead in my car. We didn't have a desperate time limit and we were on site all the time, otherwise it would have been very stressful coordinating everything and everyone. The only problem was the plumber, who was a nightmare. It took a year to build, but we moved into a building site we were so keen to be in by then, and I spent the whole summer moving rubble and painting with the new baby asleep in the corner of the kitchen.

'We do have some regrets. Because we didn't use a building company we don't have any warranties, though the building regulations were complied with, but it might be a problem if we come to sell. We cut a few corners too – the doors were all cheap – but we couldn't afford better ones, and they're only cosmetic details. We can upgrade them when we can afford to. We still have things to do, and have only surfaced the drive this summer. But everyone who comes here says the house has a lovely feel, so we must have done something right. We had no choice but to build if we wanted to carry on farming, but we were very lucky. It cost £80,000 to build and because land was cheaper then and grain prices high, we were able to do it. If we'd waited a year, we would only have been able to afford a two-bedroomed bungalow!'

work out what type and weight of joists are needed and/or whether steel beams are necessary to take the loads of the roof and floor depending on the types of materials being used in the build. They may also be necessary to advise about the construction of the foundations, which depend on the land. If your architect is only drawing up design plans (elevations) and not organizing the building-regulation drawings, then you'll need to ask if a structural engineer's calculations are necessary and pay for these separately.

WORKING WITH BUILDERS

This is the most important relationship of any self-build project. (*See Chapter 9 for advice on finding, appointing and working with builders successfully.*)

TIP *All the best-laid plans: things will inevitably go wrong, but if you're flexible (and keep a sense of humour) they're not insurmountable. On one self-build everything was going swimmingly until the contractor fixed the gutters on a low-hanging roof. Then the owners tried to open the upstairs windows . . . After a hasty rethink, the windows had to be adjusted so they opened inwards.*

USING A PROJECT MANAGER

The secret to any successful self-build project is to do it within the budget and within the time. A project manager is a professional who coordinates all the elements of the build, and it's a service offered by architects, surveyors, building contractors or professional project managers. Their fees will be between 3 and 10 per cent of the cost of the build, which sounds like a lot, but an experienced project manager will save you time and money in the end.

If you're overseeing the job yourself, you may think you can do without a project manager. It will inevitably save you money, but only if you do it well. Running a project takes skill, forward planning, people skills, decisiveness, the ability to anticipate problems, and immense skills of coordination. To do it successfully you'll need to understand how contractors work, to keep everyone briefed at each stage and to juggle subcontractors, who may be tied up on another job just when you need them. It's not a task for the faint-hearted.

INSURANCE

Several insurance policies should be in place before you begin your self-build project:

- *Site insurance*: this is essential and should include public liability cover in the event of damage to a third-party property, or injury to people (except employees) while they're on your site.
- *Contract works insurance*: to protect your investment against damage to or theft of materials from your site or damage to the building in the course of construction.
- *Legal expenses insurance*: so you can pursue any action arising from the project through the courts.
- *Accident cover*: compensation to provide for your family against temporary or permanent disablement caused through accidents that occur as a result of the project.

- *Cover for loss or damage to plant and equipment.*
- *Structural warranties (see below).*

You should ensure that any contractor you appoint has adequate insurance cover too, including public liability insurance, so he can compensate anyone should an accident occur during the building work or should any neighbouring building be damaged. It should also cover any damage to mains drainage or road reinstatement. If you're carrying out the build yourself, but are employing others to help you, then you'll need employer's insurance too, to indemnify you against your legal liability to pay compensation for bodily injury, disease, death, or nervous shock sustained by your employees, arising out of the building work.

> **TIP** *If you're carrying out work on a property when you're living there (see Chapter 9), you'll need to inform insurers about the building work, and let them know when it's complete, in case there's any damage caused to the existing building or its contents.*

Warranties

These are guarantees, provided by an impartial building warranty provider, that your house has been constructed correctly and to specific guidelines, and the warranties will insure you against structural defect (usually for a period of 10 years). In fact, your mortgage lender will insist you have them. But even if you don't need a mortgage, you'll need warranties to show potential buyers (and their lender) that the house has been built to an acceptable standard. In order to secure a warranty, you'll need inspections by the warranty provider at certain stages of the work (*see below*). Typical cover includes the following:

- Repair of major damage caused by a defect in the load-bearing structure or by ground movement.
- Any defect or damage in a flue or chimney serving a heating appliance or fireplace, which at the time of claim represents an imminent danger to the physical health and safety of an occupier of the home.

- Repairing defects that cause the underground drainage systems to malfunction.
- Damage to tile or slate roof coverings of a pitched roof, external tile hanging or rendering, and floor decking and screeds.

The National House Building Council (NHBC) is a leading warranty and insurance provider for new homes in the UK, and is a good place to find out information about policies and warranties you'll need. Go to the web site of the NHBC www.nhbc.co.uk or call 01494 735760. During the build an NHBC inspector will check the work at each stage, and then issue a warranty once he or she is happy with the quality of the work. Other warranties acceptable to self-build lenders include architects' certificates.

Several insurance companies have tailor-made insurance packages for self-builders. Go to www.ebuild.co.uk for a list.

> TIP *Even if you have an architect's certificate – his or her guarantee that the work is of adequate quality – it still pays to have a warranty. In most cases any certificate exists only between you and the architect and does not extend to people who buy the property from you.*

RECLAIMING VALUE ADDED TAX

One big advantage of self-build is that you can reclaim the VAT on goods and materials used at the end of the project. You can make the claim if the new house is to be a private domestic residence (i.e. not for business or to be let out), and you must keep detailed proof of all the goods on which you've paid VAT during the project. The claim needs to be submitted within three months of completion, and you get only one chance to claim. You cannot however claim for:

- carpets and curtains;
- white goods (washing machines, fridges etc.);
- trees and plants;
- burglar alarms;
- professional services;
- equipment hire;
- transport of materials and tools used.

HM Customs and Excise have a useful guide called *VAT Refunds for Do It Yourself Builders*, under notice 719 (www.hmce.gov.uk/forms/ notices/ 719.htm). If the build is complicated, then it would be a good idea to employ a VAT expert.

USEFUL CONTACTS

HOUSEBUILDING ADVICE AND
INFORMATION:
Asba Architects (site listing architects
who specialize in self-build, renovation
and conversion)
Freephone 0800 387310
Web: www.asba-architects.org.uk

**Association of Plumbing and Heating
Contractors** (APHC)
14 Ensign House
Ensign Business Centre
Westwood Way
Coventry CV4 8JA
Tel.: 02476 470626
Web: www.licensedplumber.co.uk

EBuild (advice on UK self-build, DIY and
renovation, and self-build mortgage links)
Web: www.ebuild.co.uk

Buildstore (Self-Build Advisory Service)
Unit 1
Kingsthorne Park
Houstoun Industrial Estate
Livingston
Scotland EH54 5DB
Web: www.buildstore.co.uk

Council of Registered Gas Installers
(CORGI)
4 Elmwood
Chineham Business Park
Crockford Lane
Basingstoke
Hants RG24 8WG
Tel.: 01256 372 200
Web: www.corgi-gas.co.uk

Design for Homes (advice/portal site incorporating the Design for Homes Architects Group, RIBA's linked society for architects in housing)
Web: www.aih.org.uk

Electrical Contractors' Association
(ECA)
ESCA House
34 Palace Court
Bayswater
London W2 4HY
Tel.: 020 7313 4800
Web: www.eca.co.uk

Housebuilding site for self-builders:
Web: www.housebuilding.co.uk

Housebuilding and Renovation
(magazine and web site)
Web: www.homebuilding.co.uk

Federation of Master Builders
Gordon Fisher House
14–15 Great James Street
London WC1N 3DP
Tel.: 020 7242 7583
Web: www.fmb.co.uk

Landbank Services
Web: www.selfbuildcentre.com

The National Federation of Builders
Construction House
56–64 Leonard Street
London ECA 4JX
Tel.: 020 7608 5150
Web: www.builders.org.uk

Royal Institute of British Architects
(250,000 pages of useful information about architecture, architects, and the Royal Institute of British Architects)
Web: www.architecture.com
Homebuilder (a Scottish web site for anyone involved in, or planning to embark upon, a self-build, extension or renovation project. Find the products, suppliers and information resources you need)
Web: www.homebuilder.co.uk

MORTGAGE INFORMATION:
Council of Mortgage Lenders (the trade association for mortgage lenders in the UK; its members undertake around 98% of UK residential mortgage lending)
Web: www.cml.org.uk

The Ecology Building Society (a mutual building society dedicated to improving the environment by promoting sustainable housing and sustainable communities)
Web: www.ecology.co.uk

LAND INFORMATION:
Land for Sale
Web: www.advice-landforsale.co.uk/self-build-land-for-sale.htm

Property Auction Guide
Web: www.property-auctions-guide.co.uk

UK Land Directory
Web: www.uklanddirectory.org.uk

Greenbelt Land For Sale
Web: www.greenbeltlandforsale.co.uk
Web: www.selfbuildland.co.uk/index.html

USEFUL LISTINGS OF LAND SEARCH
COMPANIES:
Web: www.uklanddirectory.org.uk/
Land-for-Sale-in-UK-Directory.htm

MORE SOURCES OF INFORMATION:
Tony Booth and Mike Dyson, *Build Your
Own Home: The Ultimate Guide to
Managing a Self-Build Project*, How To
Books

Murray Armor and David Snell, *Building
Your Own Home*, Ebury Press

Mark Brinkley, *The Housebuilders Bible*, 5th
edn (, Ovolo Publishing,). (Freephone credit
card orders: 01487 824704.)

The National Homebuilding Show
(usually in March each year at Birmingham
NEC, with regional shows throughout the
year)
Web: www.homebuildingshow.co.uk

The Scottish Homebuilding Show (usually in May each year at SECC Glasgow)
Web: www.homebuildingshow.co.uk

KIT-BUILD HOUSES:
Alpine Timber Frame
Tel.: 01435 868898
Web: www.alpinetimberframe.com

Benfield Green Dream Homes
Tel.: 01291 437050
Web: www.adtimtec.com/html/Green_
Dream_Homes.htm

Cedar Self-build
Tel.: 01244 661048
Web: www.cedar-self-build.com

Deckhouse
Tel.: 020 7350 2345
Web: www.deckhouse.com

English Heritage Buildings
Tel.: 0870 728 0649
Web: www.ehbp.com

Gryffe Development
Tel.: 01505 875171
Web: www.gryffedevelopment.co.uk

Potton
Tel.: 01480 401401
Web: www.potton.co.uk

Rayne Construction
Tel.: 01464 851 518
Web: www.rayne-constructionltd.freeserve.
co.uk

Robertson Timber Kit
Tel.: 01343 549786
Web: www.timberkit.co.uk

Skyhomes
Tel.: 01478 611211
Web: www.skyehomes.co.uk

HOLIDAY AND SECOND HOMES

A croft by the sea. A thatched cottage with roses over the doorway. A villa on the Med. For years and for those who can afford it, owning a second home has been immensely popular. You have a familiar bolt hole you can escape to for holidays and weekends, full of your own furniture and effects – a home from home. You light the fire or jump in the pool and it's yours to enjoy. Then, when you come to sell it, hopefully you'll have accrued a healthy asset, the proceeds of which will keep you in your old age or provide a nest egg for your children.

However, with a second home comes a great deal of responsibility, whether you intend to buy in the UK or abroad. They're expensive to purchase and expensive to run. Some second-home owners let out their holiday homes to relatives and friends at a low rental to cover these costs. But, for others, a second home can be a viable business and a means of earning valuable additional income, so they invest in a second property with no intention of staying in it themselves. What you do with your second home will affect how you're taxed when you own it and the way you borrow money to buy it.

BUYING IN THE UK

What are the advantages?

- You have a familiar place not too far away to go to for your holidays.
- You won't be at the mercy of airlines (nor will you have the cost) and you can simply jump in the car.
- You're saving yourself the cost of expensive holidays here or abroad, while still owning a property asset.

- It might make you money or at the very least earn its own keep.
- You're dealing with a familiar property system and in your own language.
- There are some valuable tax advantages with holiday lets over buy to let. For example capital gains tax on profits when you sell is lower with holiday lets and you can claim more of your rent to reduce the income tax bill you owe (*see pages 193–4*).
- You have a valuable asset in an attractive location, which will, one hopes, increase in value by the time you come to sell. However, the rise in property values is not guaranteed.

The same principles apply for choosing and buying a second home as they do for your main one (*see Chapter 3*) – but there are additional factors you need to think about:

- Because your second home will inevitably be left empty for long periods, it's vulnerable to break-ins. You might want to think about buying in a village, or close to other houses that are permanently occupied, or buy a flat in a part-occupied property (*see pages 195–6 about insuring a second home*).
- Accessibility and practicality: is it near enough to local amenities, transport routes and leisure facilities to be convenient for you (and won't take hours to reach in the Friday evening rush hour) and would also appeal to potential tenants? (*See 'Finding Suitable Properties', pages 177–8.*)
- Maintenance: a second home can be hard work. The issues of maintenance if you're letting it out are dealt with below, but even if you have the property for your own use only, think hard about the issues: could you get to it quickly in an emergency (frozen pipes, damage to the roof, after a break-in)? Do you want to spend every holiday and weekend there mending things and repainting, even mowing the lawn? You might want to think about a low-maintenance house or flat rather than a country cottage if DIY does not appeal.

- Will the house suit everyone? A seaside property may be fun now, but will you tire of it as your family grows up? Will a quaint, low-beamed cottage be practical as you grow older?

- If you intend to let, are you comfortable with the idea of people you do not know living in your house and sleeping in your bed? You'll also need to lock away your personal possessions. Do you mind having to hide your wetsuit and golf clubs every time you leave?

- Letting will also restrict the times you can holiday there. The summer season and school holidays command the highest rents, and you may find you miss out on enjoying the best times of year.

How to Finance Buying a Second Home in the UK

There are two considerations about raising the funds to purchase a holiday home, and they depend on what you intend to do with it:

OPTION 1: *Using it for your exclusive use, or renting it at a low rate to friends and relatives.* It can be difficult to borrow money to buy a holiday home, especially if you have a substantial mortgage on your main property. For this reason, most people remortgage their main home, once they've reduced their existing mortgage enough to afford to borrow further funds. This means you can buy the property outright, or at least put down a substantial deposit. Others see buying a second home as a capital investment – a means to invest money as an alternative to the stock market – and will therefore buy the property outright with cash.

A handful of lenders, however, do offer mortgages to people wanting to invest in second homes for their primary use:

Abbey National (who will lend up to 95 per cent of the property's value)
Alliance and Leicester (who will lend up to 85 per cent)
Nationwide (who will lend up to 85 per cent)
NatWest (who will lend up to 95 per cent)

TIP *Paragon Mortgages have a scheme for people wanting to buy a second home. Although it's called buy-to-let, it's available even if you do not intend to let the property at all (go to www.paragon-mortgages.co.uk).*

To cover maintenance costs and utility bills, owners can rent the property out for the odd week or weekend to friends and relatives at a low rate. Lenders would not consider this to be a commercial venture. As far as the Inland Revenue is concerned, however, this is income, and you have to declare the income on the 'land and property' pages of your tax return, even if you made no profit.

OPTION 2: *Using it for your holidays, but renting it out at other times of the year at a market rent to guests unknown to you.* Because you will occupy the holiday home for part of the year, it's not possible to get a buy-to-let mortgage (*see Chapter 1*), as this precludes you from living in the property yourself.

However, if you intend to invest in a second home and run it as a business, not only to cover costs but also to earn you income, then a lender will view this as a commercially viable business loan. A mortgage may be easier to arrange than it is for Option 1, but you'll need to convince the lender you're a good lending risk and your business is viable.

Setting up a Business

Though letting out your holiday property may sound like a part-time venture to earn a bit of cash to cover costs when you're not using it, you're running a business and will need to declare the income on your tax return. It's better to be organized and approach lettings seriously and correctly.

You're running a holiday letting business if:

- your accommodation is available for letting to the public for at least 140 days of the year, and actual letting must be at least 70 days;
- any one occupier (or group) stays for no more than 31 days in any period of seven months, but they can do so for the remaining five months.

If you're borrowing money to buy your holiday home, your lender will need to see a business plan of how you expect it to make money and to see if you're a good lending risk. But you should consider the questions they'll ask (most have their own plan layouts) anyway, even if you aren't borrowing to buy:

- *What is your business and your objective?* This needs to cover the location and description of the property, the level of service and quality you're offering and the rent you'll be charging.
- *Who is your target market and how will you reach it?* You'll need to outline the type of people you'll be hoping to attract and your marketing strategy (advertising, Internet presence etc.).
- *What is your financial forecast?* You'll need to make a realistic guess at how many guests you'll have in the first and subsequent two years, projected revenue and return bookings.

You'll need to prepare:

- a profit and loss account – showing how much profit you plan to make over a certain period, after deducting costs and depreciation;
- a balance sheet – showing your assets and liabilities and the funding for your business;
- a cash-flow forecast – showing how funds coming in will cover bills going out.

HOW TO CALCULATE THE YIELD

Purchase price of the property: £XXX,XXX

Projected annual rental income: £XXX,XXX (*err on the side of caution*)

Deduct Expenses (including mortgage repayments, maintenance, services and utilities): £X,XXX

= Net annual rental £X,XXX

Plus the cost of renting an equivalent holiday property yourself

Total annual yield: £X,XXX

Once your business is up and running, you'll have to keep good records, which you'll need so your accountant can prepare your accounts for your tax return. These should include details of:

- income;
- money owed to you at the year end (debtors);
- details of expenditure, capital equipment you've bought and capital expenditure on the property, and details of any money you owe at the year end (creditors);
- chequebook stubs, paying-in books, bank statements, interest you've paid or received, mortgage statements.

All sound a bit daunting? There are several places you can go for help with business start-up, including your bank, Business Link (www.businesslink.org), StartUps UK at www.startups.co.uk and enterprise agencies.

Managing your Property

Before you get carried away with the dream of buying a second home in the UK, and imagine yourself relaxing in your country idyll, which will be earning you lots of cash when you're not there, ask yourself a few hard questions about the practicalities. Second homes run as a business are a responsibility and the financial rewards can be slim:

TIP *Be realistic but not over-optimistic when preparing a plan for your mortgage lender. You need to show the business is viable, but not so wonderful it will be floated on the stock market in no time! Ensure you're borrowing enough to cover starting up and equipping the property – you don't want to have to go back to the lender and ask for more.*

1   Do you have enough time to market the property and deal with enquiries and bookings?

2   Do you live near enough to it to be able to clean it between lets and see in new guests at the beginning of their stay?

3   Are you prepared for the safety and legal issues of running a lettings business?

4   Are you able to get there quickly if there's a problem when guests are staying or when it's empty?

5   If you live too far away to get there easily, is there anyone who lives locally who can manage it for you, and are they reliable?

6   Should you employ a letting agency, and pay their fee?

7   Income from rental may cover your mortgage repayments (if you have them) and basic maintenance and costs (insurance, council tax etc.), but could you afford it should the roof, boiler, washing machine, bathroom suite or electricity wiring need replacing?

8   Could you still afford it if tenants were few and far between?

Only you can answer points 1–6 (*see pages 183–4 for your obligations as a holiday 'landlord'*). If time is short, or distances are too great, you might want to consider using a letting agency.

You could have more control over points 7–8. Naturally, you need to be realistic – you may not have the property let as often as you would like, but you can help to ensure it's let as often as possible by buying the right property in the right area.

TIP *Most letting agancies have links with insurance companies that can sell you a public liability policy, which is essential if you're letting your property to the general public.*

Finding Suitable Properties

Location

This and the type of property you buy are almost one and the same. If you need to let the property to make it pay, then its location should be a large consideration. Guests looking for holiday destinations in the UK (often through the Internet – *see pages 187–8*) will be looking for well-known and appealing regions. These are the 10 most popular holiday areas:

1   The Cotswolds
2   The Lake District
3   Dorset
4   The Yorkshire Dales
5   The Peak District
6   South Devon
7   South Cornwall
8   North Norfolk Coast and Norfolk Broads
9   West Scottish Highlands
10   Wales – Snowdonia and the Pembrokeshire Coast

Not surprisingly, these are popular areas with second-home buyers – so the choice may be restricted – but then that's obvious, because these are the types of places you would want to spend your holidays!

Types of Property

In order of preference, people contacting holiday letting agencies look for the following:

1   Detached cottage or house
2   Semi-detached cottage
3   Terraced cottage
4   Bungalow

> TIP *If you're tempted to buy outside a popular destination, it will be harder to rent out your property, unless it has some added attraction such as a superb location or an indoor swimming pool.*

LETTING AGENCIES

These can be the saviour for property owners who live far away from their holiday homes, or don't want the hassle of managing the property themselves. There are two types of letting agencies and you'll need to appoint the one that suits you best.

Letting and Management

These are usually located in popular holiday destinations, and may well be a department of a local estate agent. For a fee of around 20 per cent plus VAT of the rental, they'll:

 Advise you on a suitable property to buy in the area and the standard you should equip it to;

 Inspect your property to ensure it's suitable for rental to guests; set a market rent;

 Advertise the property (both locally, in a brochure and on the Internet);

 Arrange bookings on the property, take deposits and rental from holiday-makers, and pay you the balance of the rental monthly, less their commission, directly into your account;

 Often find you a cleaner, but certainly administer cleaning of the property and installation of guests on handover days;

 Organize emergency maintenance and give you information on local builders, plumbers, electricians and so on, for general maintenance.

It's up to you to equip and maintain the property generally, and to keep it up to a high standard.

Letting Only

There are hundreds of this type of letting agency. For a fee of around 20 per cent of the rental plus VAT, they'll:

Advise you on market trends and improvements you can make to your property;

 Grade your property by size, number of beds, amenities and facilities;

 Advertise your property, either in a brochure, national and local press or on the Internet (or both), usually using colour photographs and full details of the property;

 Arrange bookings on the property, take deposits and rental from holiday-makers, and pay you the balance of the rental monthly, less their commission, directly into your account;

 Inspect your property, usually annually, to check it's maintaining the standard at which it's advertised.

It's up to you to arrange property management, cleaning and maintenance. A good portal site is www.like2stay.co.uk, which lists agencies by area around the UK, and www.cottageline.com, an association of privately owned agencies.

Look through any of the brochures and web sites that advertise cottages, flats and houses to let and you'll see the variety of choices there are.

Seaside: the obvious option is to find a holiday property (house or flat) near the sea. This will be popular with guests, especially those with children looking for a bucket-and-spade holiday experience, and the closer it is to the sea the higher the rental it can demand. But there's a flip side too: properties by the sea are often more expensive to buy, as they carry a premium for their location. Though they'll be popular during the summer season (Easter to September), seaside properties are harder to let during the winter months, and you'll have the responsibility of maintaining a property that will be subject to the ravages of the British weather. Your maintenance costs may well be higher than other types of property.

REAL-LIFE ACCOUNT

Becky and Mike Hill live in Padstow in Cornwall and, four years ago, bought outright a two-bedroomed fisherman's cottage about 15 minutes' walk from the beach to let out to holidaymakers.

'Our success has been a combination of location and the house. It's right in the heart of Padstow, and we were told when we were viewing properties that there was a shortage of houses for two people who found it too expensive to rent a bigger property. We've worked hard to make it a very comfortable place to stay, with everything in it you would have at home. When people arrive after a long drive, they want to open the door and think, "Yes, this is nice." We provide bed linen and towels, fresh flowers and a bottle of wine on arrival, and information both about the cottage and current brochures about local events. We've also added umbrellas, torches, windbreaks for the beach and buckets and spades, and things in the kitchen like salt and pepper, tea and coffee. In four years we've never had any trouble or damage, but we believe that if you present a holiday property to a high standard, then people will respect it. We even include bin liners, sandwich bags and a thermos for hot drinks.

'When we equipped the cottage, we used all new furniture and carpets – people don't like shoddy and second hand – and each year I renew the bed linen and towels. We have also included a TV and video and a CD player, and all the obvious things in the kitchen – washing machine and microwave. There's no room for a dishwasher, and we were advised that as there wasn't room, not to bother trying to put one in. We already have four star accreditation [see page 188], and we wouldn't get five, because we aren't big enough.

'One secret is to have a fantastic relationship with your letting agent. Nicky Stanley at Harbour Holidays knows the cottage is to a high standard and we know she markets it well. It's important to check all the details before the brochure goes to press. But a combination of our efforts and hers have meant we are let for 48 weeks of the year.'

Country cottages: these are popular too, especially with town dwellers looking for a peaceful sojourn in the countryside. Properties not too far from a major town can often be rented out at weekends throughout the year (though the summer months will be the most popular), and proximity to leisure facilities will make them appealing (*see Chapter 10*). Typical rural cottages may also attract foreign tourists keen to experience British country life. There's no need to buy an old property – a more modern one in a lovely part of the country is infinitely better than an olde worlde cottage close to an urban conurbation. But remember that older properties often need more maintenance and may be more expensive to purchase.

Town properties: think too about a place in town. These are increasing in popularity, though the property needs to be in a heritage city centre like York, Bath, London or Edinburgh. It may not fit the bill for you as a holiday option, but if you make regular visits to London or another major city, a flat or house can be a useful pied-à-terre, which you can then let out to guests wanting to sample city life for short breaks. You're less likely with this type of property to fill it for two-week holiday rentals, but as the seasons are not so sensitive in town, you may be able to have it occupied throughout the year.

Quirky properties: guests often find more unusual properties very appealing, and it might be worth looking into buying an old windmill or water mill, a converted chapel or folly. (*See Chapter 8 for more information on how to do this.*)

What you want from the property is important – it needs to suit your holiday needs too – but it's worth doing a bit of your own market research in an area you have your eye on to find out how rentable holiday properties are in the area.

- Is there a good selection of holiday properties to rent?
- Are there too many? The market may be saturated. Many popular destinations have holiday letting agencies (*see pages 179–80*) based in local towns. Are they busy? Go in and ask them how full their holiday let properties are and what the demand is. They'll usually be happy to advise you on types of easy-to-let properties and market rents, and as most are part of a local estate agents, they may well have properties to buy on their books that would make ideal holiday lets.
- Are there plenty of leisure facilities and places in the vicinity to visit? Guests will like to have options, especially when the weather is bad.
- Is there a market for out-of-season guests – that is, those without school-aged children?

What Guests Want

Whether or not you're running a business operation, guests these days expect a high standard of comfort, including all the things they would have at home, and even a bit of luxury – it's their holiday after all. Just because your property is quaint, rural and picturesque and you're offering a 'countryside experience', it doesn't mean you can get away with providing tatty furniture and chipped crockery!

Experienced letting agents will tell you that open fires, four-poster beds, included linen and towels, walking distance from a pub, close proximity to the sea or rivers, a dishwasher, a washing machine and tumble-dryer, the acceptance of pets, short breaks available and fuel and power included are all high on the list of customer requests.

> TIP *Think about buying a property that has already had a successful history of holiday letting. You'll then be buying the 'goodwill' that comes with the property, and may be able to negotiate with the vendor for a list of previous guests who use it.*

What to Provide

- As with buy-to-let properties (*see Chapter 1*), it's better to provide good-quality new furniture that you can replace than second-hand furniture. Furniture must comply with safety regulations (see Appendix 2), but it will endure quite a bit of wear and tear, and it's better to view it as something you throw away after a few years and replace. New furniture looks smarter anyway.

- The house must be clean and be heated in the winter months.

- Kitchens must be well equipped with enough plates, cups, glasses and cutlery to cater for at least the number of beds you offer. Provide enough saucepans and serving dishes too. Guests will also expect a washing machine, freezer, microwave and dishwasher, if possible.

- Beds must have good-quality mattresses, which conform to 1988 Furniture and Furnishing Safety Regulations (*see Appendix 2*), clean soft pillows and plenty of blankets for colder weather. Washable duvets are a good idea, as are mattress covers. Remember to include bedside lights, wardrobe space and mirrors.

- Bathrooms should also be well lit, and have a shower attachment as well as a bath. Separate shower would be ideal.
- Sitting-room suites and covers should also conform to 1988 regulations, and be comfortable. Lighting should be good and it should have a heat source like an open or gas fire. Try to add personal touches like pretty pictures, dried flowers and ornaments (though not your most precious).
- The dining area should include enough chairs for the household to be seated comfortably.
- If you have a garden, it must be safe – ponds are not a good idea if you plan to attract families – and pathways should be paved well. Make sure too it's low maintenance enough that it won't look untidy if you or a gardener cannot get there to maintain it. It's a good idea to include garden furniture, and a barbecue will be popular.
- Make sure the house is well aired, without any musty smell, and that the entrance to it is well lit – some guests will arrive in the evening.
- Include smoke alarms, a fire extinguisher and a fire blanket in the kitchen.

Marketing

Unless you're using a letting agency, it will be up to you to convince potential guests that your house/flat/cottage is the *only* place they should be spending their holiday. Think about the best way to reach your target market, and how to do it as cost-effectively as possible. There's no point spending hundreds of pounds on advertising if you won't see your money back in the rentals you receive. It may be a question of trial and error to find out which advertising route suits you best, but whichever you choose, you'll need to provide as much information as you can within your chosen medium (which is where a web page is ideal). The secret, though, is to make your property as appealing as possible. Essential information to include:

TIPS THAT WILL HELP SELL (AND RESELL) YOUR PROPERTY

 Don't make your property non-smoking, unless you have very strong feelings about it. In a party of four there may well be a smoker and you don't want to lose sales because you won't allow it.

 Nearly 40 per cent of British holidaymakers take their dog with them. Exclude dogs and you're ruling out a large number of potential guests. (You're obliged by law to accept guide dogs.)

 Send guests clear directions to the property. They may well never come back if they take hours to find you and end up tired and frustrated.

 Supply extra keys – guests may return at different times during the day.

 Slot meters for the electricity are the single biggest turn-off for potential guests!

 If your property sleeps six or more, guests will expect two toilets.

 Older people represent the biggest share of the holiday letting market, so bear that in mind when equipping your property. They like baths!

- the location;
- number it sleeps;
- contact details.

But beyond that, you should find a unique selling point and stress the assets of the property:

- Is it quiet and peaceful?
- Would it appeal to walkers, artists, golfers, surfers, people looking for a beach holiday, or families?
- Do you do short breaks?
- Does it have facilities for the disabled?
- Does it have a swimming pool? (This will have a dramatic effect on lettings, but maintenance and safety are up to you.)

- Is it luxurious, with en suite facilities and so on?
- Does it have heating or open fires? (Important in the UK winter!)
- Has it been star rated (*see page 188*)?

Marketing Possibilities

Local and national press: this is the traditional advertising route and there is a mass of publications in which to place your ad. You might want to use a general publication – a local or national newspaper or a country-orientated magazine. Have a browse around the newsagents: if your property would appeal to garden lovers, ramblers or bird watchers, find out which specialist magazines there are and look at the types of advertisements they include.

Newspapers and magazines have two types of advertising: display and classified. A display ad will be bigger, can include a photograph (colour or black and white), but will be more expensive. Classified ads will be lineage (words only), so you'll have to be more inventive with your sales pitch, but are inevitably cheaper. Some bigger publications will break classified ads into sections, and have details such as self-catering properties available in particular areas of the country. Publications will provide you with rate cards, copy dates and a readership profile, and often give discounts if you take a series of ads over a period of weeks or months. It's a good idea to put together a 'brochure' with pictures of the property, complete information about what it contains and local amenity information, which you can mail out to people who respond to your ad. The more detail you can include, the better (*see below*).

> **TIP** *Don't include the rental rates in your advertising copy. Get readers interested enough in the property to call you, and you're then in a position to negotiate the rent if they think it's too steep, and to do a bit of a sales pitch.*

Tourist guides: these are usually annual publications, and you can get details about them from your local tourist office or by looking in your local bookshop. Some are specialist – around activity holidays and children – but might be effective in narrowing down your target market. They can be relatively inexpensive to advertise in, but you may have to provide copy months ahead of the publication date. Local tourist offices also produce smaller accommodation booklets (which include hotels and B&B) and will include self-catering properties.

The Internet: this advertising route is growing in popularity and can be very effective. Potentially you have a whole world 'readership'. You can often include your property in a another site such as your local tourist office web site or a local community web site that covers your area (using the name of the local town, search for it via a search engine). On these web sites look for the page with advertiser information, and there will be a fee scale for display or lineage ads.

You could also build your own web site, with your own domain name and e-mail address hosted by your Internet service provider or a web host. This involves an annual fee to host the domain name and most offer an all-inclusive package including a site-creator with design templates where you simply fill in the relevant information about your property. The problem with having your own web site is ensuring that you reach the target market. Search engines such as Yahoo! and Google search by keywords in the text on the web site. You'll need to ensure yours includes all the important words to make sure your site is listed high on a search engine listing. For example if your cottage is in Devon, make sure it includes the words 'Devon',

TIP *Using pictures: it may be too expensive to include a photograph in a press advertisement, but in a tourism guide or on the Internet they're cheaper and highly effective. Pictures will help 'sell' your property over and above any words. If guests like the look of the place, they'll read on. It might be worth having pictures taken by a professional photographer, especially the interior shots, which need good lighting. But if you're confident enough to take them yourself:*

 Try taking pictures at different times of day, and stage-set the pictures so you include as much detail as you can.

 Use a 35 mm transparency film, as the result will be of far higher quality than a print, and more likely to be accepted by a magazine.

 Better still, use a digital camera. This way you can take many more pictures, and delete the ones that are no good. Computer image editing software enables you to improve the pictures, and you'll then be able to e-mail the pictures to the relevant publication.

'south-west', 'cottage', 'cottages', 'holiday', 'holidays', 'letting', 'self-catering', 'seaside', 'country' and so on. To get advice, contact a web design company – you'll find names in your local Yellow Pages – or look on the Internet under 'web hosting', or 'web design'.

Star Ratings

This is a British Tourist Authority initiative for self-catering properties and ranges from one star to five. Although it's voluntary to have your property rated, it's a good idea, as it gives guests a yardstick of what to expect, and some guides insist you're rated before you can be included. To be assessed for a rating, contact your Regional Tourist Board (information at www.visitbritain.com), which will send you a pack that includes a standards booklet (this outlines the criteria of what needs to be included in your property to achieve a certain rating) plus the fee scale for assessment and an application form. Once you've completed and returned this, an assessor will visit the property. Inspections are annual.

Brochures

These may not be necessary if you're running a fairly low-key operation, with occasional lets. But if you depend on the income from rents, then a well-designed brochure will be an essential part of your marketing campaign. With a bit of skill, you may be able to create your own on your PC, and the best way to start is to look at other similar brochures and pick out what you think works.

- Keep the design and the font (typeface) simple.
- Make sure pictures you use will print out well at the correct resolution. You may want to stick prints on to the paper, but make sure the paper is thick enough to carry them.
- Keep copy straightforward and informative. Guests will want information about the property and the surrounding area, not flowery, poetic descriptions. Ask yourself what you would want to know.

> TIP *Proofread your copy carefully and make sure the information you include is not going to be out of date next season. You don't want to collect 250 brochures from a printer, only to discover there's a spelling mistake or the phone number is about to change.*

Unless you're planning to send out many brochures, you should be able to print them out from your computer as and when they're requested. If your operation is bigger, then a professional designer might be the answer. They'll be able to produce a slicker brochure, in colour, and the more they print the cheaper it will be.

You and your Guests

First impressions are very important. Whatever the size of your lettings business, you'll have to 'sell' your property to potential guests from the moment they make contact. They're obviously interested, or they wouldn't have responded to your advertisement, but from that moment you'll have to take over with the sales pitch. There's more to it than expounding the benefits of the property, however. If you're helpful, friendly and positive, they're far more likely to want to take their holiday in your property.

- Make sure contact is easy. Inform the whole family that phone calls might be potential guests, so they know how to answer the phone, and use an answering machine with a friendly message or a call-minding service if you can't get to the phone.

- Try not to use a fax number – potential guests prefer a conversation. Faxing is a bother. But if it's unavoidable, make sure the fax is available at all times.

- If you include an e-mail address, respond quickly to brochure requests.

- Think in advance about what you're going to say. Have information written out on a piece of paper by the phone, or close at hand, so you're ready with answers to any questions callers may have.

Tenancy/Holiday Agreements

Holiday lets are not covered by the 1988 Housing Act (*see Chapter 1*). Before it came into force many landlords let their properties as 'holiday lets' to bypass the laws regarding security of tenure. But these days a holiday let is just that – a property let to one tenant for no more than 31 days. If you renew the agreement for another month, you're technically breaking the law.

The contract between you and your tenants is finalized when you exchange letters where they place a deposit (*see below*) and you confirm the booking. You'll need to provide certain services for it to count as a holiday let – a cleaning service and change of linen, for example, though you can state if these are not included; but the rental should include utilities such as gas, electricity, water and council tax. You'll need to come to an agreement about use of the phone, or install a payphone. Make sure you've included in your brochure (or over the phone when they book) all the details of what the rental includes, and repeat them in your confirmation letter, along with any requests such as cleaning, if you expect guests to clean, and clear directions to the property. Too much information is far better than too little and avoids misunderstandings.

Payment

To secure the booking, you can ask guests to send you 20 per cent of the rent and a refundable damage deposit (*see below*). You can then ask for the balance of the rent to be paid no later than six weeks before they're due to take the property. If they cancel before the six-week deadline, you can retain the deposit, and still have time to sell a last-minute booking.

> TIP *Damage: when they leave, you'll need to collect the keys and check that the property has been left intact. Though most holiday tenants are clean and careful, some are less so. You're entitled to reclaim the cost of any breakages, but this can be hard to do. The safest option is to ask for a refundable damage deposit of £50, which you return after you've checked for any damage and deducted the costs where necessary.*

REAL-LIFE ACCOUNT

The Staines family had a holiday cottage on Anglesey, which had been in the family for years. They would use it for their family holidays, but rented it out in a low-key way during the rest of the year.

'We didn't need the income, but needed to cover costs such as maintenance, insurance and utilities, so we rented it out at a below-market-rate rent to friends and friends of friends. We found that if people knew us, they treated the house with more respect, knowing that it was our home that they were simply staying in. Also because the rent was not high, people did not complain if crockery did not match and it wasn't "perfect". We didn't leave our personal things at the house, but our books were on the bookshelves and there was beer in the cupboard. This helped to make people feel more at home, and we worked on a system of "replace what you use".

'Rebooking is essential, and at the beginning of each year we would send out a letter to past tenants telling them the rental and encouraging them to book. Because the house was pretty, we would often find letters through the door asking if we would consider renting, but we weren't keen to let it to people we didn't know. The responsibility was too great.

'The only problems were that we lived a three-hour drive from the house, and we had to rely on local people when there was an emergency. We had a cleaner, who was also on an annual retainer. We could call her if there was a problem, and as she had a key she could let in plumbers, electricians and painters when necessary. We also asked her to keep an eye on the house during the winter months. Security was not a problem, despite the secluded location of the house (though we made sure there was nothing of any value left there), but it was reassuring to know someone could let us know if the roof blew off!'

Dealing with Holiday Tenants

If you're using a full-management agency, their fee will include handling changeover days, and any problems your guests have during their stay. If not, and you've taken on management yourself, you can help by pre-empting any problems before they occur. You'll still have to ensure the property is cleaned between lets, and that nothing has gone missing or been broken by previous tenants. This will be hectic if you have more than one property in the same area, and you'll need to be organized. You also need to be there to greet them on their arrival, but it's worth putting together a comprehensive welcome package for them. This could include:

- a bottle of wine and/or some flowers;
- a pint of milk and a loaf of bread (local and crusty, not sliced and white!);
- a local delicacy – fudge, cake, cider;
- lights and heating on during the winter months;
- essential items such as toilet paper, bin liners and kitchen towels, and cleaning products as an incentive for them to leave the property as they found it;
- details about the house, how things work (oven, washing machine, microwave, TV), where things are kept;
- emergency details such as the fuse box, mains water inlet, stock of candles in case of power cuts;
- information about local tourist attractions and leisure pursuits (most produce brochures you could include);
- details of local shops and restaurants with opening times and phone numbers;
- emergency numbers such as the nearest doctor, hospital, dentist;
- an emergency contact number.

Put yourself in your tenants' shoes: what would you like to know if you were staying in your house for the first time? These touches will all help to oil the wheels of a happy and unproblematic tenancy. If you're thoughtful and helpful, perhaps your guests will be too.

Tax Issues

Some of these apply to Option 1 and Option 2 (*see pages 173–4*).

Council Tax

A 50 per cent discount on council tax applies to both second homes and long-term empty properties. From April 2004 local authorities will be able to reduce the second homes discount to 10 per cent (making the tax payable 90 per cent) and the empty homes discount to 0 per cent (making the tax payable 100 per cent). Consult your local authority to ask about council tax liability. For information about council tax in Scotland, go to www.scotland.gov.uk/library3/localgov/ctlg-00.asp.

Income Tax

Holiday lettings are recognized as a business (generating earned income) by the Inland Revenue, unlike other forms of property lettings, which are classed as investment (unearned) income. But you must fulfil the following rules:

- Your accommodation must be available for letting to the public for at least 140 days of the year and actual letting must be at least 70 days.
- Any one occupier (or group) cannot stay for more than 31 days in any period of seven months, but they can for the remaining five months.
- You cannot claim the tax incentives when you use the accommodation yourself and when the property is unavailable for letting.
- The property must be fully furnished.
- The lettings must be at full market rent, not a peppercorn rent to friends and relatives.
- Your rental income is subject to income tax, but all expenses are allowable including:

  - repairs and maintenance
  - decorating
  - heating and lighting
  - legal and letting agent's fees
  - management fees and cleaning costs
  - insurance
  - mortgage interest payments

- If the business makes a loss (which it may well in the first few years) you can offset this against any other income you may have and thereby reduce your overall tax bill.
- Married couples can maximize tax allowances by having the property in the name of the lower earner.

Even if you're only running a low-key operation, you'll still need to declare the income on the land and property section of your tax return.

Capital Gains Tax

- When you sell your holiday home you'll be subject to capital gains tax (CGT) but at a more advantageous business-asset taper relief rate.
- Under certain circumstances the gain arising from the sale of qualifying commercial furnished holiday letting accommodation in the UK can be 'rolled over' if you invest the proceeds of the sale into another qualifying business asset, including another commercial furnished holiday letting property in the UK, within 36 months of disposing of the old property (or within 12 months prior to the disposal). If you use all of the sale proceeds you receive from the disposal of the old property in acquiring the new one, the whole of your gain will be deferred until you sell the new property. This is done by deducting the 'rolled over' gain from the cost of acquiring the new asset when computing the gain arising when the new asset is sold. If you only use part of the proceeds, then only part of the gain will be deferred. See your tax advisor or find out more information from IR290 at www.inlandrevenue.gov.uk.

Note: rollover relief does not apply to commercial furnished holiday letting accommodation outside the UK.

Value Added Tax

You must register your business for VAT if your turnover exceeds the current VAT threshold – though this is quite high and most small holiday let operations will not reach this limit. If you're VAT registered you must charge VAT on the rent for your property, and at the end of each quarter you owe Customs and Excise the VAT you've collected, less the VAT you've paid on goods and services bought for the business. Speak to your tax advisor if you're unsure of the VAT process, or go to the Customs and Excise web site at www.hmce.gov.uk.

Employee Taxes

If you're employing anyone to take care of your property – a cleaner, gardener or manager – then you as their employer are responsible for collecting income tax through the PAYE system, for deducting National Insurance contributions and for paying employer's contributions. The Inland Revenue site at www.inlandrevenue.gov.uk will help with information, as will the Department of Work and Pensions (www.dwp.gov.uk).

Insuring your Second Home

Insurance policies will have an impact on how you let your properties.

Option 1: For your Primary Use

As with your main home, you'll need to ensure that the property has adequate buildings insurance cover (*see page 49*) – something your lender will insist on if you're buying it with a mortgage of course – and adequate cover to replace the contents. But be warned: insurance premiums can be higher for second homes than for main residences.

Insurance companies use postcodes as part of their risk assessment, and if the property is close to the sea or a river, where storm and flood damage risk is high, it may affect your buildings insurance premiums. Contents premiums on second homes can also be more expensive if the property is unoccupied for periods longer than 30 days, even if the value of the contents is reasonably low – it's unlikely that you'll keep your valuable art collection, dazzling jewellery and expensive widescreen TV there after all – and many insurance companies will have exclusions within the policy. You may well find you're not covered for 'escape of water' (the risk of pipes freezing and bursting is higher if you're not there), vandalism and theft. Be prepared: compared to your main home insurance costs, second home cover on:

- buildings insurance could be 20 per cent higher;
- contents insurance could be 50 per cent higher.

Option 2: As a Business

Because you're letting the general public use your property, you need to ensure you have adequate insurance cover. This includes:

- *Buildings cover*: your mortgage company will insist on this, but if you own the property outright, you'll need to have such a policy in place to cover you in case of damage to the building itself.
- *Contents cover*: you'll need to insure your own contents against accidental damage, but you do not have to cover the contents belonging to your guests.
- *Public liability*: this will cover you for civil actions brought against you should a guest injure themselves while on your property, and lettings agencies will insist you have a policy in place.
- *Employee liability*: you'll need this if you employ anyone, even casual labour, on your property. This is a legal requirement.
- *Loss of rental income*: this is optional and can be had for a small sum.
- *Cancellation insurance*: in case guests cannot take the property and you lose the rental for that period.

Caravans and Mobile Homes

A static caravan or mobile home run as a holiday-let business works in much the same way as a house or flat. You need to agree a rental – you could ask site owners what their going rate is, depending on the season – and send an agreement letter asking for a deposit as above. You'll need to include any restrictions you have (i.e. number of persons who can sleep in it), information about the caravan site on which your vehicle is situated, and inform them of any restrictions set by the site owners.

But make sure you take a close look at your insurance policy. Most caravan policies cover only the owners and their immediate family. Bakers of Cheltenham, however, have a policy that automatically covers anyone staying in the static caravan or mobile home. They can be contacted on 0800 496 1516 or at www.bakersofcheltenham.co.uk.

> TIP *Shop around for different policies, as premiums can vary enormously. Some insurers will give you a discount on the policy for your second home if they already insure your main home.*

Go to www.caravan-insurance-uk.org.uk for other specialist insurers.

BUYING PROPERTY ABROAD

Can't you just see it? The long summer evenings, the unspoilt beaches, the unpretentious local wine, the vibrant street markets full of other Brits trying to pursue the dream of property ownership abroad. It's a small world all right, particularly if you're British. More than half the UK population is keen to buy abroad, driven from our shores by the crummy weather and the overheated property market.

Although the weather may be better abroad, house-buying is no quicker and the procedures are usually more expensive. Add to that a foreign language, different legal and tax systems and it's a wonder any of us seriously considers buying overseas. There are bargains to be had out there, at least compared to UK prices. But for the unwary there are also legal and financial demands that have to be met, and practicalities to consider before you even start your search for the ideal little bolt hole. The rules governing title, tax, insurance and most aspects of the buying process are very different from those in the UK; so make sure you get expert advice and don't get carried away by the romance of it all. Here, almost more than anywhere else, you must make your head rule your heart.

A CASE IN POINT: FRENCH LEGAL COMPLICATIONS

Under French law, siblings have a five-year period after their parents' death to stake a claim in a property – even if it was not left to them in the parents' will. So you need to find out if the vendor of an inherited property has any brothers or sisters before you buy.

Is Buying Abroad Right for you?

This is the first question you need to ask yourself. It's not for everyone. Think about how you're going to use your property abroad, at various times of the year, or when your circumstances change – as children grow up, and as you grow older. Look realistically at how you're going to pay for it, and whether you expect to make anything back. Coming from a country where buying property is a valid form of speculation, and you're pretty much bound to make money every time you sell, it's hard to get your head around the fact that this simply isn't the case in many other countries (until the Brits come over and create a market). Is all the hard work, stress and expense going to be worth the enjoyment that having your own property abroad will bring you, or would you really be better off paying for holidays every year?

How Much Will it Cost?

How much you have to spend will be an essential factor in deciding where you look for your property and what kind of purchase you can make. Obviously, in the most popular holiday destinations like the South of France, the Algarve or Costa del Sol you'll pay more than for a similar property in, say, one of the Greek islands or one of the newer destinations, such as Croatia. So once you've set your financial limit you can start looking in earnest. There are various ways of financing a property purchase abroad, all with advantages and disadvantages.

> TIP *Often buyers get carried away and believe everything the agent or vendors say. Remember: the estate agent will be acting in the vendor's best interests and not yours!*

Decide the maximum amount you're prepared to spend, including fees, taxes and miscellaneous expenses. House-buying is generally more expensive abroad than in the UK, so make sure you have a clear idea of how much of your budget you'll have to allocate to these inevitable costs. Notary fees, local taxes and VAT can bump up the cost of overseas purchase, adding 10 per cent in Spain and Portugal, and 10 to 15 per cent in France and Italy, and there's more on top of that. What's left is what you can spend on the property. However tempted you may be, don't exceed this amount.

According to John Howell, a lawyer specializing in the purchase of property abroad, you should plan your finance before you go to look at property. In a seller's market, where buyers must be ready to move quickly when they find a property they'd like to buy, if you're unable to do so, the danger is that you'll lose the property to someone else. It helps you move quickly if you've thought about various things, such as the following, before you start looking at properties.

Do you Need a Mortgage?

When interest rates are low, many buyers decide to borrow to pay for at least part of their purchase abroad, keeping their own money invested elsewhere. This will almost always involve getting a mortgage.

Whether you intend to borrow in the UK or through a foreign lender, it's a good idea to get preliminary confirmation that you'll be able to borrow what you need *before* you go looking at property. The criteria used overseas to calculate your entitlement to a mortgage are very different from those in the UK and it's embarrassing and disappointing to have to cancel a purchase because you can't raise the money. Worse still, it could put you in breach of contract and you could lose your deposit.

Having your finance in place can also give you a tactical advantage when bidding for, or negotiating the price of, the property. See your lawyer or a specialist mortgage broker to get preliminary clearance. For most countries this can be obtained in about a week.

Should you Take out a UK or a Foreign Mortgage?

There are advantages and disadvantages both ways. If you extend your existing UK mortgage to buy abroad, the administrative costs will be small or negligible as there will be no additional legal or Land Registry fees but, generally, the interest rates will be a little higher than many Continental rates.

There are relatively high set-up costs for overseas mortgages – as much as 3 to 4 per cent of the amount borrowed in some cases. The interest rate at which you make your repayment will, however, probably be lower than in the UK and you'll not tie up your UK assets. Another potential advantage is that having the mortgage reduces the net value of your home overseas, which would reduce the overseas inheritance tax (IHT) payable when you die. If the IHT rate in the country where your second home is located is higher than in the UK, this will be an important consideration.

The biggest risk, however, is the exchange rate if you're going to repay the mortgage from your UK earnings. If sterling drops against the euro, the difference in how much you'll pay can cancel out any advantage conferred by the lower interest rate. For example if sterling falls and rises in value between 1.40 and 1.74 against the euro, a monthly repayment of 600 euros could cost anything between £428 and £344, and the capital value of a €100,000 mortgage would vary between £71,428 and £57,471. This doesn't matter so much if you have income coming in – perhaps from rentals – in *local currency* to pay the mortgage, but it's a problem if you're paying from your UK earnings.

There are companies that can offer up-to-the-minute currency advice and deals to help when you're financing your purchase, in which the currency exchange can be fixed at a certain rate; another option is to fix low and high limits to allow for tolerable fluctuations; and another involves a trigger mechanism to buy currency when it reaches an agreeable rate.

> **TIP** *If you've taken a euro mortgage (benefiting from the very low interest rates), consider letting your property to earn a rental income in euros, thereby counterbalancing the negative effect of a strong euro. In some countries, if you're renting your property, you'll be allowed tax relief against the rental income in respect of the interest on a local mortgage, but not on the cost of any money borrowed in the UK.*

PAYING THE DEPOSIT

When looking for property, rather than paying by cheque any deposit required while you're there, it's better to pay the likely sum into your lawyer's or mortgage lender's client account before you go. This makes it very hard for the estate agent to persuade you to sign a contract without getting it checked first! Even 'preliminary' or 'reservation' contracts have far-reaching consequences and should be checked by an independent expert before you sign them.

There can be tax problems in the UK as well. Overseas mortgage documentation must comply not only with local law but with UK tax law as well. This is such a potential minefield for investors that the only sensible course of action is to take advice from a lawyer or a specialist international mortgage broker about which type of mortgage will suit you best – it can save you a lot of money. (*See addresses on page 215.*)

Where, when, what and how?

So now we come to your first big decision: location. Theoretically, the world is your oyster, but the practicalities will guide you. There's no point buying a property that you'll come to regard as a liability rather than the pleasure it should be. Most people choose to buy in a country they've visited on holiday, and this is a good starting point. At least you have an idea of how long it will take you to get there. But getting there as a one-off is a very different matter to slogging there regularly throughout the year.

If you're tied to travelling at weekends and school holidays, you don't want long flights and crossings or complicated transfers. Even cheap flights from regional airports can end up adding a considerable amount to your holiday bill and, if you're picky about when you can travel, the price will always be higher. Base your calculations on door-to-door times, so include driving to the airport, parking and checking in at one end, clearing customs, picking up your car and driving to your destination. If, on the other hand, you're looking for somewhere to overwinter, then distance is less important and long-haul destinations become a possibility.

If good weather is important to you, try to visit at different seasons of the year. It may be ideal in July, but will it hit the spot in February? If you're a lizard and crave year-round sun, then France and the Med probably won't satisfy and you'll have to resign yourself to longer flights. Be specific about the area when you're researching, as conditions can vary a great deal. For example, in Madeira there are many little microclimates. The Bay of Funchal, protected as it is by the highest peaks, enjoys the best of sunshine, except in the months of February and March when an enveloping cloud known as the capacete (the helmet), blocks out the sunlight. Further down the west coast at Ponta do Sol and Calheta, backed as they are by the lower hills of the Paul da Serra, the sun shines brighter during these months, but they're less protected from the sea winds.

Now you're ready to think about the kind of property you want, and this is where you have to remain grimly practical. It's a romantic idea that few can afford to indulge anymore in the UK, but buying a wreck abroad and doing it up is still a possibility, at least in terms of purchase price. But the logistics involved in renovating remotely, not to mention the hassle and cost, could turn your dream into a nightmare. At the other end of the scale, there are serviced apartments to be had complete with pool cleaners, caretakers and maids on site, but you'll pay for the privilege with a yearly fee. Make sure you read the small print before you commit yourself.

Far better to pay more for a small property that you can access easily and that fits in with your lifestyle, than to fall for a fixer-upper with scores of useful outbuildings in a remote area, with all the problems of trying to oversee repair and renovation work when your home is hundreds of miles away. Time to ask yourself some questions:

- Do you prefer town or country?
- Do you want to be inland or on the coast?
- How much garden or land do you want?
- How close do you want to be to your neighbours?

- How close do you want to be to shops, bars and restaurants?
- Where's the nearest public transport, how often does it run, what time does it end?
- Will you need to hire or buy a car?
- How far is the beach?
- How far is it to sports facilities, golf, tennis, swimming and so on?
- Arts and entertainment: what's available in the area?
- Do you want to be around other Brits or would you prefer local culture?

Finding a Property Abroad

There are different ways of going about this but, before you start, work out how much you're prepared to spend, set about making sure the money is in place and get yourself some expert legal advice.

To find property abroad you can;

- visit a UK estate agent with an office in the country of your choice;
- contact a buying agent to look for you (*see below*);
- go into high street estate agencies in the country of your choice and, if you've chosen an area popular with buyers from the UK, you may even find some managed by expats (*see below*);
- take an organized inspection trip with an British agent (*see below*);
- start buying a specialized magazine, such as *Homes Overseas*;
- use the Internet;
- or attend an exhibition (*see below*).

Buying Agents and Property Finders

Sales or estate agents proliferate in the UK and abroad. They take a commission from the sale of properties that they hold in their portfolio. But buying agents and property finders do things differently. They take a fee from the buyer – and hence should act more in your interest and have a duty to find exactly what you're looking for. Here are some well-known firms' web sites:

Property Network International www.wefindhouses.com
County Homesearch www.county-homesearch.com
Live France Group www.livefrancegroup.com
The Property Finders www.thepropertyfinders.com

Tips for Visiting a Property Exhibition

These can be useful starting points, even if you haven't yet decided on a country or area to target, as you'll find a huge volume of information and expertise assembled in one place, from developers to tourist boards, estate agents to property finders. They're usually advertised in property magazines and on foreign property web sites. Here's how to get the best result:

- *Prepare in advance.* The sheer volume of exhibitors will be daunting, so try to have some idea of where and what you're looking for. Take along a list of questions you want answered.
- *Visit both large and small stands.* Different companies offer a different kind of service. Small may mean a more personal service, for example.
- *Treat the exhibition as a fun day out.* Don't feel pressured. Take your time and don't get stressed. There's no need to rush into anything. Collect information, brochures and business cards. Then go away and think about your options.
- *Make the most of the seminars and talks.* These experts can offer you invaluable legal, financial and lifestyle advice.
- *If you want to develop the process further, you can organize an inspection trip at the exhibition and meet a lawyer.* Many people will also buy property there and then.

A Word about Agents

- Only negotiate with agents who are officially registered and hold a licence.

- Make sure you feel comfortable with the agent and look at as many properties as you can.
- A good agent will help you through the whole purchasing procedure. Remember, if you feel the agent isn't right look for an alternative who will give you the service you expect.
- Ensure the agent is acting in your best interests by advising you of all properties available, rather than a select few with whom they may have connections. In the excitement of the moment you might get carried away, particularly if you feel you're about to miss an opportunity, so try to keep a cool head. Remember that the estate agent will be acting in the vendor's best interests and not yours!
- In the UK make sure any agent you deal with is a member of FOP-DAC (the Federation of Property Developers, Agents and Consultants, www.fopdac.com.

Inspection Trips

Organized property inspection trips can be a mine of information, if you approach them with your eyes open. They tend to be subsidized or part-funded by developers and agents, and some also offer reimbursement against a future sale once completed.

Some trips operate at set times each week or month, while others offer individually tailored travel to suit your availability. Generally, each trip allows you an opportunity to view a pre-planned 'hotlist' of properties that match your criteria.

TIP *Having a bit of background knowledge about the property market will prove invaluable once you're checking out some potential homes, so do some research before you go. Swot up on prices and always take a notebook, a pen and a camera. And make certain that you've defined the basics, such as what, how much and where. Use your notes as a prompt to make sure you cover all the issues. It will prove invaluable at the end of the trip when it comes to reviewing all you've seen, and it's always a good idea to put your agent on the spot a couple of times.*

Timeshare Properties

Timeshare can be an excellent method of enjoying the use of a property abroad without the expense and responsibility of buying. The idea is that you buy shares in a company, entitling you to the use of a property for a given period each year. You can usually resell or change this period according to your personal needs. Unfortunately, timeshare has a bad reputation to overcome, created by unscrupulous companies resorting to pressure sales methods and contracts that grant less than satisfactory title for the interest bought. Many timeshare schemes have the property held through off shore companies and you could end up with nothing but the possibility of suing a 'shell' company incorporated in some Caribbean or South Pacific island. Before you commit yourself it's much better to have the contract looked at in Britain on your return, and don't sign anything despite lavish promises of discounts, free gifts, champagne lunches and other sweeteners.

Legal Considerations

Find an English-speaking lawyer to advise and help you in the country where you're buying, or, in the UK, a lawyer specializing in purchases abroad. Before you decide on a property it's important to be fully aware of the entire legal process and all the associated costs involved in your property purchase, including the on-going charges for local taxes. Often the total cost of the transaction will be up to 15 per cent above the actual selling price of the property (*see page 199*).

John Howell has more good advice on the legal points to look out for. Since many of these have financial implications too, it's worth thinking them through well ahead of purchase:

- Take advice from your lawyer *before* you go to look at property. If you deal with all of the following points before you go, you'll know that you're ready to go ahead and we will not have to deal with them in a hurry when you're under pressure to sign a contract.
- If you want to let the property – or to alter or extend it – you'll

probably need certain permits or licences. In some places these are hard to obtain. Sometimes there are easy ways of avoiding the problem. If there's likely to be a problem, it helps to identify it early.

- Who should own the property? This is the most important decision you'll have to make. There are lots of options – you alone, you and your partner, you and your children, your children alone, a company (UK, local or 'offshore'), a trust and so on – if you put the property in the wrong names you'll pay massively more tax than you have to, both during your lifetime and on your death. Also, in countries (such as France) where there are restrictions on who can inherit your property, putting the property in the wrong name will mean that the wrong people will inherit it. Once you've signed a contract to buy, it's generally too late to change your plan, so you need to get advice early on. Half an hour's work here can save you many thousands of pounds, even on a modest holiday apartment.

- What would you like to happen to the property if you die? This will have important tax consequences. Also in some countries (particularly France) you're not allowed to leave your property as you please. Certain categories of relatives have priority claims to it. This can be a problem for people in second marriages or who live together unmarried.

- Few people bother to have their overseas property surveyed, and this can be a costly mistake. If you're buying an older or unusual property, a survey is particularly essential. Finding out what kinds of survey are available in your country of choice will help reduce delays when you find the property you want.

- Always use an independent lawyer when you buy. He or she will need

TIP *You can't assume that the laws will be the same as in the UK. For example in the UK, inheritance tax starts on assets worth around £250,000 (2003/4 figures), but in some countries the threshold starts at £10,000. Transfers between husband and wife are exempt from inheritance tax in the UK, but may be taxed elsewhere.*

to make a series of checks and will probably have to advise you about all sorts of unforeseen things that can crop up in a property purchase. To do this effectively he or she will need to be familiar with the law of the country where the house is located, and UK law. What you do in one country will have an impact in the other. Lawyers and notaries in provincial areas abroad with few foreign buyers are unlikely to understand UK law as thoroughly as you would like!

- If you're busy and unlikely to be around for the purchase process, it may be necessary to grant Power of Attorney to the lawyer.

- Before you sign any documents or pay any money, ask a qualified advisor to confirm that what you're doing is correct. In some countries payment of a deposit commits you to the purchase (*see page 201*).

- Is the contract clear, legal and fair? Some contracts offered by foreign estate agents are so badly drafted – particularly when translated into English – that they're nearly useless. Some are grossly unfair and, probably, illegal. Signing a contract of this kind can often lead to trouble.

- Does the property have all the necessary permissions and licences? A surprising number do not. This can cause you lots of problems later.

- If you're buying in a new development which has not been finished, how is your money protected? If you're paying by instalments, what happens if your developer goes bust and cannot finish your apartment? Do you lose your money or is it protected in some way? In most countries it's possible to protect it. Your lawyer should check that this is being done.

- Does the property have good title? There are defective titles in every country, including Britain. This must be checked by your lawyer or, in some countries, by the notary who witnesses the signing of the title deed.

- Are the boundaries clear? Often they're not, particularly in countries such as Spain that do not base title deeds on maps. This is particularly important if you're buying a rural property or a property where there is, for example, a separate parking plot or storeroom.

- Is the property burdened by any debts? Debts can be attached to a property. Your lawyer will check to make sure yours is 'clean' or arrange for any existing debts to be paid off.

- You'll normally be paying for your property in the currency of the country where it's located, in many cases euros. By law, the full price of the property should be declared in the title, and tax should be paid based on that amount. In many countries there's a tradition of under-declaration. Sometimes you'll have no choice but to go along with this. Under-declaration can be very dangerous and result in heavy penalties, and increased capital gains tax liability when you come to sell, because of the apparent gain in value.

- There are various ways of converting and sending money abroad. Some are much better value and much cheaper than others. Generally a specialist currency dealer will give you a better exchange rate than your bank. Your lawyer will probably get a better rate than you will.

- Take out the right property insurance. Depending on how you intend to use your property, you'll need different types of property insurance. In particular, holiday homes that are going to be empty for long periods need special policies. Similarly, if you intend to let your property you'll often need special insurance. If you take out the wrong type they won't pay out if you make a claim!

- Make a local will. This is not strictly necessary but it will save your heirs money. If they have to rely on your UK will, the expenses of dealing with the inheritance will be far higher. In addition the provisions of your UK will, while excellent in the UK, are probably very tax inefficient in Spain, France or wherever, so you'll pay more tax than is necessary. If you're buying a house, make a will at the same time. If you don't do it then, you won't get round to it later!

Insurance

You can take out insurance with a company either in the UK or in the country where your property is, but whichever you choose make sure you understand the terms fully. Even if your command of the language is good enough for everyday purposes, the official language used in legal documents and insurance policies is likely to be hard for you to follow. This can create complications when you try to translate the conditions and discover what is actually covered by the policy. Specialized policies provided by UK companies might answer your needs perfectly.

- Make sure any policy is tailored for the way you're going to use the property, so there are no exclusions during periods of unoccupancy or when you have tenants.
- You'll need Third Party Legal Liability cover to indemnify both the owner and the occupier. In some countries it's an offence not to have at least a minimum form of this cover from the moment of purchase, and fire insurance too.
- If you're relying on rental income, you can arrange to cover loss of pre-booked rental income and/or the cost of alternative accommodation following loss or damage.

Tax Implications

There's no doubt your tax situation will be affected if you buy property in a foreign country, and you should get expert advice at the earliest possible stage from a professional who deals with this complicated area. You need to understand fully your liability to taxation in the UK, capital gains tax, inheritance tax, foreign taxation, and the possibility of double taxation. What you don't want to do is pay tax twice. The UK has signed treaties with many countries to prevent this, including the EU, US, Australia, and South Africa. Check the position for your chosen location.

The most common reasons for buying a property abroad are to use it as:

- a holiday home;
- a permanent or occasional retirement home;
- an income-producing investment or an investment for capital growth.

In reality, most people use their property abroad for a combination of these.

Buying a property as an occasional holiday home and leaving it unoccupied for the remainder of the time is an expensive way of taking holidays, but if you've bought the property with a view to selling at a profit at some time in the future, the gain will be liable to capital gains tax in the UK when you come to sell. If you hold on to it until death,

> **TIP** *Any rents you receive from overseas properties are treated as a separate letting business from any UK rental income you may receive. You cannot set expenses or losses of one against the other. If you do pay tax in a foreign country, it's likely to be allowable as a deduction against any liability you have in the UK. Consult your tax advisor.*

it won't be subject to CGT but will be added to your estate, and may become liable to inheritance tax (*see Appendix 4*). This is one of the reasons why it's vital to make a separate will in the country where you buy your property.

If you let your property for part of the year, either to friends and family or on a more commercial basis, you're unlikely to make a substantial profit, especially if you've had to borrow to buy. The rent will be liable to UK income tax, but you'll be able to claim a proportion of the expenses against it, including the interest on any loan taken out to purchase or improve the property, costs of maintenance, utilities and repairs, agents' fees and so on.

Before you Buy

- Always allow yourself a cooling-off period, even if you see a property that seems ideal. Don't pay a deposit there and then.
- Open a bank account in your chosen country and make sure you get a 'certificate of importation' for the money you bring in from your home country.
- Set up standing orders in a local bank account to meet bills and taxes. Failure to pay your taxes in some countries, such as France, Portugal and Spain, could lead to court action and possible seizure of your property.

REAL-LIFE ACCOUNT

Dick and Lynn Shone sold a family holiday home in Norfolk and decided to use their share of the proceeds to fulfil a long-held ambition to buy somewhere in the South of France.

'We were interested in the area around Perpignan because it just seemed to offer so much – beaches, skiing in the Pyrenees, unspoilt scenery and towns with enough life to keep our teenagers amused, and all at far lower cost than Provence. That part of France has loads of regional airports too, so getting there isn't going to be a problem. We're trying out different routes to find the most convenient one.

'As soon as we decided to start looking, we subscribed to a property magazine, *French Property News*, and it was tremendously helpful for background information about everything we would have to do during the buying process. We started going down to the area and gradually narrowed down the area we were interested in to, essentially, three towns. Through friends, we met an Englishman, Richard, living near Marseilles who basically facilitates housebuying for Brits. He introduced us to a terrific estate agent and briefed her thoroughly about what we were looking for. This was great because we didn't waste any time looking at unsuitable properties.

'Richard takes a cut, but from the agent, and it's been terrific having his help. Although we both speak enough French to get by, there's no way we could handle the kinds of negotiations that buying a house entails. It helped that we didn't need to borrow money. We made sure we had euros ready and waiting so we could move quickly when we found the right house, and we had transferred the proceeds of the sale of the other house into a euro account in Jersey, which paid interest and allowed us to withdraw money with minimal notice. We've now opened a French bank account to pay utilities and local taxes and we transfer money over as we need to.

'We're planning to use the house mostly during the winter, for skiing, so we'll try to let it out during the summer, when demand should be highest. That way, we hope it will cover its costs. There's work to be done on it, but I'm happy to do that gradually so that the house is never too much of a mess to use. I just wish I had more time off work to spend there.'

Medical Care

Within the EU, state health provision is good, although just how good varies from place to place. If you have a holiday home in an EU country that you'll be visiting for three or four weeks at a time, you'll be covered by EU emergency arrangements. Make sure you take form E111, available from a post office, with you when you travel.

Although you're entitled to emergency treatment, it's worth making plans for less urgent problems that could, nonetheless, spoil your holiday. It's sensible to take out a multivisit or annual travel insurance policy that will cover medical contingencies, as well as repatriation costs and loss of luggage. These policies are not expensive, but check the small print carefully, however, as cover may be limited to individual visits of specific duration – typically 30 or 90 days. However, private health cover is recommended for added reassurance.

Outside the EU, private health insurance is vital.

THE ROAD LESS TRAVELLED

Not everyone wants to follow the trend, although there are plenty who do. The Costa del Sol has been identified as the area with the fastest growing population in all of Europe, with 2.5 million people living on the coast. In 10 years it's reckoned that number could have quadrupled. If that's enough to bring you out in a rash, then try to identify the up-and-coming hot spots and get in first.

Croatia, Turkey and Bulgaria are all growing in popularity. According to Guy King, of *Homes Overseas* magazine, if you have limited funds and a spirit of adventure, these and other less popular destinations give best value for money. But there are risks as well as rewards for pioneers: the infrastructure and health-care system are likely to be much less developed than in more conventional destinations and, since you're entering relatively uncharted territory, it won't be so easy to find legal and financial experts with experience in those markets. But what you'll find is unspoilt countryside, great bargains and a traditional way of life untarnished by expat expectations.

Safer bets are countries that are already EU members or are close to becoming so. The less popular areas of Italy, Portugal, Spain and France, and Cyprus are all very attractive. Where new road systems are being built and regional airports begin connecting flights to the UK, you can bet your bottom euro, the crowds will follow.

Letting Property Abroad

Planning to defray your costs by renting? Very similar criteria apply to letting in the UK as outlined earlier in the chapter, but a local management agent will be essential.

NIGHTMARE IN PORTUGAL

The recent problems with legislation affecting foreign property owners in Spain and Portugal underline how vulnerable they are to sudden changes of policy. In Portugal the problems stem from the fact that some 75 per cent of foreign property owners bought their homes through offshore property companies, which seemed the most tax-efficient vehicles at the time, saving both on the Portuguese purchase tax known as the *Sisa*, which can amount to 10 per cent and avoiding CGT liability in the UK when the property is sold. Now the proposed law will force an annual charge of 5 per cent of the value of such properties – on a house valued at £500,000, this works out at an annual bill of £25,000 – more than enough to make the pips squeak.

USEFUL CONTACTS

United Kingdom:
Web: www.landlordzone.co.uk/holiday_
lets.htm

Association of British Chambers of Commerce
Manning House
22 Carlisle Place
London SW1P 1JA
Tel.: 020 7565 2000
Web: www.britishchambers.org.uk

Association of British Insurers
51 Gresham Street
London EC2V 7HQ
Tel.: 020 7600 3333
Web: www.abi.org.uk

British Tourist Authority
Thames Tower
Blacks Road
London W6 9EL
Tel.: 020 8563 3186
Web: www.visitbritain.com

BusinessLink Helpline: 08456 045678
Web: www.businessadviceonline.org

The Camping and Caravanning Club
Greenfields House
Westwood Way
Coventry CV4 8JH
Tel.: 024 7669 4995

Abroad: useful information about anything from jobs to education to immigration:
Web: www.britishexpats.com

Up-to-date currency information and advice
Web: www.moneycorp.com or www.hifx.co.uk

Detailed information about every country in the world
Web: www.cia.gov/cia/publications/factbook

Homes Overseas **magazine**
Web: www.homesoverseas.co.uk

Information for British buyers abroad
Web: www.newskys.co.uk

Federation of Overseas Property Developers, Agents & Consultants
(FOPDAC)
Lacey House
St Clare Business Park
Holly Road
Hampton Hill TW12 1QQ
Tel.: 020 8941 5588
Web: www.fopdac.com
In Spain www.fipe.org and in Portugal www.afpop.com can check whether there's debt outstanding on a property

Hamptons International
Tel.: 020 7824 8822

UK-based company specializing in property in the Roussillon region of France:
Web: www.proprietes-rousillon.com

Web: www.spanishproperty-site.co.uk

John Howell's law firm specializing in property purchase abroad:
Web: www.europelaw.com

Type in a postcode or place name to find a relevant map of any UK or European area, also includes aerial photos:
Web: www.uk8multimap.com

BUYING INTERESTING PROPERTIES

If your ideal home is a new build on a spanking new estate, this is not the chapter for you. If that old proverb about an Englishman's home being his castle is something you take literally, then read on. To find a home (or a castle) with character, you sometimes have to look outside the box (in more ways than one), but with quirky homes come quirky problems too. You may be straying off the beaten track but, if you're careful, you needn't end up in uncharted territory. Let's start with finding your unusual property.

FINDING INTERESTING PROPERTIES

There are many alternatives to a traditional home. What about a converted factory, hospital or barn, disused church, school, tower, barge or even a converted railway carriage? The possibilities are almost endless, but don't expect to find much in an estate agent's window. To find your unique property, you may have to think laterally, and look for unusual properties in unusual places. For more conventional listed and period properties, try the more upmarket agencies, but expect to pay an upmarket price. And remember that the restrictions surrounding listing can make them all too interesting to buy and sell.

FINANCING YOUR PURCHASE

Banks and building societies follow strict criteria when deciding whether to offer you a mortgage (*see Chapter 2*). If you wish to buy a converted wind-mill or houseboat rather than a more conventional home, you face a whole new set of demands.

People who want to buy unusual properties are probably well aware that they cannot walk into the local branch of a high-street lender, sign on the dotted line and have the loan secured within 20 minutes. The mortgage lender has to be certain of the property's value and that it could be resold if it had to be repossessed. How many other people would want to live in an ex-nuclear bunker? Unusual properties are outside lenders' normal field of experience. When looking for finance, learn to expect delays.

However, it's possible to secure financing on virtually any property if you know how to go about it. Look at the recent ludicrous market for beach huts if proof were needed. You may have to make more of an effort to find a willing lender and, in some instances, be willing to pay more for the privilege, but your persistence will be rewarded in the end.

If you're turned down by one lender, don't assume the property is unmortgageable. Different lenders are prepared to accept different risks. Talk to a couple of brokers. They'll know which lenders are likely to be sympathetic in particular cases. You may be turned down flat by counter staff at your local branch, but a broker can talk to more senior staff and present additional information to help persuade them to accept the risk. People can secure mortgages against a variety of assets. So long as a lender thinks the asset will retain its value over the life of the loan, you're still in with a chance.

Lenders asked to consider more unusual risks often ask for a larger deposit. Expect to be asked for 25 per cent or more of the asking price. But, once they've agreed to lend the money, they'll generally offer you access to their full range of mortgage products, so you're unlikely to have to pay loaded interest rates.

FINANCING CONVERSIONS

If the property you want was originally built for a different purpose, you may run into difficulties when seeking a mortgage. The lender will want to see from the survey that any conversion work has been carried out competently, and to building regulations, and that the building is habitable. The other main issue will be its resale potential. Barn conversions in rural areas are now common, and office blocks, schools, factories and churches in urban areas have been converted into flats. More lenders are willing to look at these types of property, particularly if they're quality conversions in affluent areas.

Fewer lenders will be prepared to offer mortgages on more unusual properties, such as lighthouses, offshore forts or underground bunkers, where location is clearly an issue.

Your bargaining position will be strengthened if the property is already inhabited and has been bought and sold in the past. The longer it has been used as a residential home, the less worried the lender is going to be.

CAPITAL ALLOWANCES ON FLAT CONVERSIONS

Normal developers don't get tax relief for the conversion expenditure on their property, but the Government has recently introduced a system of 100 per cent allowances for certain conversion work, with the aim of bringing back into use flats over shops that have fallen into disuse. To obtain these allowances you must make sure that:

 The building has been disused, or used only for storage for at least a year prior to conversion;

 It must be used as a business on the ground floor, and the upper floors must have been used as dwellings;

 There must be no more than four storeys above the ground floor;

 The building must date from before 1 January 1980.

If you're planning to convert an unusual property yourself, however, lenders are likely to be more nervous. Rather than lending all the money up front, they'll tend to release money in tranches, with a fresh valuation each time to prove the value of the property is in line with the mortgage. You're unlikely to get access to the cheapest loans on the market for this type of mortgage, but you shouldn't be charged extortionate rates. Expect to pay about 1 per cent over base rate (*see Chapter 6*).

BUYING A CONVERTED PROPERTY

If you're buying a property that has been converted from some other previous use, or from house to flats (or vice versa), then it should have shown up on the deeds at time of purchase, as planning consent is required for such changes, although often people ignore the need for planning consent. The risk is that, if planning consent was not gained, you, the new purchaser, might be served with a 'compliance notice' by the local authority within 10 years of the change. It will oblige you to reinstate the property to its original condition, although there is little the local authority can do to compel the owner to do this. Most people comply simply because it makes it difficult to sell the property if no planning permission was granted.

LISTED BUILDINGS

The Grading System for Listed Buildings

English Heritage recommends buildings for inclusion on statutory lists of buildings of 'special architectural or historic interest' that are compiled by the Secretary of State for Culture, Media and Sport. The older a building is, the more likely it is to be listed. All buildings built before 1700 that survive in anything like their original condition are listed, as are most built between 1700 and 1840. After that date, the criteria become tighter with time, so that post-1945 buildings have to be exceptionally important to be listed.

The Grades

These are different in Scotland and Northern Ireland. Listed buildings are graded to show their relative architectural or historic interest:

- Grade I buildings are of exceptional interest.
- Grade II* are particularly important buildings of more than special interest.
- Grade II are of special interest, warranting every effort to preserve them.

Listing protects 500,000 or so buildings, of which the majority – over 90 per cent – are Grade II. Grade I and II* buildings may be eligible for English Heritage grants for urgent major repairs. You're extremely unlikely to get any sort of grant for a Grade II listed building.

Rather than individual features being listed, buildings are listed in their entirety; so if a house is listed, it's listed throughout. Being listed means that any alterations, either outside or inside, must be carefully considered before they can be made; so in addition to planning permission you would also need listed building consent from your local planning authority before any work could be done. Obviously, anything that detracts from the period detail that makes the property so special will not be allowed, but alterations, extensions and even partial demolitions are not out of the question. The following alterations would need listed building consent:

- changing windows and doors;
- painting over brickwork;
- removing external surfaces;
- putting in dormer windows or rooflights;
- putting up aerials, satellite dishes and burglar alarms;
- changing roofing materials;
- moving/removing internal walls;
- making new doorways;
- removing or altering fireplaces, panelling or staircases.

In some cases, repairs and alterations may need to be carried out with materials in keeping with the original buildings, which could prove expensive, although if your building is Grade I or II* listed there may be grants available to assist with the work (*see above and page 249*).

Buying Listed Buildings

If all the disadvantages of owning a listed building haven't deterred you, then at least proceed with caution and consult experts before you even think of making an offer. You need to understand the grading system, as there are significant differences in what you can and can't do with properties of different grades. As the owner, you'll be responsible for the upkeep of the original condition of the house, though changes and alterations are possible with listed building planning consent. Although this is a separate issue from planning permission, it can be applied for at the same time through the local planning authority.

It's best to talk through any potential plans with the planning office so you can get a good idea of whether consent would be granted or not before you go ahead with the purchase. You also need to make sure that any changes the previous owners have made complied with all the regulations – if not, you could have to apply for 'retrospective' permission and will be liable for putting right anything that was done wrongly or without permission.

You can find out about listed buildings in your area and obtain copies of individual entries at your local council planning department, county council offices and most local reference libraries. The full English national list is kept by English Heritage at the National Monuments Record, Kemble Drive, Swindon SN2 2GZ. Listed status should be included in property details, but if not, the solicitors' search will uncover it.

How to Apply for Listed Building Consent

This is similar to obtaining planning permission, although it's more flexible, and 90 per cent of applications are granted. Your first step should be to contact your local authority before you make the application. A conservation officer will tell you whether your proposals are likely to be accepted. This could save you time and money. It's often best to employ an architect who is used to working with listed buildings. Your application will need to include enough information to show clearly what you intend to do, with detailed drawings and photographs.

Local authorities deal with all listed building consent cases and will give you the appropriate form for making your application. The majority of cases are dealt with by the local authority, but the most important cases are referred to English Heritage (Notifications) and sometimes to the Department of Culture, Media and Sport (Referrals).

> **TIP** *Heavy responsibility: maintaining a listed building is up to the owner. If a local authority considers that a property is not being looked after properly, they may serve a repairs notice that must be complied with. This drastic measure is rarely applied and, in fact, local authorities can be a great source of help and advice in maintaining listed buildings in their area.*

Note: Carrying out unauthorized work to a listed building is a criminal offence punishable by a fine or a prison sentence, and the local council can require you to put the building back as it was ('reinstatement').

Grants for Listed Buildings

(*See Chapter 9, page 249.*)

Value Added Tax and Listed Buildings

Some listed buildings enjoy a more favourable position as regards VAT than do unlisted buildings.

What should and should not carry VAT is extremely involved, and many owners end up paying more than they should, simply because it's so hard to fathom out what should be zero-rated. VAT is payable on running repairs and maintenance, but many approved alterations, such as changing an internal wall, installing central heating for the first time, building an extension or adding a conservatory should be zero-rated. Even installing an Aga is tax free provided it's part of an approved alteration to create a kitchen where none existed previously.

The problems often arise because it's down to the contractor to decide at the outset whether to charge VAT or not, and most play safe by charging VAT rather than face an unexpected bill later on. Obviously, getting expert advice is the safest option and, according to Peter Anslow of the Listed Property Owners Club (*see page 239*), one homeowner saved £24,000 after discovering that 'underpinning' could be regarded as an extension (downwards) and was therefore exempt from tax.

Until recently, Customs and Excise did not extend this concession to the conversion of outbuildings, but following a test case, provided the outbuildings remain part of the house, the VAT relief applies.

Want to Get your Building Listed?

For advice on this, or on listing in general, contact The Department of Culture, Media and Sport (DCMS) (*see below*). When a building is listed, it's immediately protected by law, so don't forget about obtaining listings consent for changes.

Appealing against a Listing?

You might think that your listed property doesn't deserve its rating. Again you can write to the DCMS and they'll consider your proposal, but they'll base their decision only on the qualities of the property and will not take into account any other circumstances. Don't bother applying to be delisted as a way of getting difficult planning permission passed without a hitch. Applications for delisting are not normally considered if a building is the subject of an application for listed building consent or of an appeal against refusal of consent, or where a local authority is having to take action because of unauthorized work or neglect.

Further information can be found on DCMS web site: www.culture.gov.uk/historic_environment/Listing.htm.

APPLYING FOR CHANGE OF USE

Change of use is a complicated issue. Some changes of use are permissible under 'permitted development rights', but if you want to change the use to which a building or a piece of land is put in a material way, you'll need to make a planning application for change of use.

If you're buying a commercial property or other non-residential property and hoping to use it as a dwelling, you would be well advised to make an inquiry before you buy it, to see if change of use is likely to be granted. You can make a formal application for planning permission before you own the property, although this costs over £200. If you fail to buy the property, you'll have wasted your money. Alternatively, you can ask informally by writing a letter to the planning office, explaining the situation and including a site plan with as much information as you can muster to support your case. You could expect an opinion within three to five weeks, but it would not be binding.

For guidance on whether or not you need change of use, you can consult the Town and Country Planning (Use Classes Order) 1987, Government Statutory Instrument 764 at your local planning office.

COVENANTS AND RESTRICTIONS

A covenant is a promise made by a previous owner to a third party that certain things will not be done on or to the land: these might include building development, restrictions on animal husbandry, or use as a business. A covenant will show up on the deeds. Easements, on the other hand, are third-party rights allowing someone to do something on your land, such as access to their property by crossing yours. These, and any restrictions, are now listed at the Land Registry.

The law on adverse possession has recently changed. In simple terms this means 'squatters rights', or 'possession is nine-tenths of the law'. It used to be the case that if you used a piece of land for in excess of 12 years and had it fenced to keep others out, you could claim possessory title. The new law means that this right is extinguished in favour of a more complicated formula, by which you can still claim possession, but the paper owner can tell you to leave, no matter how long you've been there. However, if the paper owner doesn't tell you to leave within the subsequent two years, you can have another go – and this time you're guaranteed to succeed.

Many people mistakenly think that any land not registered at the Land Registry can be claimed by this process. Rather a lot of land is simply *unregistered* because no sale has taken place since the local Land Registry has been established, yet the ownership cannot be disputed.

BUYING PROPERTY IN A CONSERVATION AREA

According to the Civic Amenities Act 1967, Conservation Areas are 'areas of special architectural or historic interest the character and appearance of which it is desirable to preserve or enhance'. Local councils can designate Conservation Areas, and they give broader protection than listing individual buildings because all features within the area, whether listed or not, are recognized as part of its character. Conservation areas, consequently, look tremendous, and properties in them will often attract a premium price, but you'll be limited as to what you can do to your house and garden.

For example demolishing a building, fully or partly, needs Conservation Area consent. Planning permission is needed for changes to buildings that would normally be permitted elsewhere. Changes requiring consent include cladding a building, inserting dormer windows, or putting up a satellite dish visible from the street.

Anyone proposing to cut down, top or lop a tree in a Conservation Area, whether or not it's covered by a Tree Preservation Order (TPO), has to give notice to the council (*see page 272 for information on TPOs*). Fruit trees are not protected, and if a tree is dead or in a dangerous condition, it will not be protected; but it's best to check with the council Tree Officer before going ahead. Even if you're certain that you do not need permission, notifying the council may save the embarrassment of an official visit if a neighbour contacts them to tell them what you're doing. The council considers the contribution the tree makes to the character of the Conservation Area, and if necessary it will make a TPO in order to protect it. Breaching these regulations is a criminal offence.

This does not mean that development proposals cannot take place, or that works to your property will be automatically refused; but the local planning authorities will have to consider the effect of your proposals on the character of the area. Many need more information than usual for planning applications within or even adjoining a Conservation Area. This may include a:

- site plan to 1/1,250 or 1/2,500 scale showing the property in relation to the Conservation Area;
- description of the works and the effect (if any) you think they may have on the character and appearance of the Conservation Area;
- set of scale drawings showing the present and proposed situation, including building elevations, internal floor plans and other details as necessary.

For major works you may need to involve a conservation architect with experience of working in Conservation Areas.

THE INTERESTING PROPERTIES TO BUY

Buying a building that was not previously used for residential purposes is another way of finding an unusual home; but be warned that applying for change of use and converting to create a satisfactory family home is not always easy.

Churches and Chapels

With these, in particular, there are usually restrictions on the kind of use you can make of the building or on what you can do to the exterior. Services and

TIP *One fact to bear in mind, though, if you're buying property on Church of England land is that under some circumstances you can be regarded as a 'lay rector' and, under the Chancel Repairs Act, be expected to pay towards the upkeep of the church. In a recent case one couple found themselves with a bill for nearly £100,000, so it's well worth asking your solicitor to include a Chancel Repairs search with the normal search.*

utilities are rarely up to standard, which may be expensive to put right; and what you can do with the interior is often strictly controlled. For example you're not permitted to interfere with the windows, so ceilings have to remain very high. To top it all, there is a good chance that your garden will be full of dead bodies – to which surviving relatives must be permitted access. Despite all this, redundant churches usually fetch a high price, particularly in urban areas, although it's still possible to buy remote chapels relatively cheaply.

Redundant churches are subject to normal planning, listed building and conservation area controls. Planning permission is usually required for a change of use and listed building consent for any significant alterations to a listed building. You're advised to contact the local planning officer to discuss your proposals as soon as possible.

The local planning authority may already have agreed a development brief on likely permitted uses. Occasionally planning consent for change of use is already in place. The Church of England is best set up for disposal of its churches and has a list of redundant churches available all over England. This information is updated regularly and includes details on whom to approach in the area. Go to www.cofe.anglican.org/rcsale. For churches and chapels of other denominations, make contact locally.

Covenants

Purchases of redundant churches and chapels will inevitably include these to make sure that:

- they're used only for purposes authorized by the vendor: this excludes worship, gambling or 'immoral' business activities;
- they're protected from any unauthorized alterations or demolition;
- interested parties can tend or visit any graves at agreed times;
- there will be no disturbance of any human remains, tombstones, monuments or memorials.

Schools

In areas where school rolls are falling, schools sometimes find their way on to the market and can make wonderful homes, although Government policy is now that schools in rural areas should be kept open wherever possible. There's no central register of school buildings for sale, and when they do come on to the market, they're generally placed with local agents. In your area, schools threatened with closure will be easy enough to find through the local grapevine, but it may be worth contacting the Property Services department of a Local Education Authority to inquire if they have any buildings to dispose of. Parish councils may handle the sale of Church of England schools.

There may be complications with contracts, though. In one case, the new owners of the disused school had to agree that if they built anything on the site of the playground, they would give the parish council one third of the value of the building – despite the fact that they had bought the freehold!

Pubs

Pubs frequently come on to the market, but as going concerns. The possibility of change of use to residential will arise only if the pub is failing and is being sold by the publican or the owning brewery. If the pub can be shown to have a future, planners are more likely to consider it as a local amenity, and protect it accordingly. But if it isn't viable, there's no reason to stand in the way of the change-of-use permission upon those grounds, although there may be other grounds – perhaps it has a particularly historic exterior or interior.

Planners will take into account, among other factors, population density, visitor potential, competition, the flexibility of the site, parking, public transport, local case studies for comparison, the business at present, its future potential and the terms of the sale. To find a redundant pub to buy, contact the estate manager of a brewery.

Barns

Buy an old barn, convert it to a house and you've done your bit saving a historic building from falling to pieces, creating a wonderful original home for yourself in the process. Hold on – it's rarely that simple. Converting a barn needs a lot of thought. One of the biggest hurdles will be convincing local planners that a barn conversion is a good idea. Local authorities are under pressure from central government to find new uses for old buildings to keep the rural economy healthy, but many barns are miles from shops, schools and other local amenities, which doesn't make them sustainable as residential dwellings. Avoid the barn blues with these tips:

- Before you buy, check the barn's planning status carefully. It may already have planning permission for change of use, in which case be prepared to pay a premium price. In many cases, authorities would rather have barns converted to another commercial use because this brings more to the local economy than a dwelling; and if they've already been persuaded, you're being saved a lot of work.
- If it hasn't got change-of-use permission, you'll need to find an architect or builder, preferably with experience of converting barns, to draw up conversion plans and discuss them with the local planning officer. Don't buy anything unless you get a positive response; otherwise you could end up with a useless, derelict building on your hands.

- The barn may well have electricity, but probably won't have gas, phone or water and mains drainage. If it's miles from anywhere across fields, it'll be very expensive to get connected.

- Budget on having to use quality materials. Planning officers will give permission for a barn to be made into a home only if the architect plans something that retains character and is in keeping with the surroundings. Suggesting plastic windows, kitsch front doors or brash brick chimneys will get you turned away double quick.

- Is the existing barn in a reasonable structural state? If it's falling down, you may end up having to rebuild the whole thing, which rather destroys the point of a conversion.

- Be warned: barns were originally built for animals not humans. They rarely have foundations, and will invariably need underpinning.

- Get detailed costings before you exchange contracts and commit yourself to buying.

- Check with your architect and builder that the existing structure will stand being knocked about to insert doors and windows where you want them.

Each local authority interprets the government guidelines for themselves, but if you only have outline planning permission, you'll also need full planning permission later on. To obtain full planning permission, you have to submit detailed forms, with detailed sets of drawings, site location maps, floor plans and elevations (*see Chapter 9*).

Listed Barns

Some barns are listed as being of special architectural or historic interest (*see page 221*). Conversions of these will require extra sensitivity, and you may have to retain the internal features, such as roof trusses and framing, so that they can be seen. A separate application for listed building consent will also be required.

Barns Converted without Permission

Planning officers can enforce action against people who've gone ahead without planning permission and owners could be forced to reinstate the barn to its original condition at their own cost. Planning officers have a period of 10 years after work is completed to enforce this, but once the time limit's over, they cannot compel the owner to comply. After that time it would still be wise to regularize the situation by applying retrospectively for planning permission, because failure to do so would be a stumbling block if you came to

---

REAL-LIFE ACCOUNT

Peter and Louise Wingate-Saul live in the Downs of Cuckmere Valley in East Sussex in a house they converted from a cart-shed in 1990.

'We were looking for something to build, but it's very hard to get planning permission in a rural area like this, so we had to find a dwelling to replace or something to convert. The shed, which was single story, flint built and open fronted, is part of a group of buildings, and when we bought it, it already had detailed planning permission on it. But securing it had been a struggle for the vendor. The local authority thought the buildings were worth saving, but refused permission for them to become residential property. The vendor went to appeal, and the Planning Inspectorate finally ruled that the local authority had been unreasonable, but the whole process took about six months.

'The building is an unusual shape – about 65 feet long by 15 feet. However, we didn't like the plans that were finally approved – they were very basic – so we redesigned it with an architect to incorporate two bedrooms, living room, kitchen, bathroom and utility, and resubmitted. It helped that I have some hands-on experience of how buildings are constructed, having converted flats in Brighton in the past, but we consulted experts about the shed. The roof gave away its age. It's pitch pine and the timbers had been machine sawn, so it couldn't have been more than 120 years old because timbers were not sawn before that date, and, any older, it would probably have been oak-framed. The planners worried about us

sell. Anyone who bought the barn from you would inherit the problem when they took on the title to the property.

Houseboats and Canal Barges

It's cheaper to buy a boat than it is to buy a home, but beware of just comparing the purchase cost. Most high-street lenders flatly refuse to provide a mortgage for a floating home, regardless of whether it's permanently moored or

maintaining the character of the building, but that is hard to do when it was once a shed and was to become a house! It helped that the building wasn't listed or in a conservation area, and it was an advantage that the clay-tiled roof was in place. The only major design consideration was the large windows which run down one side.

'Naturally we had to comply with building regulations, and ensure, for example, that the roof was insulated – which is difficult with skeilings [sloping ceiling] and it had to be done from outside. It's so important to have a good relationship with your buildings inspector, especially in a complicated job like this. They can be tough to start with but, once they know you really are trying to do things right, they will be a help.

'A major consideration was getting services like water and electricity to the house, and we had to reserve rights of way over the vendor's neighbouring property to access his private drainage system. I wasn't working at the time and did a great deal of the heavy work myself. The hardest project was digging a 1-metre trench all the way round to underpin the building, as it had no foundations, and that took me a whole winter! We then employed contractors like the electricians, plumbers, bricklayers and plasterers as and when we needed them. It would have been exhausting to line everyone up in time to do their particular job if I'd been working full-time.

'The land cost £92,000 in 1990 – expensive, but this is Sussex – but the conversion only cost us £30,000. By the time we finished it was worth around £180,000, and now that we have added a single-story extension with a further bedroom and bathroom, it's worth considerably more. The most satisfying part is not the value, though. It's the fact that we're living in a place we converted ourselves.'

free to travel the canal network. Boats are chattels, so you can't mortgage them. This means you need to get an unsecured loan, which costs more than secured loans (*see Chapter 9*). In addition, houseboats don't have the investment potential of properties solidly rooted on land, and expenses can rack up pretty quickly. You'll still have to 'rent' your moorings, usually for a four-figure sum per annum, and you should check this out first, as there is plenty of competition for the best locations. Expect to pay a premium for a mooring in a desirable city-centre area – prices relate to local property values and there are long waiting lists.

British Waterways can provide you with a list of moorings around Britain and will tell you what they cost, what facilities are available, and if there is a mooring available. They have their own web site, www.britishwaterways.co.uk, or can be contacted on 01923 201120.

Services to Boats

There are surprisingly few residential moorings in Britain, but most provide access to electricity and telephones, and you buy gas in bottles. The postman and the milkman will usually deliver. If your boat has an engine, you'll no doubt have an oil tank, and a set of 12-volt batteries that the engine can charge. Power cuts will be a distant memory.

TIP

- *It's illegal to live on a houseboat without a licence to do so, and without being registered with the local authority.*

- *Before you buy a houseboat or canal boat, try spending some time on one, particularly in winter, so you're fully aware of just how grim it can get.*

- *You should get the boat properly surveyed, which will cost you about £300 and will make it easier to get both your mortgage and insurance.*

Most moorings are operated by British Waterways, which gives only 30 days' security of tenure. You don't rent the space your boat floats on: you're granted a licence that can be terminated with 30 days' notice. However, despite this, you still have to pay council tax. The British Waterways Board issues residential houseboat licences. With this licence, you can live permanently on your boat; but without it, you're allowed to stay on the boat only for weekends and holidays to travel up and down stretches of canal and river. Useful info from the National Association of Boat Owners at www.nabo.org.uk.

Bunkers

As Cold War paranoia becomes a distant memory for most people, underground bunkers are coming to be seen not as vital life-saving installations, but as potential living spaces. Being underground, they're hard to spot, but there are more there than you would imagine.

Local authorities and the Ministry of Defence (MoD) have been selling off underground bunkers since the end of the Cold War. Now considered 'surplus to requirements' by cash-starved authorities – the big ones cost thousands of pounds a year to keep ventilated and free from damp – they're being snapped up by businesses and individuals looking for secure storage or somewhere safe to go in the event of some as yet indiscernible attack.

When bunkers first started to be sold off in the mid-1990s, they were extremely cheap, but interest has grown and competition for them is heated, with interest from residential as well as commercial clients. If you fancy the idea of living underground, they can be sourced through the MoD.

Eco-housing

For houseowners with an interest in the environment, eco-housing is the best way to live according to your convictions. By definition, these tend to be new builds and they're rarely cheap to buy, but the reduced running costs mean that there will be long-term financial savings, quite apart from environmental ones.

The kinds of features you could expect include solar panels to heat water, recycled newspaper insulation, bath water recycled for toilets, an energy-saving kitchen and solar gain flooring. Many are designed with excellent hi-tech facilities, such as networked PCs and TVs, 'intelligent' cabling in internal walls and the potential for remote-control heating, curtains and audio systems.

As far as possible, local materials are used alongside reclaimed materials – everything from timber and boarding to reclaimed steel joists, wherever possible. But eco-friendly insulation and features like solar heating remain expensive unless built in bulk – and without the tax breaks used to encourage builders in Scandinavia, British developers are reluctant to dent their profit margins.

Martello Towers

These circular forts used for coastal defence during the Napoleonic wars were based on the design of a fortified tower at Mortella Point in Corsica, which had put up a prolonged resistance to British forces in 1793.

Quite a few of the towers are still left along the south coast of the UK, and they occasionally come up for sale, usually creating a huge amount of interest, partly inspired by some mistaken folklore that the towers can be snapped up for as little as a pound.

In fact, prospective purchasers will have to make offers, outline their proposals and show they have the financial backing to carry out the necessary renovation and conservation work under the watchful eye of English Heritage, as all the towers are listed buildings, and some are scheduled as ancient monuments too.

This means you can do little to alter their appearance, though in some instances you'll be allowed to add a single-storey building alongside the tower. You'll not be allowed to increase the number or size of the windows. Repairing them costs a fortune, and they're also notoriously difficult to sell. Still keen?

Thatched Properties

Of the 30,000 thatched buildings in England, 24,000 have been listed by English Heritage, and most of these fall into the Grade II category.

Thatch has to be replaced from time to time, but not as frequently as many people suppose. It can quite easily be 30 to 60 years between thatchings, but there are often local planning restrictions on the materials that can be used and the style or pattern. In a conservation area (*see page 251*) you'll have to maintain your thatch in a way that accords with local criteria and at your own expense, as grants are small and hard to come by. You may also be liable to restrictions even if the property is not listed or in a conservation area.

Make sure you're able to undertake the work legally, and get permission before starting. The owner and the roofing contractor will be held liable for the reinstatement of any work carried out without it.

Thatched properties are slightly more expensive to insure than normal roofed ones, but fires are not as common in thatched properties as you may fear. Take advice from your local fire authority and from the recommendations given in *The Care & Repair of Thatched Roofs* published by the Society for the Protection of Ancient Buildings and the Countryside Agency (www.thatch.org/listing.htm).

Reclamation Suppliers

For period and unusual houses a quick trip to the DIY superstore just isn't going to do it. Enter the reclamation supplier. A survey of this trade, conducted in 1998, revealed annual sales of around £1 billion, 2,500 businesses with an average annual turnover of £400,000 and a crew of 40,000 employees scouring demolition sites for the best of the rest. The demand just keeps on growing, fuelled by television makeover programmes and the perennial fascination for antiques and curiosities and a passion for restoration.

And it's not just the usual stuff – antique fireplaces, Art Deco doorways, marble worktops – you might expect, but reclamation yards sell the more basic elements too: beams and floorboards, bricks and boards, even reclaimed loos.

Conservationists are concerned about the provenance of the items. Removing them may cause damage and they may even be removed illegally from buildings at risk. There are many reputable firms, but the fear is that some dealers are less interested in the source of the materials than in their availability.

In 1990 Salvo, the main agency organizing the trade, established a simple code for dealers, which is to give buyers confidence that items have not been stolen or plundered from listed buildings. Salvo's web site features a theft alert that publishes details of stolen items.

USEFUL CONTACTS

Auction sites:
www.auctions.co.uk/property
www.auctionhammer.co.uk
www.propertyauctions.com
www.insolvency.co.uk

Finding unusual property:
www.heritage.co.uk
www.defence-estates.mod.uk/property_sale/index.htm
www.windmillworld.com/mills/forsale.htm
www.property.org.uk/unique/ch.html

Listed buildings:
Architectural Heritage Fund
Clareville House
26–27 Oxendon Street
London SW1Y 4EL
Tel.: 020 7925 0199
Web: www.ahfund.org.uk

Architectural Heritage Society of Scotland
The Glasite Meeting House
33 Barony Street
Edinburgh EH3 6NX
Tel.: 0131 557 0019
Web: www.ahss.org.uk

Department of Culture, Media and Sport
1a Cockspur Street
London SW1Y 5DH
Web: www.dcms.gov.uk

English Heritage
23 Savile Row
London W1S 2ET
Tel.: 020 7973 3000
Web: www.english-heritage.org.uk

The Georgian Group
6 Fitzroy Square
London W1P 6DX
Tel.: 020 7387 1720

Listed Property Owners Club
Hartlip
Sittingbourne ME9 7TE
Tel.: 01795 844939
Web: www.listedpropertyownersclub.co.uk

Period Property (helps users find period
homes and offers advice on maintaining
them)
Web: www.periodproperty.co.uk

The Residential Boat Owners' Association
Tel.: 07710 029247
Web: www.rboa.co.uk

**Society for the Protection of Ancient
Buildings**
37 Spital Square
London E1 6DY
Tel.: 020 7377 1644
Web: www.spab.org.uk

The Twentieth Century Society
77 Cowcross Street
London EC1M 6EJ
Tel.: 020 7250 3857

The Victorian Society
1 Priory Gardens
Bedford Park
London W4 1TT
Tel.: 020 8994 1019

(*See also Chapter 9*)

IMPROVING YOUR HOME

If more space is what you need, the obvious answer is to move to a bigger property. But that's not always possible or the best option. You may be very happy where you are: it's near schools or work, and you have a good group of friends and neighbours. There's also more to moving than just a hike in your mortgage repayments. Moving house itself is expensive, with surveys, stamp duty, legal fees and removal costs to meet, and these can be upwards of £25,000. The solution could be to stay put and improve what you already have.

According to the Council of Mortgage Lenders, the level of remortgaging (*see page 247*) rose from £12.9 billion in 1997 to £83.5 billion in 2002. And of those who remortgage and don't intend to move, 89 per cent of the borrowing is being spent on home improvements – from replacing windows to building new extensions. The Abbey National has calculated that people are borrowing an average £20,000 (2003) to spend on home improvements to create better living space. You might have a big enough garden for your children, but they're having to share a bedroom – an extension would be a bonus. The loft is spacious and unused and you need home office space – could you convert it? You need more light and a place for a dining table in a cramped kitchen – a conservatory would be ideal.

Improvements don't always have to be structural. Renovation is also an important part of home improvement – whether it be gutting and recreating the existing space, or simply putting in new wiring.

Home improvement isn't just about benefiting yourself while you live there, however. If done well, these types of improvements can only add to the value of your home. With the slowdown in the property market, many homeowners are working hard to unlock the value of their properties, rather than relying on an increase in the intrinsic value of their homes to make them money. But before you go mad with any ideas, you need to think about whether you really are adding value.

Here are some hard and fast rules to home improvement:

- Make sure it's done well – don't skimp on materials and quality of work. It's a buyer's market and, as the market slows, there will be more chains and more time for people to think very hard before buying. The gap between good and inferior will make all the difference.
- Make sure you have the right planning permissions, or you'll have problems when you come to sell.
- Make sure an extension blends in with the rest of the house and doesn't look like an add-on – the flat-roofed extensions of the past are an example of this.
- Make sure the rest of the house can work with the added space – if you add two new bedrooms, do you have big enough reception rooms and enough bathrooms to cope?
- Make sure you're not creating an oddly shaped property, which will stick out like a sore thumb next to those around it. (Your local planning office will probably ensure this doesn't happen!)
- Don't overdevelop for the type of house and its location – if the average house in your road is a three-bed semi, and you make yours into six bedrooms with extensions and a swimming pool, it will be an unwise move. The average price for an area will tend to dictate valuations, and can pull down the value of your property.
- Don't spend more on doing the work than you would reap back when you come to sell. Some properties are overvalued already and investing further in your property may not be a good idea. Check with local estate agents before you proceed with your ideas.
- Most important of all: unless you're planning to sell immediately after you've done the improvements, do the work to make life more enjoyable and comfortable for you. People may warn you that you won't earn back the money you spent on installing an expensive kitchen (*see page 246*), but if it's important to you and your lifestyle, and you're going to enjoy it, then go right ahead!

WHAT ADDS VALUE

Estate agents basically value a property based on location, number of bed-rooms, reception rooms and size of garden. So bearing in mind all the above, improvements that give your home more generous living space will, one hopes, increase its value, make it appeal to potential buyers when you come to sell, and put you ahead of the competition. But what in the experts' view are improvements worth doing?

- *Loft conversions*: the roof space is an obvious area to develop. Most houses with pitched roofs have a wealth of wasted space that simply houses the water tank and the odd suitcase. Access into roof space has to be easy, so before you go any further with your plans, think about where a staircase would need to go – ladders are not a good idea and are against building regulations anyway (*see page 261*). Consider too whether it would make the house top heavy, especially if you plan to heighten the roof and put in dormer windows (something for which you'll need planning permission); and, as we said before, would the size of the rest of the house cope with the extra load on space and bathrooms that a further bedroom would create?

- *Cellars*: if you can't go up, then is it worth looking down? Cellars are another wasted space in many older houses, but there are obvious drawbacks. Cellars were originally designed for storage, not living space, and there may be problems in terms of ensuring enough light and damp control. Make sure you have a cellar conversion done well, and to regulations (cellars with light wells will require planning permission). If it isn't done properly, an agent will only be able to put 'cellar storage' on the particulars of sale. Basement rooms can be created where no cellar exists. Victorian and Edwardian properties often have suspended timber floors and hall coal cellars, but excavating a modern property may be more difficult.

- *Heating/insulation systems*: this may not be glamorous, but a good central heating system can only add to the value of your home, though most buyers will consider that there should be a good heating system anyway. With the sellers' pack looming on the horizon (*see page 106*), properties will have to be energy efficiency rated, and good rating on your property may help swing a sale if buyers are looking at similar houses in the same area that aren't so favourably rated.

- *Extension*: ideal in terms of creating larger living space, especially if you build a two-storey extension with access on both floors. Carefully thought out and planned, it will undoubtedly add to the value of your property, especially if you're creating a larger kitchen, adding an extra bathroom and bedroom, playroom or office space, downstairs loo or shower room.

But, whatever its size, an extension is a big undertaking: it will be complicated in terms of construction – it will need foundations – and will usually need planning permission before you proceed. Think about how it will sit with the rest of the house, and whether it will eat into too much garden space. If you have a family house, a good-sized garden is a strong selling point and you won't want to lose that. Families need gardens, anyway, and there's little point in transforming a four-bedroomed house into a five-bedroomed one, if there's no space left outside to play.

- *Garages*: these are a major bonus, even though they don't create more living space. As far as buyers are concerned, they add vital parking facilities (especially important in towns), security for the car (garage parking can help reduce insurance premiums) and extra storage space. A single garage may add up to 6 per cent to the value of your property.

- *Side-return extensions*: this is the development of the 'lost space' at the back of terraced housing between the typical kitchen extensions at the back and the garden fence. However, in some areas of London, at time of writing, houses with

> **TIP** *If you're planning a loft or cellar conversion or extension, make sure your existing boiler can cope with the extra load on the central heating system. You'll undoubtedly need more radiators and pipework, and you'll need to factor into your budget the cost of this and, at worst, a more powerful boiler*

side-return extensions command about the same increase in value as the price of doing the work, which doesn't leave much of a margin if you overspend.

- *Conservatories*: these are a link between house and garden, but they'll add value only if they're in an appropriate style to the rest of the house. Be sure that what you spend you can reap, because a good conservatory can be expensive to construct properly. Think too about where you're going to place it. If the only space is against a north facing wall, is it really worth having one at all?

- *Good maintenance*: the elements will play havoc with the outside of your house, but keeping an eye on the exterior, keeping brickwork well pointed, paintwork fresh (including window frames), guttering secure and the roof in good order will all help to make a good first impression on potential buyers – kerb appeal – and might put you ahead of the competition.

- *Renovation*: whether you're renovating your property in order to sell it, or simply bringing it up to date, renovation *done well* will add value – even if it's in terms of quality of life. For a checklist of the order of priority for adding monetary value see below.

- *Outline or detailed planning permission*: even if you don't intend to do the work, it can help add value (and ease a sale) if you have plans for extensions, loft conversion, outbuildings or another house on the plot already approved by the local authority. Most planning permissions have a five-year limit, so ensure there's plenty of time left on it when you put your house on the market. But if you have outline planning permission (OPP) or detailed planning permission (DPP) for a plot in your garden, think about what effect development will have on the value of your house. Take proper advice from a good estate agent.

> **TIP** *It's worth noting that if your home improvements add significantly to the value of your property, it may move it into a different council tax band and you'll have to pay a higher rate.*

See over for more detail about carrying out these sorts of improvements.

WHAT DOESN'T ADD VALUE!

- *Kitchen*: a good-looking kitchen in keeping with the style of the house will appeal to buyers and may clinch a sale, but it won't necessarily add to the agent's *valuation*. You might spend £30,000 on a state-of-the-art version with all the gadgets and units, but it will not add £30,000 to the price. It will simply be a selling point. The same applies to bathrooms. However, if you want to sell, have a nice house, but the kitchen/bathroom is outdated, it might help a sale if you install a simple up-to-date kitchen – just don't go mad on the cost.

- *Swimming pool or hot tub*: this is a lifestyle choice and again expensive to install and maintain. While it may sound appealing on the sale particulars, it won't recoup the amount you spent installing it. It can even work against you and put off potential buyers who like the house but don't want the bother of the pool.

REAL-LIFE ACCOUNT

Richard and Sally Travis bought a Victorian house in the middle of Chester 15 years ago. It had light, spacious rooms, but the kitchen and dining area were at the back of the house, at basement level, and were quite dark.

'We decided to take out the floor, to create a tall dining room with a bannistered gallery above it. We already had a good-sized sitting room at the front of the house, so the room above the dining area was not much used, but essentially we had lost a room. It looked fabulous. The work cost £11,000 – and was all done to building regs thank goodness – but we were intending to stay in the house for a while. Then I was offered a job in Sussex and we had to move quickly. The people who came to look at the house all thought it was "very interesting" but were clearly horrified. We couldn't buy in Sussex until we had sold the Chester house, and we had to rent at huge cost. The house was on the market for well over a year before it found a buyer, a couple who were being relocated by their company and had plenty of money to spend. They reinstated the floor straight away.'

- *Overdecorating*: unless you're planning to stay in the property for a while, if you're wanting to improve to sell, keep decoration neutral and simple.

- *A landscaped garden*: having your garden planned and landscaped for your own enjoyment is fine, but avoid doing it just to try to sell your property. Gardens are a matter of taste. Better to have it tidy, with a mown lawn and weed-free beds, than to spend thousands on hard landscaping and design just to secure a sale. You won't see your money back.

- *Anything unusual*: it's better to do what you think other people will want, not just what you fancy at the time. Also avoid ripping out original features such as fireplaces, panelling, doors. They might not suit your taste, but houses with 'original detail' appeal to buyers.

> TIP *Speak to a local estate agent before proceeding with any major work – he or she will have a good idea of what appeals to potential buyers, and what is especially popular in your area.*

FINANCING HOME IMPROVEMENTS

Unless you're lucky enough to be able to pay for work on your property through income, savings or a legacy from Great-Aunt Maud, you may well have to borrow the money. There are several ways to do this:

- *Extending your existing mortgage*: you can ask your lender to increase the amount you're borrowing so long as they have proof you can cope with the increase in monthly repayments.

- *Remortgaging*: this means moving your mortgage to a new lender, either to increase the loan or to get better repayment terms. Lenders are keen to attract remortgage business, and you'll receive a competitive interest rate for a certain period to encourage you to move your mortgage to them.

- *Home improvement loan*: these are not offered by all lenders and may only be possible if you have a mortgage with a lender who offers this type of loan. Terms usually mean they'll lend up to a certain percentage of the value of your home, depending how much you still owe on your mortgage, and the monthly repayments are added to your mortgage repayments.

- *Unsecured personal loan*: you can usually borrow up to £25,000, and you do not have to specify the purpose of wanting the loan. However, as it's not secured against your home, you'll pay a higher interest rate for borrowing the money. You don't always have to have a mortgage with your personal loan lender – though you may get preferable rates – so shop around. APR (annual percentage rates – the interest you pay on the loan) can vary enormously.

- *Secured personal loan*: although you can usually borrow up to about £25,000, this type of loan is secured against your home (so it's at risk if you cannot keep up the repayments), but the interest rate you'll pay will be lower than if it were unsecured. It's separate from your mortgage, however, and you can repay over a different period if you want to. There are not usually penalties if you pay the loan off early either. Most lenders recommend payment protection insurance.

- *Equity Release Loan*: if your house is worth more than the mortgage you owe on it, some lenders will offer this type of loan whereby you can borrow money against the property and repay it over a period of between 5 and 30 years. The money doesn't have to be for home improvements, nor does the lender have to be your mortgage lender, but you'll pay a higher interest rate if it isn't.

HOME IMPROVEMENT PROJECTS IN DETAIL

Renovation

This most definitely comes under the heading 'home improvement'. If you've bought, or have been tolerating, a rundown property with outdated fittings, rotting windows, dodgy wiring and a suspect roof, then any quality work you carry

GRANTS FOR IMPROVING AND RENOVATING LISTED PROPERTIES

Grants for repairs to listed buildings (*see page 223*) are becoming increasingly hard to find as money for them becomes short, so don't buy a listed property in the expectation of getting a grant. In fact many grant-making bodies will assume that when you bought the property you factored in the cost of repair and renovation.

Policies may vary slightly among England, Scotland, Northern Ireland and Wales, but they're broadly the same. For private owners the main options are as follows:

 English Heritage (*see page 274*), or equivalent, offers grants to aid 'outstanding' buildings, which means those listed Grade I or Grade II*, but not Grade II buildings outside Conservation Areas. It's currently reviewing its grant system, but awards are most likely to go to important houses, buildings at risk, and some country houses that have been in the same hands for a long time. Grants tend to be around 40 to 60 per cent of the costs, and you're normally required to provide some public access or opening. It does run some schemes that may provide grants for private owners of Grade II buildings, particularly ones that have been in the same family for at least 30 years and where the project involves work urgently needed to keep the building structurally stable and watertight.

 CADW, Historic Scotland and the Department of the Environment (Northern Ireland) have their own grant schemes (*see page 274*).

 Local Authority Historic Building Grants: though local authorities have the power to offer grants for listed buildings, including Grade IIs, few have the money. It's worth enquiring, but do not hold out much hope, and any grant you're lucky enough to receive will be small.

 Local Authority House Renovation Grants: these are not specific to historic buildings, and are generally designed to bring properties up to an acceptable level of hygiene and safety. A building would have to be severely neglected and rundown. Local authorities can help with rescuing a historic building, but may well require you to renovate it to modern standards that would not be in keeping with an old building.

 Heritage Lottery Fund cannot normally help private owners, though it can assist Building Preservation Trusts in the rescue of a building that eventually passes into private ownership.

Further Information: The Architectural Heritage Fund (*see page 274*) has a web-based directory of funds for historic buildings www.ahfund.org.uk.

TIP *VAT is payable on repairs to all buildings, but if your building is listed, you may not have to pay it on approved alterations (see Chapter 8). The basic principle is that approved alterations for which you've been given listed building consent do not attract VAT. In practice there are grey areas, not least because of the differing judgements by local planning authorities on what may or may not require listed building consent. Whether or not you have to pay may depend on your local Customs and Excise office.*

out to bring it up to date will be an improvement. Be aware, though, that what you do should be in keeping with the age of the property, and if your property is listed (*see page 222*), there will be restrictions to the work you can carry out and the style in which you do it. Architectural salvage yards are ideal for sourcing original materials, there are magazines that specialize in period renovation, and you can get advice from an architectural society (*see pages 274–5*).

Renovation should have a two-pronged effect: you should do improvements that will make life more comfortable and enjoyable for you and your family, and which will add value to the property when you come to sell. The two are sometimes one and the same, but as there's nothing certain in this life, and you may find yourself in a situation where you have to move quickly, it might be wiser to prioritize the 'value' improvements first.

As a rule of thumb, here is the priority list for renovation:

- *Central heating, insulation and wiring*: you'll need the first two to keep you warm and to keep your fuel bills down, and good wiring to be safe. As this sort of fundamental installation involves laying pipes and wires under floors and inside walls, it can be messy and disruptive, so it's a good one to get out of the way before you start decorating. Ensure you use a qualified installation expert.
- *Windows and roofs*: many companies supply windows, and with attractive deals. But before you're seduced by offers such as 'pay for the front windows and get the back windows free', think hard. A building can be ruined by poor-quality budget windows. Think too about the

style of the property, and the windows of other similar properties nearby. Good roofing is essential to the quality of your renovation job. Don't be tempted to scrimp: take the advice of a renovation specialist and/or a surveyor for the most suitable materials to use. Be especially careful if you live in a Conservation Area. Contact the Institute of Roofing at www.instituteofroofing.org.uk, and the National Society of Master Thatchers at www.nsmt.co.uk.

- *Good bathrooms*: well-designed bathrooms are a pleasure to have, and appeal to buyers. Again, installing the pipework can be disruptive, so it's work best done early. Think about where waste pipes will need to go before you get carried away with placing the toilet/shower/bath (you won't want them coming down the front wall of the house if possible), and look at the style of suite that will maximize space. If space is tight, a power shower above the bath will be space-saving, rather than a separate cubicle. Plain white sanitaryware is cheaper, will not date so quickly and will look good.

- *Kitchen*: this room is often the centre of the house. The bigger the kitchen, the more useful, and the more appealing to potential buyers. Look at the space. Could you incorporate another room, and create dining space, with the removal of a wall? Think too about the location of waste pipes, where to place windows and the electricity supply. Plenty of designs are sympathetic to the period of your house, but incorporate all the mod cons. As we said above, it's unwise to spend a fortune on the kitchen units, unless you intend to stay in the house for a long time. Even budget kitchen suppliers have a design service (free if you buy a kitchen from them).

TIP *Most local authorities have a conservation officer. Talk to him or her about grants available locally, and it may help to get your request in at the beginning of the financial year.*

You can also go to the Citizens' Advice Bureau web site at www.adviceguide.org.uk (click on 'Housing') to find out information about getting local authority help with home improvements.

- *Garage*: your living space is obviously a priority, but a garage should be high on your list of must-dos for phase 2. It goes without saying that the garage of an older property should blend in well with the house, and you'll need planning permission for it anyway (*see page 259*).
- *Conservatory*: again this should be a phase 2 improvement, unless it's integral to the rebuild – but erecting a conservatory can be complicated. See below for further advice on conservatories.
- *Decorating*: this shouldn't be done until all structural repairs and improvements have been made. If your intention is to renovate a property in order to sell it again, then keep decoration simple and neutral. Decoration is a taste and lifestyle choice, unlike the quality of the central heating and the wiring, which are essential. Seek professional advice for ideas about decorating in a style particular to the period of your property.

Note: renovation work is not considered to be creating a new dwelling and is fully rated for VAT, unless the property has been empty for three years or more, or if you're changing the number of units, in which case it's rated at 5 per cent (*see Appendix 4*).

Structural Improvements

Before you Start

Most structural improvements – extensions, raising or extending the roof line, building a garage or outbuilding – need detailed plans. These are essential if your work needs planning permission or building regulation approval, because you'll need to submit them to the local authority planning department (*see page 259*). They're necessary too so a structural engineer can calculate exactly what your work will require in terms of load support and materials, and, most importantly, they give your builder something to work from.

Even if planning permission isn't necessary, you should consult an expert – whether it be an architect if you want drawings, or a structural engineer if your scheme will affect the fabric of the building – especially if you're removing internal or external walls. You'll need to be sure the work is done properly, so it won't fall down, be dangerous or catch the eye of a surveyor when you come to sell.

Some internal work, such as certain cellar or loft conversions, must meet building control guidelines, and you'll need plans drawn up to submit a Full Plans Application or work from a Building Notice (*see page 261*) to ensure the work is done properly.

TIP *The biggest single mistake people make when renovating property is to lose control of costs and spending. Allocate your budget and do your costings, and then keep a close eye on it. Prioritize your scheme, and have a phase 1 and a phase 2 list. Don't move on to phase 2 until you're sure you've not overspent and can afford to move on once work on phase 1 is completed.*

For these drawings or plans to be drawn up, or simply to brief your builder, you need to decide exactly what you want to achieve before you talk to anyone. In Chapter 6 there's more information about briefing an architect, but when you're adding on to or improving an existing building, you need to think about:

- what you're trying to achieve: more light, more space, modernization;
- how your ideas will affect the existing space and look of the property;
- the schedule of the work – whether you can continue to live there while work is going on;
- access to the site;
- whether you need to source old or reclaimed materials;
- your budget: what is the ceiling amount you can afford?

Extensions

As these are a big undertaking, and will undoubtedly need planning permission, you'll need to consult an expert. An architect will not only be able to advise you on the feasibility of building on to the existing property, he or she will also have input into the design. You may have strong ideas yourself, but architects have a skilled artistic vision of a building, and know what is possible as regards materials/windows/shape and what is most likely to gain planning permission. Consider the following:

- How the extension will work with the rest of the house – in terms of design, roof line and materials.
- Access to the new space, especially from the first floor.
- Drains and waste, especially if you're including a bathroom and/or toilet, or kitchen.
- Storm-water drains.

REAL-LIFE ACCOUNT

David and Fran Williams have a detached house in the Midlands, which is made up of two late Victorian farm cottages in a rural setting. The rooms were small and there were no windows on the south side of the property in the master bedroom and lounge.

'We had very strong ideas about what we wanted to achieve by adding to our house. We wanted a bigger bedroom and lounge, with plenty of light and we wanted to make the most of the lovely views. Why did we need an architect? We had even scribbled our own drawings on the back of an envelope and then approached a builder. He advised us that plans were essential, so we caved in. The architect, whom he recommended to us, listened to our ideas but came back with drawings that had taken them to a different level. He had worked out a much more feasible construction for the roof, and incorporated a fantastic bay window which would flood the rooms with light. He also recommended that we spent our money on the windows – stone sills and wooden sliding sashes – so they would fit in with the rest of the building – and incorporated a terraced area in front of the lounge to think about laying at a later date.

'The project was far more complicated than we had ever thought. We had forgotten about details such as storm drains and soak-aways, but by working with a technician to do the drawings for building regs and a structural engineer to check the roof load on the steel joists, we were able to get our plans through the planning department and building control without a hitch.

'We saved money by running the job ourselves, and only paid the architect to check the work at the end. But it was well worth paying him for the original drawings, and we finished up with a much better job than our back-of-an-envelope effort. And we've since completed the terrace!'

Loft/Cellar Conversions

As we said before, these will add value to your property when you come to sell and will add half as much space again if you live in a two-storey property, but can be expensive to carry out. At time of writing a cellar conversion in a typical south London terrace with a cellar under the hallway will cost upwards of £82,000.

Improvements to lofts and cellars are required to comply with building regulations at the very least, and if you plan to install dormer windows in a loft, or raise the roof levels, then you'll need full planning permission. Remember the property in *The Property Chain* programme that had been 'converted' without permission, so could not legally be used as living space? Oversights like this will not impress potential buyers. You'll also need to consider access – will you lose space in the existing hall or landing for a staircase/doorway?

Both lofts and cellars are important structurally. The loft mustn't be so heavy that the house can't take the load, while a cellar involves excavation underground – so structural support is essential. The advice of a structural engineer is vital (*see page 252*). He or she can also help you with party wall considerations if you live in a semi-detached or terraced property. Special rules cover structural work to walls that stand across the boundary of land belonging to different owners, or are used by two or more owners to separate buildings. You must notify neighbours about any work you intend to carry out, and the rules allow for the agreement or objection to any work within certain time limits, and compensation and temporary protection for buildings and property. The surveyor will prepare an 'award', a document that:

- sets out the work to be carried out;
- says how and when the work is to be carried out (i.e. not at weekends);
- records the condition of next door before the work begins so that any damage can be repaired and made good (this is called a 'schedule of condition');
- allows access for the surveyors to inspect the works while they're going on.

TIP *Budgeting is essential here: though you're not adding to the footprint size of your property, both cellar and loft conversions can be structurally complicated and you'll need to factor in the cost of professional advice from engineers and fees for local authority planning and building control applications.*

It's a good idea to keep a copy of the award with your title deeds in case there are questions when you come to sell.

Cellars done well will need good lighting, and natural light where possible – lightwells need planning permission. But the biggest consideration is damp. Cellars were originally designed to be functional – usually to house coal – and little consideration was given to making them waterproof. To become a habitable living space the cellar will need to be 'tanked', which involves the installation of a completely sealed lining system. You should ensure this carries a manufacturer-backed guarantee as well as the installer's guarantee.

Conservatories

These are a bit like kitchens – they come is all shapes and sizes, and budgets. Some are uPVC, others timber framed. Some can be bought as DIY kits, others are bespoke, designed to fit exactly your style of house and the space available. It isn't rocket science to work out which are more expensive, but whichever route you take, there's more to adding a conservatory than simply sticking it on to the side of the house. Like a proper extension, a conservatory needs foundations, and there will need to be a site survey to ascertain the quality of the ground. It will need to be an all-year-round living space, with good ventilation, shading, insulation and heating, and it will need to be in keeping with the style of your house.

In some cases conservatories require planning permission (if you live in a Conservation Area, a National Park, an Area of Outstanding Natural Beauty, the Norfolk Broads, the Suffolk Broads, or if your property is a listed building, you'll need to apply for planning permission for a conservatory). This will depend on several factors, including:

- the size of the intended conservatory;
- by how much it will increase the 'volume' of your house;

- whether your 'permitted development rights' have been reduced or removed under an Article 4 direction (*see page 260*);
- whether the roof line will be higher than the existing house;
- how close it is to a highway or to the boundary of your property.

You can get informal advice by contacting your local authority planning office or go to www.lga.gov.uk. But whether or not you need planning permission, all conservatories need to comply with parts, or in some cases all, of building regulations.

Whether it requires part or full building regulations approval will be determined by the Department of the Environment definition for conservatories:

1   The conservatory will be used solely for domestic purposes.
2   The conservatory is to be built at ground floor level.
3   The conservatory will not contain any sleeping accommodation.
4   A minimum of 75 per cent of the conservatory roof will be glazed with translucent or transparent materials.
5   The floor area of the conservatory will be less than 30 sq m (internal measurement).
6   The construction of the conservatory will not affect the existing drainage system.
7   The conservatory will not be 'permanently heated' (this can be achieved by thermostatic radiator valves).
8   The conservatory must be separated from the existing property by a wall, door or glazed screen.
9   No part of the conservatory shall be within 1 metre of the boundary of the property.

If your proposed conservatory meets with all of the above, it will only need to comply with Building Regulation N1, Glazing Safety in Relation to Impact. In all other instances conservatories are deemed to be extensions and will require Full Building Regulations Approval.

Most specialist conservatory companies offer a full service, including:

- handling planning permission and listed building consent;
- technical surveys;
- full damp-proofing and floor insulation;
- a choice of glass;
- full heating and ventilation;
- electrical installation;
- blinds and ceiling fans;
- flooring;
- security.

The DIY route will undoubtedly be cheaper, but it will be up to you to ensure that all the essential build details have been taken care of. If you add a conservatory without planning permission when you should have had permission, there's a danger you'll have to remove the conservatory.

Outbuildings

Again, whether or not these need planning permission will depend on the size and location of the outbuildings you're converting or building (*see below*), but buildings not intended for human habitation don't need to observe building regulations. However, even workshops and garages need to be constructed properly, on a solid base with damp-control considerations, and need to be in keeping with the surroundings and existing buildings, even if this is from an aesthetic point of view. There are three approaches:

1 A new-build construction from plans drawn up by an architect or designer.
2 A timber-framed building, which will be designed to your specification within certain design perimeters, constructed off-site and pieced together on site.
3 A prefabricated timber construction, brought to and erected on site.

Planning and Restrictions

Getting planning permission is usually a two-stage process: full planning permission and a full plans approval (or building regulations approval). You can start work without the latter, but you would be unwise to start work without the former. Some work does not need planning permission (*see below*), but most work needs building regulations approval or the equivalent – especially if it involves structural alternations. It's always worth asking the opinion of your local planning office – they're usually very helpful – but broadly speaking, you'll need planning permission if:

- you want to make additions or extensions to a house, flat or maisonette (including those converted from houses);
- you want to add dormer windows;
- you want to divide off part of your house for use as a separate home (e.g. a self-contained flat or bedsit), or use a caravan in your garden as a home for someone else;
- you want to build a separate house in your garden;
- you want to divide off part of your home for business or commercial use (e.g. a workshop), or you want to build a parking place for a commercial vehicle at your home;
- you want to build something that goes against the terms of the original planning permission for your house: for example your house may have been built with a restriction to stop people putting up fences in front gardens because it's on an 'open plan' estate (your council has a record of all planning permissions in its area);
- the work you want to do might obstruct the view of road users;
- the work would involve a new or wider access to a trunk or classified road.

You don't always need planning permission:

- to add 15 per cent to the size of less than 70 sq. m. with certain conditions (ask your local planning office);

- to carry out internal alterations or work that does not affect the external appearance of the building;
- to let one or two of your rooms to lodgers;
- to add windows flush with the house (such as roof skylights);
- for small alterations to the outside, such as the installation of telephone connections and alarm boxes;
- other small changes: for example putting up walls and fences below a certain height. These have a 'general planning permission' for which a specific application is not required (*see below*). Planning permission is not generally needed before erecting a fence or wall, provided it's no more than 1 metre in height if next to a highway, or 2 metres elsewhere. If you wish to exceed these limits, you'll need to get planning permission from the local authority. There are no planning restrictions on the height of hedges.

Development Rights

If you live in a house, you can make certain types of minor changes to your home without needing to apply for planning permission. These are called 'permitted development rights' and come from a general planning permission granted not by the local authority but by Parliament.

In some areas, permitted development rights are more restricted, and you'll need consents. If you live in a Conservation Area, a National Park, an Area of Outstanding Natural Beauty or the Norfolk or Suffolk Broads, you'll need to apply for planning permission for certain types of work that do not need an application in other areas. There are also different requirements if your house is a listed building, in which case you'll need listed building consent (*see page 222*).

You should also note that the council may have removed some of your permitted development rights by issuing an Article 4 direction. This will mean that you have to submit a planning application for work that normally doesn't need one. Article 4 directions are made when the character of an area of 'acknowledged importance' would

TIP *In certain circumstances, you can apply for Agricultural Notification (a cheaper and quicker process than full planning permission) for an annexe being constructed in your garden.*

be threatened – most common in Conservation Areas. You'll probably know from your original searches at time of purchase if your property is affected by such a direction, but you can check with the council if you're unsure.

Covenants and Private Rights

Because of restrictive clauses (covenants) in the title to your property or conditions in the lease, you may need to get someone else's agreement – a neighbour's or the freeholder's perhaps – before carrying out some kinds of work to your property, even if you don't need to apply for planning permission. You can check this yourself or consult the lawyer who dealt with the conveyancing of your property when you bought it. Some properties also enjoy historic rights. The council will not be involved in checking or enforcing your private rights such as a 'right to light'. This is a sticky problem and you should take legal advice.

Building Regulations

This a statutory requirement that must be satisfied in order for construction to be carried out, and to ensure that adequate standards of building work are met so the building is safe and healthy. Building regulation drawings will include details of the materials being used, timber sizes, size of wall cavity and insulation, roof structure, depth of foundations, ventilation, steel joists where necessary and so on. Applications can be submitted with your planning application, or once you've gained planning go-ahead. You can get technical guidance on meeting the requirements by going to www.odpm.gov.uk or buy a copy from HM Stationary Office on 0870 600 5522. (*See Chapter 6 for the building regulations process.*)

Building Notice

For certain smaller projects you can apply for a building notice, especially if you trust your builder to do a good job. No detailed drawings are necessary – you simply complete a form – and the building control surveyor will visit the site and talk through the work with you and the builder, so he is confident that the work is being done properly. On completion a certificate will

TIP *The Council for the Preservation of Rural England (CPRE) runs seminars on how to make representations at a planning enquiry, how to object to a planning application and how to influence local development plans. Call the CPRE on 020 7976 6433.*

be issued. This is a cheaper option, but is not advisable on a bigger, more complicated job. The inspector will have to visit the site more often and may well hold up a job if he or she is unhappy about certain stages.

Making a Planning Application

You apply to your council for planning permission. Planning applications are decided in line with the development plan unless there are good reasons not to do so. Points that will be looked at include the following:

- numbers, size, layout, siting and external appearance of the building;
- proposed means of access, landscaping and impact on the neighbourhood;
- availability of infrastructure, such as roads and water supply;
- proposed use of the development.

You can apply yourself, but it may be better to get the help of a professional, such as an architect, a solicitor or a builder, who will know the process well, and will ensure it's done properly for you.

Anyone can make an application, irrespective of who owns the land or buildings concerned. However, if you're not the owner or if you have only part-ownership, you have to inform the owner or those who share ownership, including any leaseholder whose lease still has seven or more years to run, and any agricultural tenant. This is the process:

- The planning officer will make an assessment of your application before putting his recommendation to the planning committee of councillors who will make their decision.
- The local authority are obliged to tell you how long they'll need before making a decision – usually around eight weeks – but it can request an extension. It has an obligation to inform neighbours and

TAKE CARE!

If you build something that needs planning permission without obtaining permission first, you may be forced to put things right later, which could prove troublesome and costly. You might even have to remove an unauthorized building. This action is known as 'enforcement'.

For full information on the planning process in England and Wales go to www.planningportal.gov.uk or www.odpm.gov.uk.

For Scotland go to www.scotland.gov.uk/planning. For Northern Ireland go to www.doeni.gov.uk/planning.

place a planning application notice on site. Don't make a fuss – confrontation will only work against you.

- You'll get notification of approval – or otherwise – within two days of the decision being made. Keep in touch with the planning office during the approval process. They may be able to give you an idea of the likely outcome.

Application Been Refused?

If you've kept in touch with the planning office, they may well have advised you already that a refusal is likely. You can either ask to defer your application for 'reconsideration of the plans' before a decision is made (that way a refusal does not go 'on the record') or withdraw your application and make a new one. If you're refused officially, you have 12 months in which to alter your plans, and you can then resubmit plans at no extra charge. You can also appeal via the Secretary of State for England and the National Assembly in Wales. All appeals are administered centrally by the Planning Inspectorate, and a planning inspector will visit the property and reassess the application. This process is laborious, and can take up to nine months. If you're refused again, it will almost certainly put an end to your scheme. Ask your local authority for a guide to the appeals process.

TIP *Planning permission has to be executed within five years of permission being granted, or you'll have to renew it.*

Dealing with Objections

Possibly the most important link in the home improvement chain is the neighbours. If your houses are close together, any work you carry out on your property will affect them, even if it's the noise and disruption as the work progresses. In Britain we have a love–hate relationship with our neighbours, and while trauma and warfare go on elsewhere in the world, it's nothing compared to the uproar that can ensue if a neighbour feels his lifestyle and his property is under threat.

The law has to strike a balance between one person's right to develop his land, and another's right to enjoy his property without disturbance. But if your work is highly disruptive to your neighbour's lifestyle, if the builders are inconsiderate or work outside 'reasonable' hours, then your neighbour may be able to make a claim of nuisance and pursue it through the courts. Neighbourly disputes can get very nasty, and who wants to fall out with the people who live just over the fence?

As soon as you decide to carry out any home improvements ensure you're absolutely certain about your boundaries and rights. Then let your neighbours know of your plans, either in person or by letter. They'll be informed by the planning office, anyway, if you've applied for planning permission, so it's best to keep them sweet and on your side right from the start, because if they object strongly and have a good case, there's a good chance your permission will be refused. Even if the work does not involve planning permission, there will be noise, mess and disruption, so warn them, and offer the goodwill that the work will be carried out as swiftly as possible with the minimum upheaval. Make sure your contractors know where to park and/or leave skips, and ask them to be sensitive to those who live close by.

TIP *Never underestimate the influence of the parish council. They'll be informed too of your planning application, and can be influential in the decision as to whether it's approved or not. It might be wise to inform them in advance and in writing of your intentions, so you're aware of any objections before they become an issue when you come to submit your plans.*

Working with Builders and Contractors

Unless you're planning to do the work yourself, you'll need a builder. Most people spend longer choosing their holiday than they do their builder, yet they're likely to be trusting thousands of pounds' worth of work to him. Builders have had a bad press for years – everyone has a cautionary tale – but for every bad one there are plenty of professional builders who take a great deal of care over their work. Everyone can see the quality of the finished product, so it's worth their while to do it well. Most building work takes a long time – there will inevitably be hitches – so it's worth ensuring you like the builder, and feel you can work well with him. Here are tips to getting it right:

- *Find a good builder by word of mouth.* Talk to friends about builders they've used, and ask the opinion of your architect. He or she will have worked with many builders and will know the good from the bad. Once you have some names, ask the builders if you can contact people they've worked for, for verbal 'references' – or better still, go and see the work. A confident builder will have no problem letting you do this.

- *Put the contract out to tender.* This means asking at least three builders to give you a written quotation for the work. Make sure you give each builder copies of the plans, a site visit and the same written brief about the project. There's an important difference between a *quote* and an *estimate.* A quote is a definite price, which he cannot change without informing you in writing first before proceeding with the additional work. An estimate is a 'ballpark figure', which he's not obliged to adhere to.

- *If you can't find a recommendation, use a respected trade body.* The National Federation of Builders (NFB) and the Federation of Master Builders (FMB) (*see page 274*) both have a directory of members, searched by area, but not all good builders are members of a federation.

- *Use your eyes too as you drive around the area.* Builders usually have boards on site. Take a look at the names and the work they're doing.

You can always put a note through the letter box of the house at which they're working, asking if the houseowner would recommend them.

- *Decide whether you want to use a large contractor, who may well employ all the people working on site himself, or a smaller builder, who will use subcontractors for groundwork/brickwork/plastering.* The latter may be cheaper (he doesn't have high employment costs) and is responsible for the quality of the work his subcontractors do, but is more at their mercy in terms of scheduling the work.

- *You may choose to employ your own plumbers, electricians or kitchen fitters.* Let your builder know from the start that this is your intention, though it may be easier to have one builder coordinate the whole job, as he will need to work alongside the other trades.

- *Don't immediately go for the cheapest quote.* Check the quote thoroughly to ensure it includes all the details; then it's a question of your preference and how comfortable you feel with the builder.

- *Once you've offered the work and the builder has agreed to do it, get it in writing.* It's worth drawing up a contract, though precious few people do it. This does not have to be done through a solicitor (the NFB and FMB have a contract you can buy for a small sum). Simply put in writing what work is to be done, the terms of payment, security and safety, catering arrangements (i.e. who's making the coffee), disposal of waste materials, hours of working and the start and completion dates. You can even specify whether they have access to your toilet. Agree that any changes to the contract must be made in writing. You should also ask to see a copy of the builder's public liability insurance. All this will help lessen the likelihood of disagreements later.

- *Depending on the size of the job, most builders will ask for part-payment at various stages of the work.* They need this to pay for materials and subcontractors, and you need to ensure the finance is in place (*see page 267*). If your builder makes a demand for cash, or payment up front, find another builder. Your final payment should not be handed over until you and your architect are happy with the work.

Be suspicious too if he isn't registered for VAT or offers you a VAT-free deal. This means one of two things. Either the builder does not do enough business per year to meet the VAT threshold, or he is avoiding his tax liabilities. You need to ask yourself, 'Is this builder large enough to be able to complete my work? Will he be around if any of the work requires repair? How can I have a valid contract if there's no proof of payment?'

- *Remember: it's up to you, not the builder, to ensure you have planning permission where necessary, and have submitted building regulations drawings.* Most builders will know the building control surveyors at your local authority, and will inform them as each stage of the building work is completed, so they can make an inspection.

- *Keep communicating and be interested.* It's better to ask what is going on if you're not sure what they're doing, than to arrive too late when something has been done wrong. Building work can be held up for all sorts of reasons, not least the weather, but if you have a good relationship and talk to your builder, you won't be left fuming if he doesn't appear on site when you expected him to be there.

- *Be prepared for mess, dust and noise.* It's impossible to build neatly and quietly, and you cannot reasonably expect builders to manage it, though you can ask that the site be left tidy and safe, especially over the weekend when they're not working.

- *Don't expect them to read your mind.* If you have a particular vision of a finished project (especially on a job that didn't need detailed planning drawings), then show them a picture from a magazine or brochure so they know what you're talking about.

- *If something happens to your financial situation and your ability to pay, let your builder know as soon as possible.* He'll have to pay for materials as he goes along, and will need to know if cuts have to be made.

- *Always talk to the 'man in charge'.* If you want changes made halfway through, don't discuss it with the subcontractors. That will confuse everyone.

- *Try not to change your mind.* Be decisive from the start, so everyone knows what is going on. It will also save you unbudgeted costs and won't delay the project.

- *However, be flexible too.* Even on jobs that involve detailed drawings, you may come across unforeseen problems that demand a compromise – positioning of pipework or vents, for example. These might not be the builder's fault and you'll need to be sympathetic to issues like that.

- *Make sure any materials, fixtures and fittings you're supplying are delivered on time.* If your builder is ready to fit the kitchen/bathroom/tiles and they're still in the warehouse, you'll end up with a bigger bill for wasted time. Check when you order such items what the maximum delivery time will be.

- *It's a good idea to retain a small sum for about four weeks until you're happy with the quality.* The final stage when you (and your architect) check over the work is called 'snagging'. The amount you retain will depend on the size of the contract, but on large jobs it's normal to have a defect liability where you can hold back 10 per cent for six months. You must specify your intention to do this in the contract or in your written acceptance of the job.

- *Book early and be patient.* Good builders have work scheduled months in advance, but quality work is worth waiting for.

Value Added Tax and Building Work

Work involved in creating a 'new dwelling' through the *conversion* of an existing building is largely free of VAT. VAT-registered builders have to charge the reduced rate of 5 per cent on the supply of labour and materials, which you can later reclaim through your local Customs and Excise Office when you complete the project. Ask for VAT Notice 719 for more information. This also applies to properties that have been abandoned for 10 years or more.

Renovation work: this is not considered to be creating a new dwelling and is fully rated for VAT, unless the property has been empty for three years or more, or if you're changing the number of units, in which case it's rated at 5 per cent.

REAL-LIFE ACCOUNT

Ten years ago, Linda and Simon George bought a Cheshire farmhouse with about 10 acres of land. Though still lived in by the farmer and his wife, it only had an outside loo, and the couple lived in one room, cooking over an open fire. Linda and Simon invested in a mobile home so they could live on site and began a massive renovation project. Last year, and now with three children, they completed a second improvement phase, including an extension, which affected almost every room in the house. There's not much they don't know about working with builders.

'Our architect put us in touch with the builder this time round, so we knew it was a reliable recommendation. He was quick, efficient and nice to have around. But it's a rare builder who's good in all respects and, as we weren't prepared to manage the project ourselves, we appointed him because this was his strength. The downside was that he was somewhat blinkered by building regulations and would take the path of least resistance, rather than suggest ideas which, though still within regs, would have been more imaginative or suitable in our circumstances.

'He knew from the start that we were going to be living in the house throughout the work, and we worked out a plan with him that would keep disruption to the minimum. He had the extension work almost complete, and we arranged it that we would be away for a week on holiday when they knocked through to the main house. But that is the only time to go away. From our previous experience during the first phase, we knew that it pays to be around when there are decisions to be made and to keep on top of the job all the time. Some days there might be 15 men on site – electricians, plumbers and plasterers. They can get through a lot of work in one day, but it's a lot to undo if they do it wrong.

'And boy are there decisions! Sometimes there are 15 or 20 a day – how high should this step be? Where do you want the plug points? This can be a real trap. You become bogged down in details when really you should keep your eye on the bigger picture. So it pays to plan ahead – envisage each room as it will look when it's finished, where the lamps/the TV/the dining table will go, so when you're asked questions, you'll have the answers ready.

'But we've still made mistakes. In future we would check out for ourselves which subcontractors the builder uses. We found out too late that the electricians our builder appointed are notoriously bad and we had to pay to have their mistakes put right. And doormats! We forgot to check that a doormat would fit under the back door when you opened it, and we should have had a small well for the mat set into the floor. It's all about thinking ahead!'

Listed buildings: work on 'approved alterations' to listed buildings can be zero-rated by VAT-registered contractors, provided you've been granted listed building consent, and the work is neither repair or maintenance. See VAT notice 708. (The Customs and Excise web site is at www.hmce.gov.uk.)

Insurance and Reducing your Liability

Contractors will – or should – have their own public liability and employers liability insurance. But don't rely on this, as it will not cover all your needs, especially if you're using more than one contractor. For larger jobs, such as renovation or extensions, it would be worth having site insurance in place, which will cover you against injury to trespassers, injury or death to others resulting from construction, theft of plant or materials and damage to the property. Speak to your insurance broker or your existing insurer.

> TIP *The building work may affect your home and contents insurance – contact your insurance company to tell them there's building work going on.*

It's a good idea to protect yourself against defects appearing after the work has been completed. If you've borrowed money from a lender to carry out home improvements, they may well insist that Structural Defects Insurance (SDI) is in place. For renovations, SDI is available through a small number of specialist insurers. Speak to your broker. The Federation of Masterbuilders also has a Masterbond Warranty for home improvements, including loft conversions, extensions and structural work/alterations. Go to www.fmb.org.uk/consumers/nrwb/masterbond.asp (*or see page 275*).

Do-it-yourself

So long as you've observed planning regulations and building regulations where applicable, there's nothing to stop you doing the improvement work yourself. It would certainly save you money, and there are several courses and seminars for DIYers (see the excellent web site www.homebuilding.co.uk or the monthly magazine *Homebuilding and Renovating*). However, building work, carpentry, plumbing and electrical work is complicated and takes skill and experience. Any incompetence on your part will be obvious to a surveyor who looks at the property when you come to sell. Although you may be able to tackle simple jobs yourself, the bigger jobs are best left to the professionals.

The Garden

This might not seem an obvious part of home improvement, but a well-landscaped garden can be the icing on the cake of a good-looking house. Estate agents will tell you that an attractive garden makes a house much more saleable. There are two types of landscaping:

- Hard landscaping: this is the framework of the garden and the exterior of your house around which the garden works, and involves the construction element: driveways, pathways, terracing and steps, walls, brick-built archways and gazebos, decking, ponds, and lighting.

  But hard landscaping is not easy. Often you're dealing with large areas, and unless you have a good eye, it can be hard to imagine what the finished effect will be. There are also a host of different materials to choose from and it's not always easy to work out which materials will blend in with the period of your house. Decisions, decisions. Either enlist the help of a landscape designer (*see page 273*) or look for ideas in the hard landscaping of gardens you admire. Some builders' merchants and bigger garden centres have show areas where terracing, edging and walls are laid out to show you the effect.

  Prices vary wildly for materials, but as with any home improvements, buying the cheapest can be a false economy. Hard landscaping in a garden will have to put up with frost, rain, snow, strong sunshine and a lot of wear and tear (especially if you have children), so it needs to be as tough as the fabric of your house.

- Landscaping: this is the organic element of garden design – the flower beds, shrubs, trees and hedges. Hard landscaping and the plants should work together, and any good landscape designer will consider the two. You'll need to think about:

- *Existing planting:* You may want to keep maturer plants and trees within your scheme (they'll help with shape and structure), and in some cases you may have to. Some trees are protected by a Tree Preservation Order. This is a statement by the local council that the tree is intended to remain unless there's a justifiable reason for its removal. You may also live in a Conservation Area (*see page 226*). However the searches your solicitor made when you were buying the property should have unearthed details like this. Anyone can apply to the council for consent to fell protected trees. But, if they're healthy specimens which contribute to the character of the area, it's unlikely consent will be granted. Each application is considered on its merits. You can also apply for consent to prune a tree. One of the council's tree officers will make an assessment of the effect of the proposals on the health and appearance of the tree. Certain procedures are considered unacceptable – topping is one of them.

- *The purpose of the garden:* are you a mad keen gardener and want lots of borders and a vegetable garden? Are there children who need a large lawn area to play? Do you plan to eat out when the weather is good? These factors will dictate what space you allot to what type of landscaping.

- *Privacy:* Is your garden overlooked? You might want to plan hedges and tree planting to provide some protection from neighbours' gardens. But there are laws regarding boundaries and trees, so proceed with caution. Check with your local Citizens' Advice Bureau or go to www.gardenlaw.co.uk.

- *The way your garden faces:* The type of plants you choose, and where you place seating areas will entirely depend on whether the garden faces north, south, east or west.

TIP *Remember when planning your garden to incorporate an area for a greenhouse, compost heap, garden storage, tool shed or bins. These areas can be screened off with hedging and/or fencing.*

- *Your soil:* Soil can be acid, neutral or alkaline, sandy, loamy or heavy clay (and everything in between). As any experienced gardener will tell you, you'll have to work with your soil type, or incorporate raised beds into your hard landscaping scheme which can be filled with imported acid/alkaline soil for plants intolerant to your garden conditions.

The expertise and plant knowledge of landscapers and designers can help enormously in creating a fabulous garden scheme. As with an architect, it's best to find a landscape designer by recommendation. You can also take up references if you're not familiar with their work. Go and see schemes they've designed, and note especially how the schemes have matured. You can also search for a garden designer through the Society of Garden Designers at www.sgd.org.uk and www.gardendesign-uk.com. The job can be done several ways:

- *Full service:* this involves a designer creating a complete scheme for you, incorporating plants and hard landscaping in their plans and then supplying a levels and soil survey. Designers will then see through the whole job (either using their own staff or subcontracting).
- *Design only:* the landscape designer will listen to your requirements; then come up with a drawing involving hard landscaping and planting schemes. You pay for these, but then employ a surveyor and the hard landscaping company yourself, who will work to the designer's drawings.
- *Landscaping only:* you employ a contractor to do the work to your design. You can then employ a landscape designer for planting suggestions and/or do the planting yourself. Alternatively, take the advice of a plantsman or garden centre who can recommend what will flourish in your soil.

For garden advice go to www.gardenadvice.co.uk.

TIP *Thanks in no small way to garden makeover shows on TV there has been a trend recently for very contemporary, quick-fix garden design. But avoid being too fashion-conscious in your garden design plans, and think long term. Garden design is expensive and needs to be done so it lasts and matures well. This year's decking may well look grotty and dated five years down the line when you try to sell the property.*

USEFUL CONTACTS

Architectural Heritage Fund
Clareville House
26–27 Oxendon Street
London SW1Y 4EL
Tel.: 020 7925 0199
Web: www.ahfund.org.uk

Architectural Heritage Society of Scotland
The Glasite Meeting House
33 Barony Street
Edinburgh EH3 6NX
Tel.: 0131 557 0019
Web: www.ahss.org.uk

Building regulation information
Office of the Deputy Prime Minister
Web:www.odpm.gov.uk/stellent/groups/
odpm_buildreg/documents/
sectionhomepage/odpm_buildreg_page.hcsp

Building Conservation.com (very good
online directory of conservation companies,
associations and advisors)
Web: www.buildingconservation.com

Builders' Merchants Federation
Tel.: 020 7439 1753
www.bmf.org.uk

CADW (information on planning for listed
buildings in Wales)
Web: www.cadw.wales.gov.uk/historic/index

Directory of Garden Designers
Web: www.gardendesigner.co.uk

English Heritage
Tel.: 0870 333 1181
Web: www.english-heritage.org.uk

Federation of Master Builders
Gordon Fisher House
14–15 Great James Street
London WC1N 3DP
Tel.: 020 7242 7583
Web: www.fmb.co.uk
Web: www.findabuilder.co.uk/index.asp

Heritage Conservation Network
Web: www.heritageconservation.net

Homebuilding and Renovating (web site and monthly magazine)
Web: www.homebuilding.co.uk

The Institute of Structural Engineers
11 Upper Belgrave Street
London SW1X 8BH
Tel.: 020 7235 4535
Web: www.istructe.org.uk

National Federation of Builders
National Office
Tel.: 020 7608 5150
Web: www.builders.org.uk

National Home Improvement Council
Web: www.nhic.org.uk

Period Property UK (web site with houses for sale and renovation tips)
Web: www.periodproperty.co.uk

The Royal Horticultural Society (RHS)
Tel.: 01483 224 234
Web: www.rhs.org.uk

Royal Institute of Chartered Surveyors
2 Great George Street
Parliament Square
London SW1P 3AD
Tel.: 0870 333 1600
Web: www.rics.org.uk

Scottish Civic Trust
The Tobacco Merchants' House
42 Miller Street
Glasgow G1 1DT
Tel.: 0141 221 1466
Web: www.scottishcivictrust.org.uk

The Society of Garden Designers
Tel.: 020 7838 9311
Web: www.society-of-garden-designers.co.uk

The Society for the Protection of Ancient Buildings
37 Spital Square
London E1 6DY
Tel.: 020 7377 1644
Web: www.spab.org.uk

Ulster Architectural Heritage Society
(has a catalogue of listed buildings which are for sale)
66 Donegal Pass
Belfast BT7 1BU
Tel.: 028 9055 0213
Web: www.uahs.co.uk

MAKING MONEY FROM YOUR HOME

You've got your property and, with any luck, it will increase in value as a capital asset over the years. When you come to sell it, you'll realize the gain and be very pleased with yourself for making such a good choice all those years before. But what if jam tomorrow isn't your style? What if you want to see some profit now? There are ways of making money from your home. Some you may have thought of already, others you may not. They all require plenty of effort and organization on your part, but if you want jam today, surely that's not much to ask?

HOUSE-SWAPS

OK, so it's not exactly making money, but the amount you could save on your holiday as a result of house-swapping will be as good as money in the bank. Most house-swaps work between countries, and obviously it's going to be easier to swap your house if you live somewhere picturesque or attractive to tourists. But you'd be surprised how open-minded house-swappers can be. House-swappers want an authentic experience of life in another country, so local colour, even if it might not seem charming for you, is what they're after. Just be realistic about what you're offering and what you want. There are pros and cons for house-swapping, and for many holidaymakers it has become a way of life.

Pros

- The standards of comfort far exceed those of a self-catering holiday, because you and your co-swappers are staying in a real home, equipped for daily living rather than just a holiday let.
- You can experience a real community in the country you're visiting, rather than being stuck with a bunch of other tourists.
- You get your own home looked after – plants watered, pets fed, lawn mowed. Also, it's not being left empty and is therefore more secure.
- You can find properties to swap with all over the world, and in areas you would probably never think of visiting otherwise. Because the accommodation is so much cheaper, you can think of longer-haul, more expensive flights to countries you couldn't otherwise afford.
- The people with whom you swap will probably leave a load of local information on places to visit, restaurants, local shopping and so on. You get an insider's insight, which is usually more accurate than a tourist guide, so you save time and get straight to the best local treats.
- You may get use of the car thrown in (remember to arrange insurance, and do the same if your swap partners are allowing you to use theirs).
- Many of the swapping agencies provide information about the family offering the swap. You can find people with similar interests or professions to yours, so you'll be sure that, if you have kids, you'll find age-appropriate toys.
- Swappees will often ask friends to drop by (probably to check that you're not wrecking the place), but they'll often offer hospitality, so you (and your kids) will have a chance to make local friends.
- Lastly (and most important) it's a bargain! The expenses involved include advertising your property through an agency, communicating with potential swap partners, and then paying for flights, insurance and living expenses. You could literally save thousands on a normal hotel or villa holiday.

Cons

- Swapping houses with strangers can be daunting.
- You may feel compelled to do a lot of cleaning – even decorating – before you swap.
- It's unlikely you'll ever meet your co-swappees, as they'll be travelling to your house as you're travelling to theirs. Ask the agency for as much information about them as you can. You'll often be exchanging e-mails and phone calls while ironing out the details, and that will give you a chance to size each other up.
- There's quite a lot of preparation to do – searching through potential swap partners and finding someone who matches your requirements and dates. Then there's the little matter of whether they want to swap with you! Your e-mail, fax and/or phone will be busy as you exchange details.
- It can be disappointing if arrangements fall through after you've invested so much time in them. And there's no refund, of course (although some agencies offer an insurance policy).
- If the country you're interested in has different school holidays to yours, finding a match can be difficult.
- It's just possible that you'll swap with a nightmare, who'll trash your house and crash your car. According to the agencies, this occurs almost never because the swappees know you're staying in their house too. It's wise to get a friend to drop round to (unobtrusively) check up on your house and make sure your swapping partners are happy and settled.

If you're tempted, browse any one of the many sites dedicated to bringing home-swappers together. You'll be amazed at what is available. They include:

Homelink International www.homelink.org.uk
Intervac www.intervac.com

The International Home Exchange Network

www.homexchange.com

www.digsville.com (mostly US)

Trading Homes site www.trading-homes.com

Echangedemaison site

www.echangedemaison.com (mostly French)

Latitudes Home Exchange

www.home-swap.com (mostly Australian)

Web Home Exchange www.webhomeexchange.com

Worldxchange www.worldxchange.net

Homebase Holidays www.homebase-hols.com

Home-swap Heaven

Here are some tips for making sure your home-swap runs smoothly:

- Be honest and accurate when describing your home. It's in everyone's interests to tell the truth.
- Don't book travel arrangements until you have absolute confirmation of dates with the household you're swapping with.
- Tell your insurer you're leaving your home in the care of others. It won't necessarily affect your premium, but it might have a bearing if you have to claim for something that happened in your absence. If you're swapping cars, there will be an extra premium to pay to add your house-swappers' names to your policy.
- Tell your neighbours that you're lending your home to other people, so as not to arouse suspicion if they see strangers letting themselves in through your front door.
- Give your home a thorough clean before you leave. Make sure you clear plenty of drawer and cupboard space so your guests can put away their own clothes, toiletries and groceries. Make up the beds, and leave clean towels.

- Lock away any valuables and important documents. If guests are going to be using your computer, back everything up before you leave and lock away important disks.

- Sort out who is paying what in terms of bills, particularly the telephone, and store-cupboard essentials. If the swap has been arranged through agents, they'll probably address these on their agreement form.

- Compile a guide to your home, complete with local information, instructions for appliances, useful phone numbers and emergency contacts.

- Give a spare set of keys to a neighbour or friend or relative who lives locally, and give your home-swappers their details in case they lock themselves out.

- Leave some wine and some basics like bread and milk in case it's too late when your guests arrive for a trip to the shops.

- Treat your temporary home as you hope your visitors are treating yours. Leave the house as you found it. And if the owners are due back imminently, leave them some groceries and a few bottles of wine.

STARS IN YOUR EYES

Having your house used as a film or TV location, or in a commercial, can be an exciting way of making extra income. Don't imagine you have to live in a manor house or a castle. Location finders need all kinds of properties and yours might just fit the bill. Of course, there are stories of property owners being approached by location finders, just like there are stories of girls who go on to be supermodels being approached by agents in airport departure lounges – but these are in the minority. The best way to set your property on the road to stardom is to register with a production company or a location finding agency ('scouts'). There are also niche property location databases that cover homes with unusual locations or stories, such as up mountains, or haunted properties.

TIP *Remember too that you may well have to move out during filming. This could be expensive if the shoot is a long one, and could be very disruptive to the family.*

The vast majority of finders will register you for free and then negotiate a share of the use fee. A few finders want up-front registration fees (typically about £200 plus VAT) but offer no advantage over their free rivals – so don't rush to pay them. Good location finders will want to find out as much as they can about the viability of your property and will send you questionnaires to complete about the period and size, parking, transport links and nearby rental accommodation. But don't imagine you're guaranteed an income. Competition is tough. Many councils in large cities now have 'location officers' dealing with public buildings and lists of private houses and they may get the first approach.

If your house has star quality and meets all the stringent requirements of the production company, daily fees will vary from about £400 to £10,000. But it's not all glamour. Film crews routinely number a hundred or more, and they may want to change decoration and even structures – so prepare yourself for huge disruption.

Before you agree to allow your home to be used, there are points you must clarify, including:

- the fee and when it will be paid;
- security for technical equipment;
- the total duration and hours of filming;
- penalty clauses for any overruns;
- whether stunts will be staged;
- legal liability, indemnity and insurance;
- exact use of the planned film or TV show;
- returning property to its original condition.

These firms search out locations:

www.highexposure.co.uk or call 01663 750160
www.medialocations.co.uk or call 020 8455 4949

www.oic.co.uk / www.location.tv or call 020 7419 1949

www.saltfilm.com or call 020 7637 7885

WHAT YOU CAN EXPECT

Annabel François, library manager at OIC Locations (*see above*), says:

'Commercials and TV are the most consistent work. We look for all sorts of properties – quite ordinary ones are just as popular as huge ones – but we use a lot of suburban houses. The essential thing is good-sized rooms to accommodate the crew. It's also important that parking and access are easy. If you live near an airport or have frequent train noise, then it won't work.

'Eighty per cent of filming takes place in and around London, because that is where the crews are based, but we need rural locations as well. We list your property on our web site if we think it's suitable, and production companies consult it and make their selection. You can expect to be paid from £1,000 per day up to as much as £5,000 a day for a really exceptional property. Often the production company will need to come in and dress the property before filming and will pay half the day rate for time spent doing that – and undoing it afterwards.

'There will be a single location manager who is your point of contact throughout the process, and you can take up any problems with them. For example if you don't want anyone to smoke in your house, or if you have light coloured carpets that need to be covered up, they'll see to it. They also sort out any problems afterwards if anything is damaged. All production companies have public liability indemnity. We take 10 per cent of your fee if the property is used.'

LODGERS

Taking in a lodger, for many people, is the stuff of music-hall jokes and sit-coms, but for those with a room to rent it's a fantastic way to make up to £4,250 a year (2003/4 figures) without having to worry about paying tax on it.

Far more people could take in a lodger than actually do. There's no doubt there are drawbacks in having someone share your house with you, and you'll want to be cautious about the kind of person you take on. It makes

CHOOSE YOUR LODGER WITH CARE

Some of the best lodgers, from your point of view, are people who need short-term accommodation while working temporarily on business in your town, but who actually live elsewhere. Rather than going to the expense of using a hotel, they would be only too pleased to stay with a conveniently placed family or household during the week. The big plus with these kinds of lodgers is that they go home at weekends.

sense to check out people's references and credit records before you let a room to them, and find out as much as you can about their lifestyle to make sure it's compatible with the way you run your home.

Under the Government's Rent-a-Room Scheme you can let out a room in your home for up to £4,250 a year tax-free, which works out at a smidgen over £80 a week in your pocket, although it also includes a share of the utility bills for the household.

If you're thinking of going down this route, you should contact your mortgage lender and your insurer to inform them of the situation. And get your lodger to sign a tenancy agreement that will enable you to let on a month-to-month basis, with both parties being able to end the tenancy at fairly short notice. Asking for an up-front deposit and a month's rent in advance will also ensure that you're covered if they leave or default on rent payment, leaving you with a massive phone bill!

TIP *It's worth advertising your room to let through the newsletter of a big local employer who may have employees looking for accommodation. Theatres also have actors or backstage staff who may want somewhere temporary to live.*

Amazingly enough, you can use the Rent-a-Room Scheme when applying for a mortgage. Some mortgage lenders will allow you to add the expected rent on to your income when applying for a loan – and if you're a first-time buyer, or trying to upgrade to a bigger property, that could make a difference to your buying power. Note that the allowance of £4,250 a year is based on the property and not per person. So if you're a couple, the allowance will only be half each.

For more information on letting to tenants go to www.inlandrevenue.gov.uk/pdfs/ir87.htm (*see also Chapter 1*).

RUNNING A BED AND BREAKFAST

'Working from home' takes on a new meaning if you decide to offer bed and breakfast. If you have a large enough property with spare rooms, preferably *en suite*, don't mind hard work, are good at frying eggs and like meeting new people, it could be an ideal way of making extra money.

Life is much simpler if you restrict yourself to letting two rooms – if you exceed this, you'll have complicated fire regulations to contend with. You don't have to register with the relevant Tourist Board, although it will probably bring in more trade if you do, as they'll probably feature you in their listings and publications and your property can be star-rated (*see page 188*). The British Tourist Authority provides a start-up pack that will help with information and ideas.

There are tax implications in running a bed and breakfast (B&B) business, which you need to be aware of:

- You can run it as a Rent-a-Room Scheme (*see lodgers*): so long as you don't earn over the threshold limit in any one year.
- If, however, you make more than this threshold, you'll need to declare the income, though you can set some of the running costs and overheads against the income.
- Some B&Bers run their ventures seriously, and there's a possibility the Inland Revenue will consider that you're running a business from your home, and that it's not exclusively a private dwelling. You'll not then be entitled to the capital gains tax exemptions. It might also make you liable to pay a business rate. Tests apply, and these include how much of your home is used for the business and how often.

REAL-LIFE ACCOUNT

Jane and William Franklin live in a substantial family house in a pretty Gloucestershire village and provide B&B in their spare rooms.

'The whole venture started by accident. We didn't realize that the people who used to live here did B&B until we got a phone call asking if we still did it. Jane said yes spontaneously, and we haven't looked back! She has a web site, and advertises in an up-market B&B book. There are definitely upsides and downsides, and unless you're prepared to do it seriously, it's not worth it because B&B will not run itself and it can be demanding. You have to be prepared to be up early to do breakfast, there is cleaning to do and beds to make, and there has to be someone around late afternoon to greet guests. You lose a degree of privacy – and we wouldn't do it if the house hadn't had a fairly separate part with two bedrooms and a bathroom. There are security worries, but we don't have a sign advertising B&B and we would never let anyone in who just arrived on the doorstep.

'The great thing is that there is reasonable money to be made and, though we've had the odd unpleasant people, on the whole guests are interesting and utterly charming, and they come back again and again.'

SHORT-TERM LETS

These have their appeal, not least because the rents you can command are far higher than for conventional residential letting. If you live in a desirable area, say in the centre of a city or near a regular sporting or cultural event – Wimbledon, Ascot, Chelsea (for the flower show) or Edinburgh – you should have no trouble at all letting for as little as a week.

If you work abroad on short-term contracts, and are prepared to put up with the inconvenience of having to maintain your property in an appropriate state for tenants to come into, it's all gain. Foreign executives in the same situation as you, who prefer a home to a hotel, are ideal – not least because short lets are 30 to 40 per cent cheaper than hotel rooms. Lettings agents are your best choice for finding a tenant. The better areas of London, including the City and Canary Wharf, as far south as Clapham, across to Richmond and Chiswick and up to St John's Wood and Hampstead are all suitable locations. Outside London, Aberdeen, Manchester, Bristol and Birmingham have smaller short-let markets.

Dozens of homeowners in London SW19 go on holiday during Wimbledon fortnight and let their houses to tennis fans and players while they're away. Given the influx of people to Edinburgh during the festival, it's no wonder that performers and culture vultures alike are desperate for accommodation. If you live in a desirable holiday area, you can organize the let to fit in with your annual holiday – and miss the crowds of tourists that drive all residents mad.

Rents on short lets are higher than normal, although letting agents' fees are higher too. But short lets are also useful for people who've bought a new house before they've sold off their existing property. A six-month shorthold tenancy would mean having to take the house off the market, but a short one allows them to continue to try to sell it while making money from it. In some cases, the money from letting is used to pay a bridging loan (*see Chapter 2*).

Short lets are also a possibility for buy-to-let investors who are finding it difficult to find long-term tenants. But these lets are not without their drawbacks. If you start short lets, properties are likely to be empty for longer overall, and agents charge a lot for their services – some as much as 25 per cent, plus a further 5 per cent for full management. This compares with about 10 per cent, plus 5 per cent, for conventional lets. Also, with the best will in the world, it's not possible to do such thorough checks on a short-term tenant as you would on a long-term one – employers' references and credit card details are not a lot to go on.

Short-term letting is slightly different from other forms of letting:

- Rent for the whole tenancy is often paid at the outset.
- Contracts/agreements are not normally for longer than three months, and sometimes much shorter – after which point the tenant must move out.
- The type of agreement you would sign depends on whether you live

in the property prior to letting it or have purchased it purely as an investment (*see Chapter 1*). The former agreement would be an assured tenancy and the latter an assured shorthold tenancy. This actually makes little difference to the tenant, who in either case is still served with a Section 8 Notice, which formally brings the tenancy to a conclusion at the end of the term.

You'll need to check that you're actually allowed to let this way under the terms of your lease, if relevant, with your mortgage lender and even with the local authority. And there will be expenses and obligations on you as the landlord (*see Chapter 1*).

COUNTRY SLICKERS

This may not be a tactic that will apply for any more than a privileged minority, but new Common Agricultural Policy (CAP) rules make it profitable to buy farms and use them essentially as homes with big farmy-looking gardens. As farmers have found it harder and harder to make ends meet, wealthy non-farmers have been snapping up farms with hundreds of acres attached so they can benefit from tax breaks and subsidies – soon they won't even have to run them as profitable concerns.

Under the new, reformed CAP farmers will not receive a subsidy for producing food; instead, they'll receive a 'single farm payment' related to the acreage of their farm and quite unrelated to any crop they may or may not produce. If your farm looks like a farm, you should qualify for public money. And the more 'environmentally friendly' your farm is, the more money you can claim. Nine billion euros have been reserved for 'agri-environmental' schemes and, though payments will be withheld for breaking environmental, food safety and animal welfare standards, not producing any food is no barrier to receiving a payout of taxpayers' money.

As a dilettante farmer you might produce nothing more than a few pints of goat's milk for your friends, but that does not matter under the new CAP so long as you can convince officials you're in the 'farming business'. But even without CAP reform, farms have become used as on-shore tax havens. Under Inland Revenue rules, farmers can pass their farms to their children free from inheritance tax. In order to qualify for the tax break, you don't personally have to drive the tractors, feed the cattle or even decide when to plant the corn, but merely show that it's you who pays the bills. In future, thanks to the EU, it will be even easier.

For more information go to the Europa site at
europa.eu.int/pol/agr/index_en.htm

and the Inland Revenue site at
www.inlandrevenue.org.uk.

USEFUL CONTACTS

Association of Residential Letting Agents (ARLA)
Maple House
53–55 Woodside Road
Amersham HP6 6AA
Tel.: 0845 345 5752
Web: www.arla.co.uk

British Tourist Authority
Web: www.visitbritain.com

Inland Revenue Rent-a-Room Scheme
Web: www.inlandrevenue.gov.uk/pdfs/ir87.htm

Appendices

1

WHO'S WHO IN THE BUYING, SELLING AND OWNING OF PROPERTY

Architect: a building design expert. The word 'architect' is a protected term and only a qualified architect can use it. He or she should be a member of the Royal Institute of British Architects.

Architectural technician/technologist: a qualified architectural draughtsman who can draw up an architect's plans and prepare drawings for building regulation approval.

Building control inspector/surveyor: freelance or employed by the local authority, the surveyor who will approve building regulation drawings and visit the site to pass each stage of a building project before issuing a completion certificate.

Chartered building surveyor: a qualified surveyor and an expert in building construction, repair, maintenance and alteration who can be instructed to carry out a full structural survey on a property. They must be a member of the Royal Institution of Chartered Surveyors to call themselves chartered.

Conservation architect: an architect who specializes in the restoration, development and maintenance of old buildings.

Contractor: a person or firm who contracts to supply materials or labour, especially for building work.

Developer: a person or company who buys up plots of land for building, with the intention of selling the property on to a third party on completion.

Estate agent: an agent concerned with the valuation, management, lease and sale of property. May well be qualified as a surveyor and/or valuer.

Freeholder: the person who has possession of a freehold (tenure by which land is held in absolute ownership).

Independent financial advisor (IFA): a qualified financial expert who will source mortgages, pension plans and insurance policies, taking commission and/or fees from the product provider. Must be regulated by the Financial Services Authority.

Insurer: a company that provides financial protection for property, life, health and so on in return for a premium.

Insurance broker: a financial expert (usually an IFA – *see above*) who will research insurance policies to source the most suitable depending on the circumstances; then take a commission and/or fee from the product provider.

Home inspector: the person who will assess properties for energy efficiency and so on, should Sellers' Packs become law.

Land agent: an agent who is concerned with the valuation, management, lease and sale of land.

Land Registry: the official record of land ownership in the UK.

Landlord: the owner who lets land, property and/or rooms to tenants.

Landscape designer: an expert in the field of exterior design, hard landscaping and planting schemes. May or may not be officially qualified.

Leaseholder: the person in possession of a leasehold property, which has been conveyed to them by the freeholder (*see above*) for a specified time, usually for rent.

Letting agent: an agent who deals with the letting, rental and sometimes management of property under a tenancy agreement or for a short-term holiday let, and who takes a percentage of the rental as a fee.

Licensed conveyancer: a specialist property lawyer, trained and qualified in all aspects of the law dealing with property.

Mortgage broker: a qualified IFA who can research the marketplace for the most suitable mortgage in the circumstances, and will then take a commission and/or fee from the mortgage lender.

Mortgagee: the person who is lent money in the form of a mortgage.

Mortgage lender: the bank, building society or financial institution that lends money in the form of a mortgage in return for repayments with interest.

Notaire: a public official in France who prepares title deeds relating to the sale and purchase of land. He or she puts on the public record the fact that the deed has been signed in his or her presence and understood by the parties concerned. He or she may act on behalf of vendor and purchaser, and makes various title checks about the property.

Notary: a public official in Spain, Italy or Portugal who puts on the public record the fact that the title deed recording the sale/purchase has been signed in his or her presence and understood by the parties concerned.

Planning Committee: a committee of local councillors who consider planning applications for acceptance or rejection.

Planning Inspectorate: works for the Office of the Deputy Prime Minister (previously the DTLR) and the National Assembly for Wales and deals with planning and environmental legislation, including processing planning and enforcement appeals, inquiries into local development plans and listed building consent appeals.

Planning officer: an official employed by the local authority to develop local planning policy and to deal with submissions for planning permission from private and commercial applicants.

Solicitor: a qualified legal expert who will deal with the conveyance of land title either on behalf of the purchaser or the vendor.

Structural engineer: a professional involved in the design and supervision of a construction, and who is involved with management, risk assessment and checking the condition of a structure.

Tenant: a person who has use of land, property or a room subject to the payment of rent to a landlord.

Tenants in common: a group of people who use land or property in equal shares and contribute equally to the rent payable.

Trading standards officer: an expert in consumer affairs, usually employed by the local authority, to ensure compliance with a wide range of UK and European legislation, and a fair and safe trading environment for consumers and businesses.

Valuer: an expert who values your property and who may or may not be a qualified surveyor.

Valuation surveyor: a qualified surveyor asked by you or your lender to advise on the valuation of the property. He or she may also be a chartered building surveyor.

Vendor: a person selling a property.

2

INFORMATION FOR LANDLORDS

The following includes regulations landlords must comply with when renting out property to tenants. It's a basic outline and the information is not comprehensive. Legislation also changes all the time, so you're advised to seek professional advice.

REPAIRS

Under the Landlord and Tenant Act, 1985, landlords are obliged to keep the structure and exterior of the property in a good state of repair. You're entitled to incorporate potential cost of repairs into the rent you charge, but you may not charge the tenants separately for repair to any of the things mentioned above. You have final responsibility for ensuring that the following areas are safe and fit for use, as well as effecting repairs when necessary to restore them to a fair condition:

- The structure and exterior of the property.
- Any hot water installations, as well as the supply of water itself.
- Basins, sinks, baths and other sanitary or drainage installations.
- Ensuring an adequate provision of lighting, heating and ventilation.
- Treating of any health-threatening damp that occurs (not to be confused with condensation, a more common but less serious problem caused mostly by poor ventilation).
- In flats and maisonettes you must also repair any other areas or

installations you own or control and whose disrepair would affect the tenant.

- Anything else you mutually agree with the tenant in the tenancy agreement.

FURNITURE AND FURNISHINGS (FIRE) (SAFETY) REGULATIONS 1988 (AMENDED 1989, 1993)(CONSUMER PROTECTION ACT 1987)

These regulations set levels of fire resistance for domestic upholstered furniture, furnishings and other products containing upholstery, acting as secondary legislation under the Consumer Protection Act 1987. See www. hmso.gov.uk/si/si1988/Uksi_19881324_en_1.htm.

Landlords and letting agents are included under the scope of the regulations. The Amendment Regulations, introduced in 1993, draw specific attention to the responsibilities of letting agents and those engaged in the 'letting of accommodation'. The regulations refer to the 'supply' of furniture and furnishings a letting agent or commercial landlord is deemed to be 'supplying in the course of business' when these types of items are included within a property.

The bulk of the regulations deal with the duties of manufacturers (and importers if manufactured abroad) in producing and supplying domestic furniture and furnishings to the required new standards for fire resistance. These standards include two tests: the match test and the cigarette test. For new furniture, any products manufactured after 1 March 1989 or sold by a retailer after 1 March 1990 must be to the new standards and will be labelled accordingly.

Landlords letting residential property are expected to ensure that any soft furniture complies with the regulations. The main provisions are that:

- upholstered articles (i.e. beds, sofas, armchairs etc.) must have fire-resistant filling material;

- upholstered articles must have passed a match resistance test or, if of certain kinds (such as cotton or silk), be used with a fire-resistant interliner;
- the combination of the cover fabric and the filling material must have passed a cigarette resistance test.

The regulations apply to the following:

- beds, headboards of beds and mattresses;
- sofa beds, futons and other convertibles;
- nursery furniture;
- garden furniture suitable for use in dwellings;
- scatter cushions and seat pads;
- pillows;
- loose and stretch covers for furniture;
- extra or replacement furniture purchased for rented accommodation.

The regulations do not apply to antique furniture or any furniture made before 1950:

- bedclothes (including duvets);
- loose covers for mattresses;
- pillowcases;
- curtains;
- carpets;
- sleeping bags.

Exclusions and indemnity:

- *Private landlords.* It's the view of the Department of Trade and Industry (DTI) that a private landlord or owner in some situations (e.g. letting a single dwelling) who lets his property on a one-off short-term basis (while, e,g., he's temporarily working away from home) is not a commercial landlord and therefore not a 'supplier in the course of business'. However, an agent when acting for such an owner is subject to the Regulations, even if the landlord is not.

- *Pre-1950 furniture*. Furniture produced prior to 1950 is exempt from the regulations.

- *Due diligence*. Section 39 of the Act provides a defence of 'due diligence'. It shall be a defence to show that a person took all reasonable steps and exercised all due diligence to avoid committing the offence. Merely asking the landlord to sign a statement that there's non-compliant furniture is not considered to be sufficient in this respect. Asking for proof of the date of purchase (i.e. receipts) would be good verification. Alternatively, the agent could ask the manufacturer (or ask the landlord to do so) whether the furniture in question complies or not, and if still unclear, the landlord should be advised to get technical advice.

- *Find tenant only*. The Department of the Environment has suggested that an agent acting only in the capacity of introducing suitable tenants to a landlord (and taking no part in the preparation of an inventory or day-to-day management) is exempted from the regulations.

The maximum penalty for non-compliance is six months' imprisonment or a fine, or both.

For further information:

Your Local Trading Standards Office

HMSO Copy of 1988 Regulations: S.I. 1988 No. 1324

HMSO Copy of 1989 Amendment Regulations: S.I. 1989 No. 2358 (available from HMSO – 0870 1502 500)

Copy of 1993 Amendment Regulations: S.I. 1993 No. 207

DTI Publication: *A Guide to the Furniture and Furnishings (Fire) (Safety) Regulations 1988*

(DTI, Consumer Safety Unit, Department of Trade and Industry, 10–18 Victoria Street, London SW1H 0NN)

GAS SAFETY (INSTALLATION AND USE) REGULATIONS 1994

These regulations were introduced in order to reduce the number of deaths in rented property caused by carbon monoxide poisoning from faulty gas appliances. The gas supply and gas appliances must be maintained in a safe condition by a properly qualified Council of Registered Gas Installers (CORGI) registered engineer. An annual safety inspection must be carried out and a service record maintained.

In the absence of a current gas safety certificate, safety checks will have to be carried out before the commencement of any new let. Landlords requiring further information are referred to publications available from the DTI, Consumer Unit, Rm. 302/303, 10–18 Victoria St, London SW1E 6RB:

Safety in the Installation and use of Gas Systems and Appliances, Gas Safety (Installation and Use) Regulations 1994 – Approved Code of Practice and Guidance.
HSE Books, PO Box 1999, Sudbury, Suffolk CO10 6FS.

ELECTRICAL EQUIPMENT (SAFETY) REGULATIONS 1994

These regulations operate in much the same way as the gas safety regulations and place a legal obligation on the landlord and his agent to ensure that any portable electrical equipment supplied as part of a tenancy is safe. Regular safety checks are required and, although no time period is specified, it's recommended that these are carried out on a yearly basis at the same time as the gas check. In general, all unnecessary electrical items should be removed from the property prior to the letting.

In the absence of a current electrical safety certificate, safety checks will have to be carried out before the commencement of any new let. Landlords requiring further information are referred to publications from the DTI,

Consumer Unit, Rm. 302/303, 10–18 Victoria St, London SW1E 6RB:

> *Guide to the Low Voltage Electrical Equipment (Safety) Regulations 1989*
> Maintaining Portable and Transportable Electrical Equipment
> HSE Books, PO Box 1999, Sudbury, Suffolk, CO10 6FS.

SMOKE DETECTORS BUILDING REGULATIONS 1991

These regulations require all properties built since June 1992 to be fitted with mains-operated interlinked smoke detectors/alarms on each floor. Properties built before that date do not have such a statutory requirement. As a responsible landlord you should ensure both smoke detectors and fire extinguishers are fitted for maximum safety.

PLUGS, SOCKETS AND SO ON (SAFETY) REGULATIONS 1994

This Act states that since August 1994 all three-pin plug tops supplied to a tenant must meet British Standard 1363 and be so marked. This standard means that the live and neutral pins must have part insulation.

WATER INDUSTRY ACT

This Act came into force on 1 April 2000. As a result it's possible for a tenant who is a water customer to have a water meter fitted, regardless of the landlord's wishes. If you do not want a water meter fitted to your property, then the water utility must remain in your name. You can then insist that the tenants do not fit a water meter.

LANDLORDS WHO LIVE ABROAD

If you're a landlord and your 'usual place of abode' is outside the UK, the Non-Resident Landlord's (NRL) Scheme Act allows you to apply for a self-assessment status in order for rents to be paid over to you without tax deducted – though this does not mean the income is exempt from UK tax. In the absence of this certificate, the agent (or tenant if there's no letting agent) is required to deduct basic rate tax from the rents and pay this to the Inland Revenue on a quarterly basis. Discuss this with your tax advisor, who can also advise on what items of expenditure can be offset against rental income. More details on this can be found from the Inland Revenue Leaflet IR140 on the Inland Revenue web site www.inlandrevenue.gov.uk, or phone 0845 9000 404.

SAMPLE ASSURED SHORTHOLD TENANCY AGREEMENT

See over for all types of residential accommodation, furnished and unfurnished

The samples are © Law Pack Publishing Ltd www.lawpack.co.uk

(N.B: These forms are reproduced as samples only and the author and publishers cannot assume responsibility for their proper and correct interpretation.)

F201E

TENANCY AGREEMENT - ENGLAND & WALES
(for a Furnished House or Flat on an Assured Shorthold Tenancy)

The PROPERTY _____

_____

The LANDLORD _____

of _____

_____

The TENANT _____

_____

_____

_____

_____

The TERM _____ months beginning on _____

The RENT £ _____ per week/month* payable in advance on the _____ of each week/month*   (*delete as appropriate)

The DEPOSIT £ _____

The INVENTORY means the list of the Landlord's possessions at the Property which has been signed by the Landlord and the Tenant

DATED _____

SIGNED _____   _____

_____   _____

(The Landlord)   _____

_____

(The Tenant)

THIS TENANCY AGREEMENT comprises the particulars detailed above and the terms and conditions printed overleaf whereby the Property is hereby let by the Landlord and taken by the Tenant for the Term at the Rent.

IMPORTANT NOTICE TO LANDLORDS:
(1) The details of 'The LANDLORD' near the top of this Agreement must include an address for the Landlord in England or Wales as well as his/her name.
(2) Always remember to give the written Notice to Terminate to the Tenant two clear months before the end of the Term.

IMPORTANT NOTICE TO TENANTS:
(1) In general, if you currently occupy this Property under a protected or statutory tenancy and you give it up to take a new tenancy of the same or other accommodation owned by the same Landlord, that tenancy cannot be an Assured Shorthold Tenancy and this Agreement is not appropriate.
(2) If you currently occupy this Property under an Assured Tenancy which is not an Assured Shorthold Tenancy your Landlord is not permitted to grant you an Assured Shorthold Tenancy of this Property or of alternative property.

Terms and Conditions

1. This Agreement is intended to create an Assured Shorthold Tenancy as defined in the Housing Act 1988, as amended by the Housing Act 1996, and the provisions for the recovery of possession by the Landlord in that Act apply accordingly. The Tenant understands that the Landlord will be entitled to recover possession of the Property at the end of the Term.

2. The Tenant's obligations:

   2.1 To pay the Rent at the times and in the manner aforesaid.

   2.2 To pay all charges in respect of any electric, gas, water and telephonic or televisual services used at or supplied to the Property and Council Tax or any similar property tax that might be charged in addition to or replacement of it during the Term.

   2.3 To keep the items on the Inventory and the interior of the Property in a good and clean state and condition and not damage or injure the Property or the items on the Inventory (fair wear and tear excepted).

   2.4 To yield up the Property and the items on the Inventory at the end of the Term in the same clean state and condition it/they was/were in at the beginning of the Term (but the Tenant will not be responsible for fair wear and tear caused during normal use of the Property and the items on the Inventory or for any damage covered by and recoverable under the insurance policy effected by the Landlord under clause 3.2).

   2.5 Not make any alteration or addition to the Property nor without the Landlord's prior written consent (consent not be withheld unreasonably) do any redecoration or painting of the Property.

   2.6 Not do anything on or at the Property which:

   (a) may be or become a nuisance or annoyance to any other occupiers of the Property or owners or occupiers of adjoining or nearby premises

   (b) is illegal or immoral

   (c) may in any way affect the validity of the insurance of the Property and the items listed on the Inventory or cause an increase in the premium payable by the Landlord.

   2.7 Not without the Landlord's prior consent (consent not to be withheld unreasonably) allow or keep any pet or any kind of animal at the Property.

   2.8 Not use or occupy the Property in any way whatsoever other than as a private residence.

   2.9 Not assign, sublet, charge or part with or share possession or occupation of the Property.

   2.10 To allow the Landlord or anyone with the Landlord's written permission to enter the Property at reasonable times of the day to inspect its condition and state of repair, carry out any necessary repairs and gas inspections, or during the last month of the Term, show the Property to prospective new tenants, provided the Landlord has given 24 hours' prior written notice (except in emergency).

   2.11 To pay the Landlord's reasonable costs reasonably incurred as a result of any breaches by the tenant of his obligations under this Agreement.

   2.12 To pay interest at the rate of 4% above the Bank of England base rate from time to time prevailing on any rent or other money due from the Tenant under this Agreement which remains unpaid for more than 14 days, interest to be paid from the date the payment fell due until payment.

   2.13 To provide the Landlord with a forwarding address when the tenancy comes to an end and to remove all rubbish and all personal items (including the Tenant's own furniture and equipment) from the Property before leaving.

3. The Landlord's obligations:

   3.1 The Landlord agrees that the Tenant may live in the Property without unreasonable interruption from the Landlord or any person rightfully claiming under or in trust for the Landlord.

   3.2 To insure the Property and the items listed on the Inventory and use all reasonable efforts to arrange for any damage caused by an insured risk to be remedied as soon as possible and to provide a copy of the insurance policy to the Tenant.

   3.3 To keep in repair

   3.3.1 the structure and exterior of the Property (including drains gutters and external pipes)

   3.3.2 the installations at the Property for the supply of water, gas and electricity and for sanitation (including basins, sinks, baths and sanitary conveniences)

   3.3.3 the installations at the Property for space heating and heating water.

   3.4 But the Landlord will not be required to

   3.4.1 carry out works for which the Tenant is responsible by virtue of his duty to use the Property in a tenant-like manner

   3.4.2 reinstate the Property in the case of damage or destruction if the insurers refuse to pay out the insurance money due to anything the Tenant has done or failed to do

   3.4.3 rebuild or reinstate the Property in the case of destruction or damage of the Property by a risk not covered by the policy of insurance effected by the Landlord.

4. Ending this Agreement

   4.1 The Tenant cannot normally end this Agreement before the end of the Term. However after the first three months of the Term, if the Tenant can find a suitable alternative tenant, and provided this alternative tenant is acceptable to the Landlord (the Landlord's approval not to be unreasonably withheld) the Tenant may give notice to end the tenancy on a date at least one month from the date that such approval is given by the Landlord. On the expiry of such notice, provided that the Tenant pays to the Landlord the reasonable expenses reasonably incurred by the Landlord in granting the necessary approval and in granting any new tenancy to the alternative tenant, the tenancy shall end.

   4.2 If the Tenant stays on after the end of the fixed term, his tenancy will continue but will run from month to month (a 'periodic tenancy'). This periodic tenancy

   can be ended by the Tenant giving at least one month's written notice to the Landlord, the notice to expire at the end of a rental period.

   4.3 If at any time

   4.3.1 any part of the Rent is outstanding for 21 days after becoming due (whether formally demanded or not) and/or

   4.3.2 there is any breach, non-observance or non-performance by the Tenant of any covenant or other term of this Agreement which has been notified in writing to the Tenant and the Tenant has failed within a reasonable period of time to remedy the breach and/or pay reasonable compensation to the Landlord for the breach and/or

   4.3.3 any of the grounds set out as Grounds 2, 8 or Grounds 10-15 (inclusive) (which relate to breach of any obligation by a Tenant) contained in the Housing Act 1988 Schedule 2 apply

   the Landlord may recover possession of the Property and this Agreement shall come to an end. The Landlord retains all his other rights in respect of the Tenant's obligations under this Agreement. Note that if anyone is living at the Property or if the tenancy is an Assured or Assured Shorthold Tenancy then the landlord must obtain a court order for possession before re-entering the Property. This clause does not affect the Tenant's rights under the Protection from Eviction Act 1977.

5. The Deposit

   5.1 The Deposit will be held by the Landlord and will be refunded to the Tenant at the end of the Term (however it ends) at the forwarding address provided to the Landlord but less any reasonable deductions properly made by the Landlord to cover any reasonable costs incurred or losses caused to him by any breaches of the obligations in this Agreement by the Tenant. No interest will be payable to the Tenant in respect of the deposit money.

   5.2 The Deposit shall be repayable to the Tenant as soon as reasonably practicable, however the Landlord shall not be bound to return the Deposit until he is satisfied that no money is repayable to the Local Authority if the Tenant has been in receipt of Housing Benefit, and until after he has had a reasonable opportunity to assess the reasonable cost of any repairs required as a result of any breaches of his obligations by the Tenant or other sums properly due to the Landlord under clause 5.1 above. However, the Landlord shall not, save in exceptional circumstances, retain the deposit for more than one month after the end of the tenancy.

   5.3 If at any time during the Term the Landlord is obliged to deduct from the Deposit to satisfy the reasonable costs occasioned by any breaches of the obligations of the Tenant the Tenant shall make such additional payments as are necessary to restore the full amount of the Deposit.

6. Other provisions

   6.1 The Landlord hereby notifies the Tenant under Section 48 of the Landlord & Tenant Act 1987 that any notices (including notices in proceedings) may be served upon the Landlord at the address stated with the name of the Landlord overleaf.

   6.2 For stamp duty purposes, the Landlord and the Tenant confirm that there is no previous agreement to which this Agreement gives effect.

   6.3 The Landlord shall be entitled to have and retain keys for all the doors to the Property but shall not be entitled to use these to enter the Property without the consent of the Tenant (save in an emergency).

   6.4 Any notices or other documents shall be deemed served on the Tenant during the tenancy by either being left at the Property or by being sent to the Tenant at the Property by first-class post. If notices or other documents are served on the Tenant by post they shall be deemed served on the day after posting.

   6.5 Any person other than the Tenant who pays the rent due hereunder or any part thereof to the Landlord shall be deemed to have made such payment as agent for and on behalf of the Tenant which the Landlord shall be entitled to assume without enquiry.

   6.6 Any personal items left behind at the end of the tenancy after the Tenant has vacated (which the Tenant has not removed in accordance with clause 2.13 above) shall be considered abandoned if they have not been removed within 14 days of written notice to the Tenant from the Landlord, or if the Landlord has been unable to trace the Tenant by taking reasonable steps to do so. After this period the Landlord may remove or dispose of the items as he thinks fit. The Tenant shall be liable for the reasonable disposal costs which may be deducted from the proceeds of sale (if any), and the Tenant shall remain liable for any balance. Any net proceeds of the sale will be dealt with in the same way as the Deposit as set out in clause 5.2 above.

   6.7 In the event of damage to or destruction of the Property by any of the risks insured against by the Landlord the Tenant shall be relieved from payment of the Rent to the extent that the Tenant's use and enjoyment of the Property is thereby prevented and from performance of its obligations as to the state and condition of the Property to the extent of and so long as there prevails such damage or destruction (except to the extent that the insurance is prejudiced by any act or default of the Tenant).

   6.8 Where the context so admits:

   6.8.1 The 'Landlord' includes the persons from time to time entitled to receive the Rent.

   6.8.2 The 'Tenant' includes any persons deriving title under the Tenant.

   6.8.3 The 'Property' includes any part or parts of the Property and all of the Landlord's fixtures and fittings at or upon the Property.

   6.8.4 All references to the singular shall include the plural and vice versa and any obligations or liabilities of more than one person shall be joint and several (this means that they will each be liable for all sums due under this Agreement, not just liable for a proportionate part) and an obligation on the part of a party shall include an obligation not to allow or permit the breach of that obligation.

   6.8.5 All references to 'he', 'him' and 'his' shall be taken to include 'she', 'her' and 'hers'.

F201S

RENTAL AGREEMENT - SCOTLAND
(For a Furnished House or Flat on a Short Assured Tenancy)

THIS RENTAL AGREEMENT comprises the particulars detailed below and the terms and conditions printed overleaf whereby the Property is hereby let by the Landlord and taken by the Tenant for the Term at the Rent as a Short Assured Tenancy.

The PROPERTY _____

_____

The LANDLORD _____

of _____

_____

The TENANT _____

_____

_____

_____

The TERM _____ months beginning on _____

The RENT £ _____ per week/month* payable in advance on the _____ day of each week/month*   (*delete as appropriate)

The DEPOSIT £ _____

The INVENTORY means the list of the Landlord's possessions at the Property which has been signed by the Landlord and the Tenant

DATED _____

SIGNED _____   _____

_____   _____

(The Landlord)   _____

_____

(The Tenant)

before: Witness _____   Witness _____

FULL NAME _____   FULL NAME _____

Address _____   Address _____

_____   _____

Occupation _____   Occupation _____

IMPORTANT NOTICE TO LANDLORDS:
1. In order to qualify as a Short Assured Tenancy the period of let must be at least 6 months and the tenant must have been given a 'Notice of a Short Assured Tenancy, Form AT5' (included in Form Pack F201), in advance of the creation of the tenancy that the tenancy is to be a Short Assured Tenancy.
2. The Tenant must be an individual (not a firm or company) who will occupy the property as his/her main residence.
3. The details of 'THE LANDLORD' near the top of this Agreement should include the full name and address of the Landlord.
4. Always remember to give both (a) written Notice to Terminate to the Tenant two clear months before the end of the Term and (b) formal Notice to Quit at least 40 clear days before the expiry of the Term. These two Notices should be sent by recorded delivery post and may be sent at the same time.

SPECIAL NOTES FOR EXISTING TENANTS:
1. If you already have a regulated tenancy, other than a short tenancy, should you give it up and take a new tenancy in the same house/flat or another house/flat owned by the same landlord, that tenancy cannot be a Short Assured Tenancy and this Agreement is not appropriate; your tenancy will continue to be a regulated tenancy .
2. If you have a short tenancy under the Tenant's Rights etc. (Scotland) Act 1980 or the Rent (Scotland) Act 1984 your landlord can offer you a Short Assured Tenancy of the same or another house/flat on the expiry of your existing tenancy.
3. If you are an existing tenant and are uncertain about accepting the proposed Short Assured Tenancy you are strongly advised to consult a solicitor or organisation which gives advice on housing matters.

Terms and Conditions

1. This Agreement is intended to create a Short Assured Tenancy as defined in Section 32 of the Housing (Scotland) Act 1988 and the Tenant acknowledges that he has received prior to the creation of the Tenancy notice to that effect in Form AT5 that the tenancy may be brought to an end by an order for possession granted by the Sheriff on the application of the Landlord or of the heritable creditor of the Landlord in any of the circumstances set out in Grounds 2, 8 or 9 to 17 inclusive in Schedule 5 to the Housing (Scotland) Act 1988 provided always that the Landlord has complied with Section 19 of that Act.

2. The Tenant will:

   2.1 pay the Rent at the times and in the manner aforesaid without any deduction abatement or set-off whatsoever;

   2.2 immediately upon occupation of the Property arrange for the Tenant to be registered as the consumer of gas, electricity and telephone services and to pay all charges in respect of any electric, gas, water and telephonic or televisual services used at or supplied to the Property and Council Tax or any similar tax that might be charged in addition to or replacement of it during the Term;

   2.3 keep the interior of the Property in a good, clean and tenantable state and condition and not damage or injure the Property and take all necessary precautions against damage by frost or flooding the Tenant accepting the Property and contents (so far as belonging to the Landlord) and (save as specified in the Inventory of Contents) as being in good tenantable order and condition at the commencement of the Tenancy, the Tenant by acceptance hereof renouncing any claims against the Landlord in respect thereof;

   2.4 yield up the Property and all and any Contents belonging to the Landlord at the end of the Term in the same clean state and condition they were in at the beginning of the Term (reasonable wear and tear and damage by insured risks excepted);

   2.5 not install or erect fixed TV aerial or satellite dish or make any alteration or addition to the Property nor without the Landlord's prior written consent do any redecoration or painting of the Property;

   2.6 not do or omit to do anything on or at the Property which may be or become a nuisance or annoyance to the Landlord or owners or occupiers of adjoining or nearby premises or which may in any way prejudice the insurance of the Property or cause an increase in the premium payable therefor;

   2.7 not without the Landlord's prior consent allow or keep any pet or any kind of animal at the Property;

   2.8 not leave the Property unoccupied for any period exceeding 3 weeks and not use or occupy the Property in any way whatsoever other than as a private residence;

   2.9 not assign, sublet, charge or part with or share possession or occupation of the Property;

   2.10 permit the Landlord or anyone authorised by the Landlord at reasonable hours and upon reasonable prior notice (except in emergency) to enter and view the Property for any proper purpose (including the checking of compliance with the Tenant's obligations under this Agreement and during the last month of the Term the showing of the Property to prospective new tenants);

   2.11 pay interest at the rate of 4% above the Base Lending Rate for the time being of the Landlord's bankers upon any rent or other money due from the Tenant under this Agreement which is more than 3 days in arrears in respect of the period from when it became due to the date of payment.

3. The Landlord will:

   3.1 subject to the Tenant paying the rent and performing his/her obligations under this Agreement allow the Tenant peaceably to hold and enjoy the Property during the Term without lawful interruption from the Landlord or any person rightfully claiming under or in trust for the Landlord;

   3.2 insure the Property and the contents of the Property which belong to the Landlord;

   3.3 keep in repair the structure and exterior of the Property (including drains, gutters and external pipes);

   3.4 keep in repair and proper working order the installations at the Property for the supply of water, gas and electricity and for sanitation (including basins, sinks, baths and sanitary conveniences);

   3.5 keep in repair and proper working order the installation at the Property for space heating and heating water.

   3.6 But the Landlord will not be required to:

      3.6.1 carry out works for which the Tenant is responsible by virtue of his/her duty to use the Property in a tenantlike manner.

      3.6.2 rebuild or reinstate the Property in the case of destruction or damage by fire or by tempest flood or other accident.

4. The Deposit has been paid by the Tenant and is held by the Landlord to secure compliance with the Tenant's obligations under this Agreement (without prejudice to the Landlord's other rights and remedies) and if, at any time during the Term, the Landlord is obliged to draw upon it to satisfy any outstanding breaches of such obligations then the Tenant shall forthwith make such additional payment as is necessary to restore the full amount of the Deposit held by the Landlord. As soon as reasonably practicable following termination of this Agreement the Landlord shall return to the Tenant the Deposit or the balance thereof after any deductions properly made without interest.

5. The Landlord hereby notifies the Tenant that any notices (including notices in proceedings) should be served upon the Landlord at the address stated with the name of the Landlord overleaf.

6. In the event of damage to or destruction of the Property by any of the risks insured by the Landlord the Tenant shall be relieved from payment of the Rent to the extent that the Tenant's use and enjoyment of the Property is thereby prevented and from performance of his obligations as to the state and condition of the Property to the extent of and so long as there prevails such damage or destruction (except to the extent that the insurance is prejudiced by any act or default of the Tenant) the amount in case of dispute to be settled by arbitration.

7. This Agreement and the tenancy hereby constituted may be terminated:

   7.1 by the parties at any time by mutual agreement in writing; or

   7.2 by either party on or after the end of the Term by giving to the other party not less than 2 months' notice in writing of termination or such shorter period of notice as the parties may mutually agree in writing.

   7.3 It is expressly agreed that if:

      7.3.1 the rent or any part thereof shall be unpaid for 14 days after any of the Rent Payment Dates whether demanded or not; or

      7.3.2 any other sum due and payable by the Tenant to the Landlord under this Agreement shall be unpaid for 14 days after the date on which it falls due and payable in terms of the relevant provision hereof; or

      7.3.3 there shall be any other breach, non-observance or non-performance by the Tenant of any of its other obligations under this Agreement then the Landlord shall be entitled forthwith to terminate the tenancy and that without prejudice to the Landlord's rights, claims and remedies for the Rent, interest, damages and expenses.

   7.4 The Tenant agrees that its liability for the Rent and for the performance of the Tenant's whole obligations under this Agreement shall subsist, unless otherwise agreed by the Landlord in writing as continuing obligations until the latest of the following dates:

      7.4.1 the end of the Term;

      7.4.2 the Termination Date;

      7.4.3 the date of the Tenant's removing from and giving the Landlord vacant possession of the Premises and restoring the items on the Inventory to the Landlord.

8. Where the context so admits:

   8.1 the 'Landlord' includes the persons for the time being the Owners of the Property;

   8.2 the 'Tenant' includes any persons permitted to derive title from the Tenant;

   8.3 the 'Property' includes any part or parts of the Property and all of the Landlord's fixtures and fittings at or upon the Property;

   8.4 the 'Term' shall mean the period stated in the particulars overleaf or any shorter or longer period in the event of an earlier termination or an extension or holding over respectively;

   8.4 the 'Termination Date' shall mean the date given by the Landlord in the Termination Notice (Section 33 Notice) and Notice to Quit being the date by which the Tenant is required to leave the Property or alternatively the date given by the Tenant in his written Notice of Termination being the date the Tenant intends to leave the Property;

   8.5 all references to 'he', 'him' and 'his' shall be taken to include 'she', 'her' and 'hers'.

9. All references to the singular shall include the plural and vice versa and any obligations or liabilities of more than one person shall be joint and several and an obligation on the part of a party shall include an obligation not to allow or permit the breach of that obligation.

10. This Agreement will be governed by and construed in accordance with the Law of Scotland and the parties submit to the jurisdiction of the Scottish Courts.

3

BUYING PROPERTY IN SCOTLAND

SCOTTISH CONVEYANCING LAW

This is very different from that of England and Wales. These are the main differences, but for in-depth information of Scottish conveyancing, you should consult a solicitor.

- Most Scottish properties are sold on an owner-occupier basis – there are no freeholds or leaseholds.
- Buyers and vendors enter into a legally binding contract at a much earlier stage.
- Solicitors are involved almost from the start, and gazumping is virtually unheard of.
- Lenders will also give a mortgage application decision ('agreement in principle') prior to an offer going in.
- Surveys of property are carried out *before* an offer is made and, indeed, help in setting the level of the bid.

MORTGAGE

Funds need to be in place only in time for the agreed date of entry. This is when you'll be required to pay the price in exchange for gaining entry to the property, but lenders will give a decision on your mortgage application before an offer is made. Buyers in Scotland do not have to provide a deposit.

Vendors in Scotland market their property on an 'offers over' basis. A guideline figure is provided and it's up to the buyer to decide what to bid. Lower bids will not necessarily be rejected, but the final selling price will depend on a number of factors, including other prospective buyers and whether the property has been on the market for a long time. Offers must be made through a solicitor and are usually pitched at between 1 and 10 per cent over, but in a buoyant market, that may not be enough to secure the property. In general terms, if an offer is acceptable, then the vendors will set a time limit for a survey to be carried out.

SURVEYS AND VALUATIONS

In Scotland, potential buyers commission the survey or valuation prior to making an offer. If a buyer decides to make an offer subject to survey or subject to contract, it may jeopardize their chances of the offer being accepted, particularly if a closing date is set. If the offer is not successful, the potential purchaser will have lost the money spent on the survey, plus any other fees, and this can be problematic in a rising market, where offers may have to be made on several properties in succession before a bid is accepted.

In England and Wales potential buyers will make an offer subject to contract and satisfactory survey. This means that neither purchaser nor vendor is legally bound to go through with the transaction until a survey has been carried out and contracts have been exchanged. If the survey is not satisfactory, the buyers will either negotiate or withdraw.

NOTING INTEREST

The potential purchaser asks the solicitor to 'note interest' to the vendor's agents. This means that if another interested party arrives on the scene the potential purchaser may be offered the chance to submit a competing formal offer. The vendor's agents, however, don't have to do this and, if an acceptable offer is made, the property may be sold without a closing date being fixed.

THE SOLICITOR'S ROLE

Buyers and vendors in Scotland must use a solicitor or authorized conveyancing practitioner qualified in Scottish law. Similarly, a Scottish solicitor cannot act in connection with the purchase or sale of a house in England or Wales. The Scottish solicitor is also likely to be acting as the estate agent, so there's just one point of professional contact throughout the whole process.

CLOSING DATE

If more than one buyer is interested in purchasing a property in Scotland, the vendor will usually set a closing date, the date by which the vendor wishes all interested parties to submit offers. No one knows what the other offers may be, and while it's most common for vendorss to accept the highest offer, this is not always the case.

At the closing date, the vendor will decide which offer to settle upon, in consultation with his or her solicitor. The solicitor will then indicate verbally to the successful buyer's solicitor that the offer has been accepted. If a property is offered at a fixed price, the first acceptable bid at that price will be accepted. At this stage it's a verbal acceptance only and not legally binding.

CONCLUDING MISSIVES

When an offer is accepted, the next step is for the purchaser's and vendor's solicitors to draw up the missives. These are a series of formal letters setting out the details of the contract and, once the missives have been concluded, the buyer and vendor have entered into a legally binding contract to purchase at the agreed date of entry and the vendor to sell. Neither side can withdraw without being liable for the consequent losses of the other party. In return for the loan, you're giving the lender 'standard security' over the land and buildings (known as 'heritable property'). The lender then keeps the title deeds until the mortgage has been repaid.

The process in Scotland is more or less as follows:

- A suitable property is found.
- The mortgage is applied for.
- The solicitor is appointed.
- The solicitor 'notes the interest'.
- The mortgage application is completed.
- Valuation or survey takes place.
- Mortgage application is agreed.
- The offer is made on the property.
- The mortgage application is completed.
- Offer is accepted.
- Buildings and life assurance are arranged and put in place.
- Solicitors conclude the missives.
- Settlement is made.

USEFUL CONTACTS

Web: www.espc.co.uk/information/pdf/espc_movers_guide.pdf

Good information on the buying system in Scotland:
Web: www.icplanning.co.uk/buying_scotland.shtml

Scottish Parliament site:
Web: www.scotland.gov.uk

4

TAX: BUYING, SELLING AND OWNING PROPERTY

CAPITAL GAINS TAX

This is the tax payable for any tax year where a person's total capital gain exceeds the capital gains tax (CGT) exempt amount (£7,900 for individuals for the tax year 2003/4). CGT is not normally payable on the gain made on the sale of your primary residence, though there have been suggestions recently that the Treasury is considering changing this exemption looking especially closely at taxing people who make speculative short-term investments in the housing market. It is, however, payable on gains on disposal of other assets, such as a second residence or holiday home. But the gain liable to CGT may be reduced by reliefs such as indexation allowance and taper relief. Consult your tax advisor. The Inland Revenue produces a booklet *Capital Gains Tax: An Introduction*.

Under certain circumstances, the capital gain arising from the sale of qualifying commercial furnished holiday lettings accommodation in the UK can be 'rolled over' if you invest the proceeds of the sale into another qualifying business asset, including another commercial furnished holiday letting property in the UK, within 36 months of disposing of the old property or within 12 months prior to the disposal. If you use all of the sale proceeds you receive from the disposal of the old property in acquiring the new one, the whole of your gain will be deferred until you sell the new property. This is done by deducting the 'rolled over' gain from the cost of acquiring the new asset when computing the gain arising when the new asset is sold. If you use only part of the proceeds, then only part of the gain will be deferred. See your tax advisor or find out more information from IR290 at www.inlandrevenue.gov.uk.

Note: rollover relief does not apply to commercial furnished holiday lettings accommodation outside the UK.

COUNCIL TAX

Council tax is a local authority levied tax payable by occupiers of residential property in England and Wales, and is banded depending on the value of the property. A 50 per cent discount on council tax applies to both second homes and long-term empty properties. From April 2004 local authorities will be able to reduce the second homes discount to 10 per cent (making the tax payable 90 per cent) and the empty homes discount to 0 per cent (making the tax payable 100 per cent). Consult your local authority to ask about council tax liability.

Under the Local Government Finance Act 1992, a single-occupancy tenant is obliged to pay council tax and the landlord is not liable. However, if there are several people occupying your property who do not constitute a single household (i.e. students, nurses etc.), then you as landlord are obliged to pay the council tax, though this may be reflected in the rent you charge.

If you're letting out part of your home as a self-contained flat, you should consult a council tax official at your local authority to see if, in their opinion, it constitutes a separate dwelling. Generally speaking, a flat or a bedsit may count as a separate dwelling if it has a cooker point.

The Office of the Deputy Prime Minister issues the following leaflets: *Council Tax: A Guide to Your Bill* and *Council Tax: A Guide to Valuation Bands and Appeals*. Go to www.odpm.gov.uk for more information.

INCOME TAX

This is payable under Schedule A on any income above the threshold of £4,615 (2003/4 figure for persons under 65 years of age). This includes income from property, in particular rents from tenants. Deductions for allowable expenses can be set against the property income received. You'll need to declare this income on the land and property pages of your tax return. Your tax advisor, a tax enquiry centre or the tax helpline will be able to advise you. Inland Revenue Self-Assessment helpline: 0845 9000 444.

INHERITANCE TAX

This is payable at 40 per cent on the value of your estate (your wealth and assets upon your death) that is over the tax-free threshold of £255,000 (2003/4 figures). (The amount up to the tax-free threshold is charged at a 'nil' rate.) A grant of representation ('probate') is needed before your estate can be distributed, unless it's small. Generally, your personal representatives will be required to settle the inheritance tax (IHT) bill in advance of probate being obtained, although tax in certain circumstances on assets, like land and buildings, can be paid by instalments. Transfers of property and gifts between husband and wife, no matter how large in value, are exempt from IHT. This is known as the interspouse exemption rule. (However, this exemption is limited to £55,000 where the spouse making the gift is domiciled in the UK but the spouse receiving the gift is domiciled outside the UK.) There are exemptions too for smaller gifts to non-spouses; for example gifts where the total value does not exceed £3,000 in any one tax year plus any unused balance of the £3,000 from the previous tax year. This £3,000 gift can be made to one person or be divided up between several people. Gifts not exceeding £5,000 to sons or daughters on their marriage are also exempt.

Outright transfers of property and gifts made during a lifetime are treated as potentially exempt transfers and are only considered exempt from IHT providing the donor survives a minimum of seven years after the event;

otherwise, these gifts are added back into the estate. When chargeable, such gifts are taken in chronological order with the amount up to the tax-free threshold being charged at a 'nil' rate and any excess at 40 per cent.

All outright gifts and bequests (such as property) to a UK registered charity are also exempt from inheritance tax. Matters such as these can be complex, so it's advisable to seek professional advice. More information about IHT (including a range of useful leaflets) can be found at Inland Revenue: www.inlandrevenue.gov.uk, or call the Inheritance Tax Helpline on 0845 3020 900.

VALUE ADDED TAX

You can reclaim the VAT on goods and materials used at the end of a self-build project. You can make the claim if the new house is a private domestic residence (i.e not for business or to rent out), and you must keep detailed proof of all the goods on which you've paid VAT during the project. The claim needs to be submitted within three months of completion, and you only get one chance to reclaim. You cannot however claim for the following:

- carpets and curtains;
- white goods (washing machines, fridges etc.);
- trees and plants;
- burglar alarms;
- professional services;
- equipment hire;
- transport of materials and tools used.

HM Customs and Excise have a useful guide called *VAT refunds for Do It Yourself Builders*, under notice 719 (Go to www.hmce.gov.uk/forms/ notices/ 719.htm). If the build is complicated, then it might be a good idea to employ a VAT expert.

Work involved in creating a 'new dwelling' through the conversion of an existing building is largely free of VAT. VAT registered builders have to charge the reduced rate of 5 per cent on the supply of labour and materials, which you can later reclaim through your local Customs and Excise Office when you complete the project. Ask for VAT Notice 719 for more information. This also applies to properties that have been abandoned for 10 years or more.

Renovation work is not considered to be creating a new dwelling and is fully rated for VAT, unless the property has been empty for three years or more, or if you're changing the number of units, in which case it's rated at 5 per cent.

Work on 'approved alterations' to listed buildings can be zero-rated by VAT registered contractors, provided you've been granted listed building consent, and it's neither repair or maintenance. See VAT notice 708 at the Customs and Excise web site: www.hmce.gov.uk.

GLOSSARY

additional security fee Or Mortgage Indemnity Guarantee policy is taken out to insure/indemnify the mortgagee (lender) against loss in the event of default on the mortgage repayment.

administration fee Fee charged for taking a building and contents insurance policy other than one that is part of the mortgage lender's package.

advance Another name for the mortgage loan.

adverse credit Term used if the borrower has a poor credit history, which might include previous mortgage or loan arrears, CCJ or bankruptcy.

agency sales fee Percentage of the property sale price paid to the estate agent as a fee.

agreement in principle Document provided by the lender to show that a prospective buyer will be eligible for a mortgage subject to valuation of a property.

agricultural restriction A freehold covenant that restricts the occupancy of a property to those engaged in agriculture.

annual percentage rate (APR) A standard basis for comparing interest rates on different forms of credit. The calculation must include the 'total charge for credit', which includes such things as arrangement fees, valuation fees and so on, and so does have some merit.

architect's certification Guarantee provided by the architect on a building project that construction is sound.

arrangement fee Fee paid to the lender in return for providing a mortgage. Usually paid on completion or with application.

arrears Overdue payments.

asking price The price of a property as it appears on the sale particulars.

assignment Document transferring rights of ownership from one person to another, including an endowment policy to the building society in connection with a mortgage. Can also be the document transferring the lease on a property.

assured shorthold tenancy The most common form of tenancy agreement for domestic lets.

ASU Accident, sickness and unemployment insurance (see also MPPI), designed to pay out to the borrower in case of accident, sickness or involuntary unemployment.

auction Public sale of a property to the highest bidder, at which the purchaser must immediately sign a binding contract and pay a deposit.

Australian Another term for a flexible mortgage.

balance outstanding The amount payable on a property purchase or a loan after a percentage has been paid.

banker's draft Cheque drawn on the bank itself against deposit of cash. Normally required in property transactions.

bonus Additional amounts paid at the end of a policy term or annually on with-profits policies.

bridging loan Short-term loan to facilitate the purchase of one property before the sale of another.

broker's fee Fee charged by an intermediary for sourcing the most appropriate financial product.

building regulations Statutory requirements that must be satisfied in order for construction to be carried out, and to ensure that adequate standards of building work are met so the building is safe and healthy.

building society Mutual organization specializing in offering a savings facility and lending money to individuals to purchase or remortgage residential properties.

buildings insurance Financial cover for the structure of a building that should be enough to cover reinstatement.

buildings/structural survey The most comprehensive survey carried out by a chartered surveyor to assess the structural state of the property and to find hidden faults.

buy to let mortgage Mortgage designed for the purchase of property to rent, with repayments based on the projected rental income as opposed to the personal income of the borrowers.

capital An asset or resource.

capital gains tax Tax levied by the Inland Revenue on profit on the proceeds of the sale of a capital asset.

cashback A payment you receive when you take out a mortgage. It may be a fixed amount, or a percentage of the amount of the mortgage.

centralized lender A mortgage lender who does not rely on a branch network.

chain A sequence of interdependent property deals that rely on all being successfully concluded.

charge Any right or interest, especially a mortgage, to which a freehold or leasehold property may be held.

charge certificate The certificate issued by HM Land Registry to the mortgagee of a property with registered title, and containing details of restrictions, mortgages and other interests. Where there's no mortgage, it's called the 'land certificate' and issued to the registered owner.

chattels Items that can be moved, such as furniture or personal possessions.

completion When the sale and purchase of the property are finalized.

conditions of sale Standard terms in a sale contract that must be met before the transaction can be completed.

contract Legally binding agreement details terms of sale/purchase or work to be carried out.

conveyance The deed by which freehold, unregistered title changes hands. If the property is leasehold and unregistered, it's called an 'assignment'. If the title is registered, the deed is called a 'transfer'.

conveyancing The legal process involved in buying and selling property.

county court judgement (CCJ) Sometimes made through non-payment of debts, and is recorded on your personal credit report.

covenant A promise or restriction contained in a deed.

credit reference agency A company that provides potential lenders with information about a credit reference on a potential borrower.

credit scoring Criteria by which lenders assess loan risk.

credit search Check the lender makes with a credit reference agency to find out whether a potential borrower has CCJs or a bad credit score.

deed A legal document that is 'signed, sealed and delivered', and by which title to both freehold and leasehold is transferred.

defects Negative factors within a property or a construction that can adversely affect its value.

deposit The percentage of the cost of a purchase paid in advance to secure the purchase.

disbursements A solicitor's expenses, which might include Land Registry fees, searches, faxes and so on.

draft contract A legal document setting out the terms of sale at the outset of negotiations.

early redemption charges Charges made by a lender if part or all of a loan or mortgage is paid off before the agreed date.

easement A right, such as a right of way, that the owner of one property has over an adjoining property.

equity The amount of value in a property that isn't covered by a mortgage.

equity release Taking a new, larger mortgage, or increasing an existing mortgage to raise capital.

excess The initial sum of money paid before an insurance policy pays out.

exchange of contracts The point at which buyer and vendor sign and swap identical contracts, and the deposit is paid on the property.

fixtures and fittings Any item attached to a property and so legally part of the property.

freehold Ownership of a property and the land it's on.

full structural survey The previous name given to a structural/building survey.

gazumping The name for the process of accepting a higher offer on a property when an offer has already been accepted, before exchange of contracts.

gazundering Whereby the buyer drops his or her offer just before exchange of contracts.

ground rent Fee that a leaseholder pays a freeholder annually.

guide price An estimate of selling price.

home buyer's report Property survey that is more detailed than a lender's valuation survey, but less detailed than a full buildings survey.

home information packs Proposed Government initiative whereby vendors and their solicitor assemble details about the property, including local searches and a survey to present to potential buyers.

income protection insurance A policy that pays out monthly in the event of accident, sickness and involuntary unemployment of the mortgage payer.

income reference Confirmation of a borrower's employment and salary from an employer, or from an accountant in the case of the self-employed.

intermediary A mortgage broker or advisor who locates the most appropriate mortgage for borrowers and arranges the mortgage on their behalf.

inventory A comprehensive list of possessions or contents of a property, which should be signed and agreed by both parties.

joint tenants Two or more people holding title to a property as co-owners, that when one dies, ownership automatically passes to the surviving tenant.

land certificate Certificate issued by the Land Registry to confirm ownership of a piece of land.

Land Registry fee Fee paid to the Land Registry to register ownership of a piece of land.

leasehold Ownership of a property (but not the land) for a set number of years.

licensed conveyancer A qualified lawyer who specializes in the legal aspects of buying and selling property.

listed building consent Permission granted by the local authority granting permission for alteration to a listed building within limitations.

listed property One considered to be of historical or architectural importance, and which cannot be altered internally or externally without listed building consent.

loan to value (LTV) Size of the mortgage as a percentage of the value of the property.

local authority search Search by buyer's solicitor to research proposed developments for the area close to the property, and to check details such as planning permissions and enforcements.

missives Exchange of letters between Scottish solicitors leading to a binding agreement.

mortgage A loan to buy a property whereby the property is put up as security against the loan.

Mortgage Indemnity Guarantee (MIG) Insurance protecting the lender against having to repossess the property and being unable to sell it to recover the loan. Usually insisted upon by lenders when LTV is over 75 per cent.

Mortgage Payment Protection Insurance (MPPI) (see also **ASU**) Policy that pays out to the lender in the event of the mortgager being unable to meet his or her repayments because of accident, sickness or involuntary unemployment.

Mortgage Repayment Protection (MRP) Insurance policy taken through the lender at the time of taking out the loan.

mortgagee The mortgage lender.

mortgager The person taking out the mortgage.

negative equity Position in which the money owing on the mortgage is greater than the value of the property.

offer The price suggested by a buyer for a property or land.

overpayment When monthly repayments on a mortgage are increased above the agreed rate. Usually the case with flexible mortgages.

payment holiday An agreed period during which the borrower can make no mortgage payments. Available to borrowers with a flexible mortgage and who've previously made overpayments.

pension A long-term savings plan to provide income at the time of retirement.

permitted development rights Rights to carry out alterations to a property without planning permission having to be granted.

Personal Equity Plan (PEP) This is a tax-free way to own shares or unit trusts. You can also use PEPs as a way to repay an interest-only mortgage with some lenders.

planning permission Official notification that development can take place within stated restrictions.

preliminary enquiries Questions asked by the buyer's solicitor prior to exchange of contracts.

public liability insurance Policy that indemnifies a business against loss or injury to a third party.

redemption Paying off your mortgage when either moving house, remortgaging or at the end of the mortgage term.

redemption penalties Charges levied by the lender when a borrower pays off the mortgage before the end of the agreed redemption period.

registered land Land including the buildings on it, the title to which has been recorded by the Land Registry.

remittance fee Charge made by the lender when monies are sent to the solicitor on completion of a property purchase.

remortgage The process of moving a mortgage to a new lender, and paying off the previous mortgage with the new one.

repayment Money paid monthly to the lender by the mortgager, and which constitutes some pay back of capital borrowed and some interest payable on the loan.

repossession The legal process by which the lender has the right to sell a property to recover the debt when the mortgager has defaulted on mortgage repayments.

sealing fee Charge made by the lender when a mortgage is repaid.

searches Investigations carried out during the conveyancing process with the local authority and other official organizations, the results of which may affect the value of the property.

self-certification loan A system whereby a self-employed person can declare their income, specifying sources and amounts to qualify for a mortgage.

service charges Charges made to a tenant or leaseholder to cover maintenance insurance and repair costs.

stamp duty Tax levied by the Inland Revenue on property purchases, and banded depending on the price paid.

standard variable rate (SVR) The interest rate a lender charges on a mortgage that goes up and down, depending on the Bank of England base rate.

structural/buildings survey The most comprehensive survey carried out by a chartered surveyor to assess the structural state of the property and to find hidden faults.

tenant A person who holds title, especially from a landlord under a lease, or who has the use of property subject to the payment of rent.

tenants in common Two or more people who hold property together, so that when one dies, the share doesn't pass automatically to the survivor but forms part of the estate of the deceased.

term The life of a mortgage.

term assurance Insurance policy that repays the mortgage on the death of the insured person, or in some cases on diagnosis of a terminal illness. Level term assurance covers a principal sum throughout the policy term and pays out the full amount on death.

tie-in period Period of time after a special mortgage deal has ended, during which the borrower is obliged to keep a mortgage with the lender, or else risk paying a redemption penalty.

title deeds Documents showing ownership of a freehold or leasehold property.

transfer deed Document transferring ownership of a property between parties.

valuation An assessment of a property to determine its value, usually for mortgage purposes.

valuation fee A fee paid to the lender by the borrower to carry out a valuation.

vendor The person selling the property.

INDEX